207 BEST SELLING AFFORDABLE HOME PLANS

HOME PLANNERS, LLC
Wholly owned by Hanley-Wood, LLC

Published by Home Planners, LLC
Wholly owned by Hanley-Wood, LLC
3275 West Ina Road, Suite 110
Tucson, Arizona 85741

Distribution Center:
29333 Lorie Lane
Wixom, Michigan 48393

Patricia Joseph, President
Jan Prideaux, Editor In Chief
Marian E. Haggard, Editor
Peter Zullo, Graphic Designer

Photo Credits
Front Cover: Andrew D. Lautman
Back Cover: Laszlo Regos

10 9 8 7 6 5 4 3 2 1

Printed in the United States of America.

Library of Congress Catalog Card Number: 00-134201

ISBN softcover: 1-881955-75-3

On the front cover: The small square footage and convenient one-level
plan of this comfortable ranch design (S2947) works well for anyone's
lifestyle. For additional information about this design, see page 70.

On the back cover: Nearly charming to a fault, Design S2488, is a great
starter home, second home or leisure cottage. For more information
about this design, see page 169.

TABLE OF CONTENTS

Editor's Note
The age-old dream of building a home is alive and as strong as ever, though perhaps modified in these financially tight times. Many are finding that with some ingenuity, creative thinking and the help of a reputable stock plan company, they can realize their dream home in thoroughly livable *and* affordable style. Contained herein is the finest collection of home plans available that addresses budgetary constraints without limiting options, versatility and comfort. The homes, though economical to build, are filled with amenities and surprising spaciousness, making them a fine value for the prospective home builder. If your intent is to build a home that is near to custom, our intent is to help you do so without the cost of custom plans.

About The Designers

The Blue Ribbon Designer Series™ is a collection of books featuring the home plans of a diverse group of outstanding home designers and architects known as the Blue Ribbon Network of Designers. This group of companies is dedicated to creating and marketing the finest possible plans for home construction on a regional and national basis. Each of the companies exhibits superior work and integrity in all phases of the stock-plan business including modern, trendsetting floor planning, a professionally executed blueprint package and a strong sense of service and commitment to the consumer.

Design Basics, Inc.

For nearly a decade, Design Basics, a nationally recognized home design service located in Omaha, has been developing plans for custom home builders. Since 1987, the firm has consistently appeared in *Builder* magazine, the official magazine of the National Association of Home Builders, as the top-selling designer. The company's plans also regularly appear in numerous other shelter magazines such as *Better Homes and Gardens*, *House Beautiful* and *Home Planner*.

Design Traditions

Design Traditions was established by Stephen S. Fuller with the tenets of innovation, quality, originality and uncompromising architectural techniques in traditional and European homes. Especially popular throughout the Southeast, Design Traditions' plans are known for their extensive detail and thoughtful design. They are widely published in such shelter magazines as *Southern Living* magazine and *Better Homes and Gardens*.

Alan Mascord Design Associates, Inc.

Founded in 1983 as a local supplier to the building community, Mascord Design Associates of Portland, Oregon, began to successfully publish plans nationally in 1985. With plans now drawn exclusively on computer, Mascord Design Associates quickly received a reputation for homes that are easy to build yet meet the rigorous demands of the buyers' market, winning local and national awards. The company's trademark is creating floor plans that work well and exhibit excellent traffic patterns. Their motto is: "Drawn to build, designed to sell."

Larry W. Garnett & Associates, Inc.

Starting as a designer of homes for Houston-area residents, Garnett & Associates has been marketing designs nationally for the past ten years. A well-respected design firm, the company's plans are regularly featured in *House Beautiful*, *Country Living*, *Home* and *Professional Builder*. Numerous accolades, including several from the Texas Institute of Building Design and the American Institute of Building Design, have been awarded to the company for excellence in architecture.

Home Planners

Headquartered in Tucson, Arizona, with additional offices in Detroit, Home Planners is one of the longest-running and most successful home design firms in the United States. With over 2,500 designs in its portfolio, the company provides a wide range of styles, sizes and types of homes for the residential builder. All of Home Planners' designs are created with the care and professional expertise that fifty years of experience in the home-planning business affords. Their homes are designed to be built, lived in and enjoyed for years to come.

Donald A. Gardner, Architects, Inc.

The South Carolina firm of Donald A. Gardner was established in response to a growing demand for residential designs that reflect constantly changing lifestyles. The company's specialty is providing homes with refined, custom-style details and unique features such as passive-solar designs and open floor plans. Computer-aided design and drafting technology resulting in trouble-free construction documents places the firm at the leading edge of the home plan industry.

Home Design Services, Inc.

For the past fifteen years, Home Design Services of Longwood, Florida, has been formulating plans for the sun-country lifestyle. At the forefront of design innovation and imagination, the company has developed award-winning designs that are consistently praised for their highly detailed, free-flowing floor plans, imaginative and exciting interior architecture and elevations which have gained international appeal.

ONE-STORY HOMES

Singularly Livable and Affordable

The one-story home has always been a popular housing choice because of its low-slung, ground-hugging profile, easy adaptability and livability.

With its unencumbered, single floor plan, the one-story takes on a variety of shapes — the most cost-efficient being the simple rectangle. With no projecting wings, bays or other protrusions — all under a straight, in-line roof — this configuration assures the most prudent use of building materials. And the facility of its construction makes it less labor-intensive — a plus at the building stage.

Low-cost construction is not the only consideration of affordability, however. While the simple rectangle may be the most reasonable to build, an overly wide house may not be appropriate for some sites. For instance, a 100-foot wide house may require the purchase of a large and costly lot. An equally livable arrangement with a 65-foot L-shaped house, or a 50-foot U-shaped house, will probably result in a smaller and less expensive building site.

Consider also the energy efficiency of a square one-story over the same size rectangle. A 20' by 80' rectangular home yields a 1,600 square foot area with 200 linear feet of wall space, while a 40' by 40' home has an equal amount of square footage with only 160 feet of wall space. This results in an obvious heating and cooling savings.

Remember, too, that the one-story need not be plain-Jane in its style. While added features such as bump-outs and protrusions are expensive, the amount of convenience and charm they provide and the quality of living they deliver may prove cost-effective in the long run. A front-facing bay window or a kitchen greenhouse could make all the difference in an otherwise boxy design.

Basements and attics are a great investment and a provident addition to the simple one-story house. Providing square footage at a relatively low cost, these bonus areas allow for increased space with less expenditure. In many areas, building codes do not permit the location of bedrooms in typical basements. However, full or partial basements are ideal for developing recreational space, hobby areas, laundries and storage facilities. Such inexpensive space can make a small or modest-size one-story house significantly more livable, incorporating economy and effective use of area. In parts of the country where basements are not practical or even possible, storage space can be allocated to garages, attics, closets and sheds.

The one-story enjoys an advantage over multi-storied houses in providing for today's indoor-outdoor lifestyles. It allows all zones — from living and sleeping areas to work spaces — direct access to patios, terraces and gardens without the expense encountered in second-floor balconies and decks. Simple amenities such as sloping ceilings, glass gable ends, skylights and sun rooms also help to open up interiors. Similarly, the U-shaped or L-shaped one-story often can enclose a pool or "outdoor room," further enhancing the economizing use of space and allowing added privacy.

Covering a diversity of sizes and styles, the one-story homes in this section are filled with amenities that enhance their appeal without compromising their affordable nature.

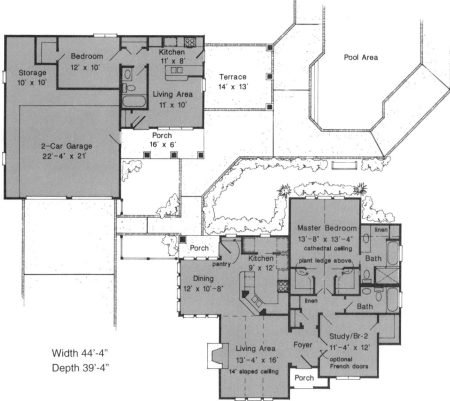

Storage
10' x 10'

Bedroom
12' x 10'

Kitchen
11' x 8'

Living Area
11' x 10'

Terrace
14' x 13'

Pool Area

2-Car Garage
22'-4" x 21'

Porch
16' x 6'

Width 44'-4"
Depth 39'-4"

Porch

Kitchen
9' x 12'

pantry

Dining
12' x 10'-8"

Master Bedroom
13'-8" x 13'-4"
cathedral ceiling
plant ledge above

linen

Bath

linen

Bath

Living Area
13'-4" x 16'
14' sloped ceiling

Foyer

Study/Br-2
11'-4" x 12'
optional
French doors

Porch

Design by
Larry W.
Garnett &
Associates, Inc.

Design S9096

Square Footage: 1,268
Guest Cottage: 468 square feet

● The perfect plan for those with a live-in relative, long-term guest or a family member who works at home, this plan allows a separate cottage with complete livability. The main house features a living room with fireplace and sloped ceiling, a glass-enclosed dining room with porch, kitchen with plenty of counter space and two bedrooms with two baths (or make one a study). The separate cottage is attached to the garage and has its own living area, galley kitchen and bedroom with walk-in closet and full bath. It also features a front porch and private side terrace. It can work as complete living quarters or a private studio or office. A bright solution to today's living patterns.

Design S9023

Square Footage: 1,373

● While relatively small in
terms of square footage, this
home possesses the design
characteristics and fine crafts-
manship of another era.
Influenced by Shingle Style
cottages, the exterior features
a sloping gable with a gentle
curve over the front porch.
Shingle siding is accented by
expansive windows surrounded with wide wood trim.
Inside, the living area offers a
fireplace and built-in media
center. Decorative columns
separate the living and dining
areas. French doors open to a
6' x 17' rear porch from both
the dining area and the master
bedroom. The well-appointed
master bath has ample linen
storage, a private water closet
and a garden tub with adjacent glass-enclosed shower.

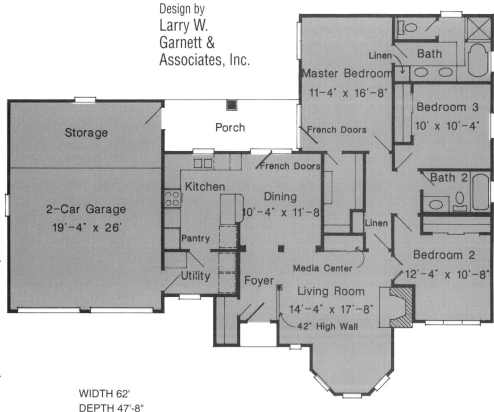

Design by
Larry W.
Garnett &
Associates, Inc.

WIDTH 62'
DEPTH 47'-8"

7

Design S9178
Square Footage: 1,706

● With a width of only 42 feet, this house achieves over 1,700 square feet in living space! Its pleasing exterior, with a volume roof and shuttered windows, provides a perfect introduction to the interior. The open living and dining rooms offer a nice atmosphere for formal entertaining. With a columned foyer as a prelude, guests won't help but be impressed. The breakfast room overlooks a side courtyard where there's room enough for outdoor dining. A utility area adjacent to the kitchen leaves room for a folding counter. Sleeping accommodations include a front secondary bedroom with a walk-in closet and convenient access to a full bath. The master bedroom offers a fine bath and a large walk-in closet.

Design by
Larry W. Garnett & Associates, Inc.

glass block

Master Bedroom
14' x 15'-4"

Util.

Covered Patio
5' x 9'

French door

Breakfast
12' x 10'

Kitchen
11' x 12'-8"

pantry

Living Room
18' x 14'-8"

Dining
11' x 13'-4"

Foyer

display niches

Porch
7' x 14'

2-Car Garage
19'-4" x 21'-4"

Bedroom 2
13'-4" x 12'
10' ceiling

WIDTH 42'
DEPTH 67'-8"

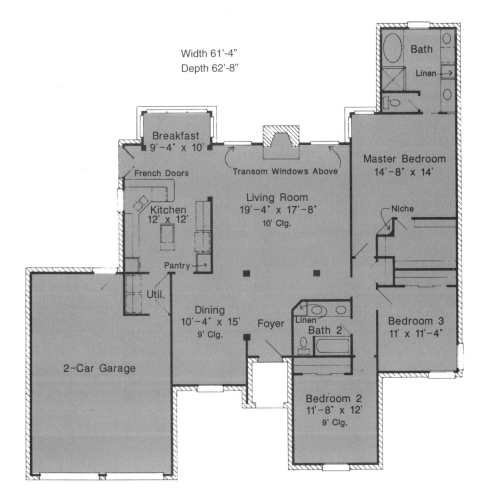

Width 61'-4"
Depth 62'-8"

Breakfast 9'-4" x 10'

French Doors

Transom Windows Above

Kitchen 12' x 12'

Pantry

Living Room 19'-4" x 17'-8" 10' Clg.

Util.

Dining 10'-4" x 15' 9' Clg.

Foyer

Linen

Bath 2

2-Car Garage

Bedroom 2 11'-8" x 12' 9' Clg.

Bath

Linen

Master Bedroom 14'-8" x 14'

Niche

Bedroom 3 11' x 11'-4"

Design S9143
Square Footage: 1,846

● While small in size, this home is rich with detail that will bring myriads of compliments. A wonderfully open living area features separation of space by the use of columns. The dining room has a 9' ceiling and is near the kitchen for easy serving. The living room has a fireplace with flanking transom window as its central focus. A glass-surrounded breakfast room has French doors to the outdoors. Bedrooms are found on the right side of the plan. The master has a large walk-in closet and its own bath with double-bowl vanity and separate tub and shower. Two secondary bedrooms share the use of a full bath with double-bowl vanities.

Design by
**Larry W.
Garnett &
Associates, Inc.**

Design S9136
Square Footage: 1,541

● A recessed entry adds interest
to the facade of this quaint home.
It leads to a small foyer that
opens directly onto the airy living
space: a living room with 10' ceiling and built-in media center. A
dining room with 9' ceiling is
adjacent to the L-shaped kitchen
and has access to the rear porch.
Three bedrooms include two
family bedrooms with ample
closet space and a master bedroom with gambrel ceiling, luxurious bath, and access to the rear
porch. The two-car garage adds
storage space to the plan.

Design by
Larry W.
Garnett &
Associates, Inc.

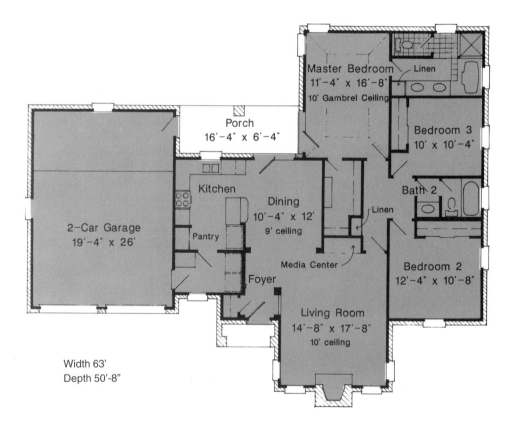

Width 63'
Depth 50'-8"

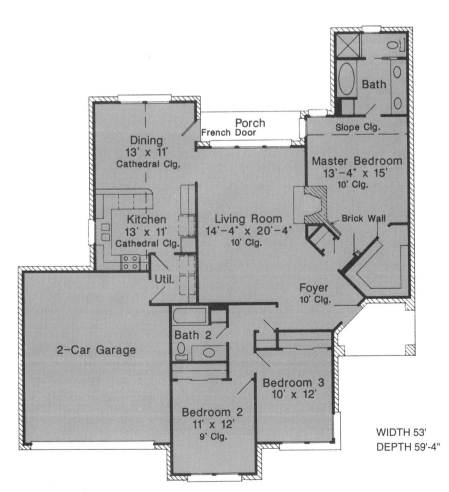

Design S9118

Square Footage: 1,661

● With the living room as its hub, this one-story is perfect for casual family living and formal entertaining alike. The entry foyer is angled and separates the master suite from family bedrooms. The dining room has a cathedral ceiling and French door to the rear porch. The two-car garage can be reached through the service entrance at the utility room which conveniently attaches to the U-shaped kitchen.

Design by
**Larry W.
Garnett &
Associates, Inc.**

WIDTH 53'
DEPTH 59'-4"

Design by
Larry W.
Garnett &
Associates, Inc.

QUOTE ONE®
Cost to build? See page 216
to order complete cost estimate
to build this house in your area!

Design S9088

Square Footage: 1,994

● This charming budget-conscious design provides an abundance of living space. Radiating around the roomy kitchen are the dining room with ten-foot ceiling and living room with French doors and fireplace. A glass-surrounded breakfast area near the kitchen provides space for casual eating. Three bedrooms, all with walk-in closets, dominate the left wing of the home. Bedroom 2 has an eleven-foot sloped ceiling. The master suite features a corner tub and a glass-enclosed shower with seat. Note the large utility room and storage space in the garage.

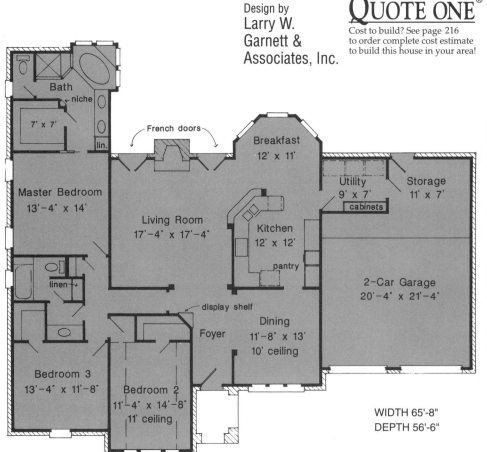

Bath
niche
7' x 7'
lin.
French doors
Breakfast
12' x 11'
Master Bedroom
13'-4" x 14'
Living Room
17'-4" x 17'-4"
Utility
9' x 7'
Storage
11' x 7'
cabinets
Kitchen
12' x 12'
pantry
linen
2-Car Garage
20'-4" x 21'-4"
display shelf
Dining
11'-8" x 13'
10' ceiling
Foyer
Bedroom 3
13'-4" x 11'-8"
Bedroom 2
11'-4" x 14'-8"
11' ceiling

WIDTH 65'-8"
DEPTH 56'-6"

Design by
Larry W.
Garnett &
Associates, Inc.

Bath

Porch

Breakfast
10' x 10'

2-Car Garage

Master Bedroom
13'-8" x 16'
11' Vaulted Clg.

Dining
11'-4" x 13'-8"
10' Clg.

Kitchen
12' x 13'-4"

42" Wall

Util.

Bath 2

Living Room
18'-4" x 17'
9'-6" Clg.

Bedroom 2
11'-4" x 10'-4"

Foyer

Bedroom 3
11'-4" x 10'-8"
10' Clg.

Width 64'
Depth 50' - 10"

Quote One®

Cost to build? See page 216
to order complete cost estimate
to build this house in your area!

Design S9028
Square Footage: 1,707

● No slouch on amenities, this plan is a popular
choice with those looking for a smaller sized
home. The openness of the floor plan makes it
seem much larger than it really is. Note, for
example the high ceilings in the living room
and master bedroom and the short front wall
defining the dining area. A bay-windowed
breakfast room opens the kitchen area (don't
miss the attached porch for outdoor dining).
Three bedrooms include a large master suite.
The laundry area is conveniently located near
the bedrooms and shared bath.

13

Design S9027

Square Footage: 1,822

● This is a beautiful one-story plan and one that will adequately serve family needs in a limited amount of space. A central living area with fireplace acts as the hub of the plan, opening up from the front foyer. Close by are the efficient kitchen and dining area. Three bedrooms are grouped together to the left side of the plan. The master suite demands close attention to its many amenities: fireplace, French doors to a rear terrace, and a luxurious bath with oversized shower. A two-car garage features utility room space and a storage area.

Design by
Larry W.
Garnett &
Associates, Inc.

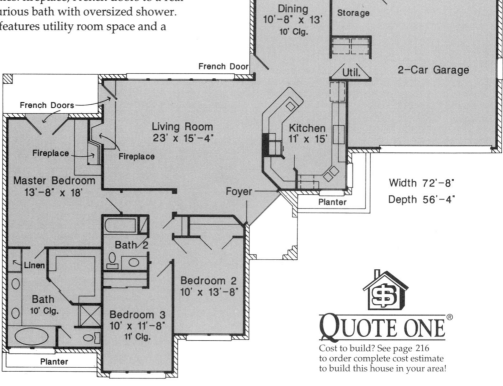

Width 72'-8"
Depth 56'-4"

Quote One®
Cost to build? See page 216
to order complete cost estimate
to build this house in your area!

Design by
Larry W.
Garnett &
Associates, Inc.

Cost to build? See page 216
to order complete cost estimate
to build this house in your area!

Design S9098
Square Footage: 1,996

● Living and working areas to the right, sleeping quarters to the left — that's the design of this home. To the rear is a long covered porch reached through the living room and master suite. The foyer is raised above the living room and dining room a few steps. A profusion of glass in the breakfast room and hall lights up these areas. Two family bedrooms share a full bath with double lavatories.

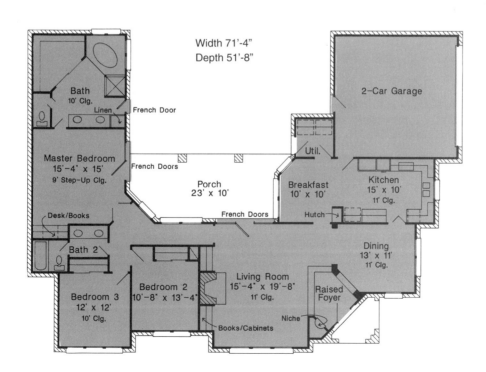

Design S9089
Square Footage: 1,849

● A wonderful floor plan is found on the interior of this cozy one-story plan. The large living room and conveniently placed dining room both open from the raised foyer. In between is the galley kitchen with huge pantry and attached breakfast area. French doors flanking the fireplace in the living room open to the rear yard. To the right of the plan is the master bedroom with walk-in closet and double lavatories. To the left of the plan are two family bedrooms sharing a full bath in between.

Cost to build? See page 216 to order complete cost estimate to build this house in your area!

WIDTH 60'
DEPTH 57'-4"

Design by
Larry W. Garnett & Associates, Inc.

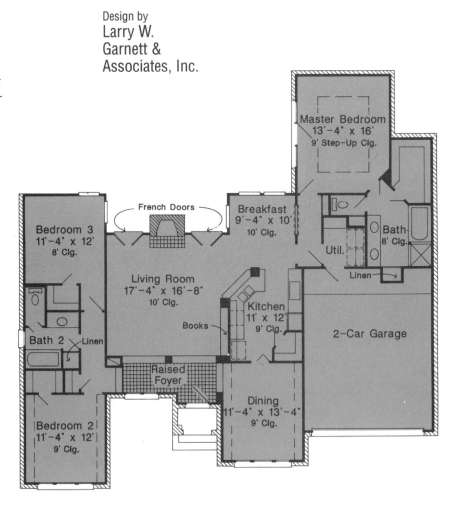

Master Bedroom
13'-4" x 16'
9' Step-Up Clg.

French Doors

Breakfast
9'-4" x 10'
10' Clg.

Bath
8' Clg.

Util.

Linen

Bedroom 3
11'-4" x 12'
8' Clg.

Living Room
17'-4" x 16'-8"
10' Clg.

Kitchen
11' x 12'
9' Clg.

2-Car Garage

Books

Bath 2   Linen

Raised Foyer

Dining
11'-4" x 13'-4"
9' Clg.

Bedroom 2
11'-4" x 12'
9' Clg.

Design S8923

Square Footage: 2,361

● The combination of finely detailed brick and shingle siding recalls some of the distinctive architecture of the East Coast during the early part of this century. The foyer and gallery provide for a functional traffic pattern. The formal dining room to the front of the home is outlined by columns and features a 13-foot ceiling. The extensive living area offers a corner fireplace. A screened porch surrounding the breakfast room is an ideal entertainment area. The master suite features two spacious closets and a bath with a garden tub and an oversized shower. Bedroom 4 can serve as a study, nursery, guest room or home office.

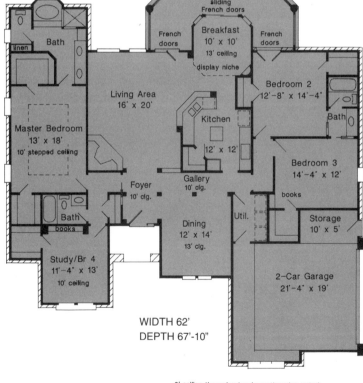

Screened Porch

sliding French doors

French doors

Breakfast
10' x 10'
13' ceiling

French doors

display niche

Bath

linen

Living Area
16' x 20'

Bedroom 2
12'-8" x 14'-4"

Bath

Master Bedroom
13' x 18'
10' stepped ceiling

Kitchen
12' x 12'

Bedroom 3
14'-4" x 12'

books

Foyer
10' clg.

Gallery
10' clg.

Util.

Storage
10' x 5'

Bath

books

Dining
12' x 14'
13' clg.

2-Car Garage
21'-4" x 19'

Study/Br 4
11'-4" x 13'
10' ceiling

WIDTH 62'
DEPTH 67'-10"

9' ceiling throughout unless otherwise noted

Design by
Larry W.
Garnett &
Associates, Inc.

Quote One®

Cost to build? See page 216
to order complete cost estimate
to build this house in your area!

Design S8611

Square Footage: 1,413

● An angled side entry to this home allows for a majestic, arched window that dominates its facade. The interior, though small in square footage, holds an interesting and efficient floor plan. Because the breakfast room is placed to the front of the plan, it benefits from two large, multi-paned windows. The dining and family rooms form a single space enhanced by a volume ceiling and an optional fireplace, which is flanked by sets of optional double doors. Both the family room and master bedroom boast access

to the covered patio. A volume ceiling further enhances the master bedroom, which also has a dressing area, walk-in closet and full bath. The plans include options for a family room with corner fireplace, fireplace with French doors or a sliding glass door instead of a fireplace. The package includes plans for three different elevations!

Design by
Home Design Services, Inc.

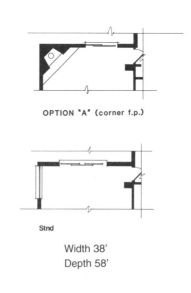

OPTION "A" (corner f.p.)

Stnd

Width 38'
Depth 58'

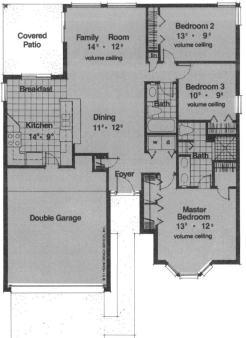

Covered Patio

Family Room
14⁰ · 12⁰
volume ceiling

Bedroom 2
13⁰ · 9⁰
volume ceiling

Breakfast

Bedroom 3
10⁰ · 9⁰
volume ceiling

Bath

Kitchen
14⁰ · 9⁰

Dining
11⁰ · 12⁰

w d

Bath

Foyer

Double Garage

Master Bedroom
13⁰ · 12⁰
volume ceiling

Design S8610
Square Footage: 1,280

● This plan is ideal for the young family that needs a house that's small but smart. As in larger plans, this home boasts a private master's retreat with lots of closet space, dual vanities and a shower. The living area embraces the outdoor living space. The family eat-in kitchen design allows for efficient food preparation. Note the interior laundry closet located close to the sleeping area. This plan comes with three options for Bedroom 2 and one option for the master bath. It also includes blueprints for three elevation choices!

WIDTH 40'
DEPTH 48'

Design by
Home Design Services, Inc.

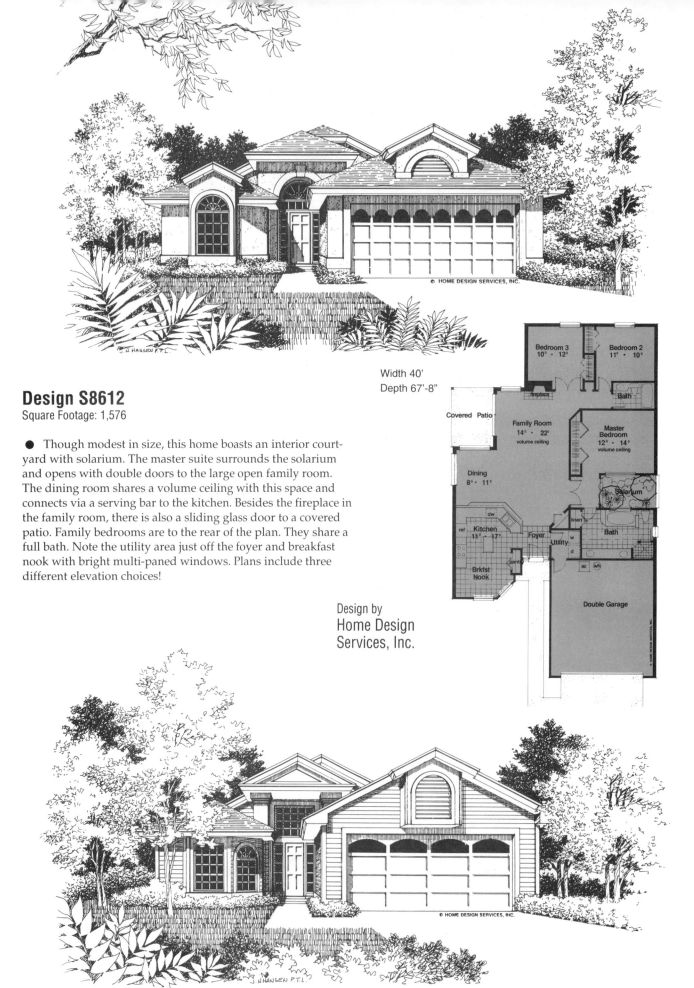

Design S8612
Square Footage: 1,576

● Though modest in size, this home boasts an interior courtyard with solarium. The master suite surrounds the solarium
and opens with double doors to the large open family room.
The dining room shares a volume ceiling with this space and
connects via a serving bar to the kitchen. Besides the fireplace in
the family room, there is also a sliding glass door to a covered
patio. Family bedrooms are to the rear of the plan. They share a
full bath. Note the utility area just off the foyer and breakfast
nook with bright multi-paned windows. Plans include three
different elevation choices!

Width 40'
Depth 67'-8"

Design by
Home Design
Services, Inc.

Bedroom 3
10⁰ · 12⁰

Bedroom 2
11⁰ · 10⁰

Covered Patio

fireplace

Bath

Family Room
14⁰ · 22⁰
volume ceiling

Master
Bedroom
12⁰ · 14⁰
volume ceiling

Dining
8⁰ · 11⁰

Solarium

dw

linen

ref

Kitchen
11⁰ · 17⁰

Foyer

Utility

Bath

Brkfst
Nook

pantry

ac w/h

Double Garage

© HOME DESIGN SERVICES, INC.

← 40'-0" →

Master Bed Rm.
13⁰ · 17⁰
vault or 10' flat

Covered Patio

Breakfast
11⁹ · 8⁴

Kitchen

Shelf @ 42"

shelf

Bath

lin

wic

Family Rm.
14⁸ · 23⁰
vault or 10' flat

Dining Rm.
vault or 10' flat

36" Pre-Fab Fireplace

Bed Rm. 2
13¹⁰ · 9⁶
vault or 10' flat

Living
vault or 10' flat

Plant Shelf Abv.

Ba.

Foyer

wh | A/C | W | D

A/C

Entry

Bed Rm. 3
13¹⁰ · 11⁰
vault or 10' flat

Double Garage

© HOME DESIGN SERVICES, INC.

Design S8613

Square Footage: 1,872

● Vaulted ceilings throughout this home suggest the innovative touches that add interest in a single-level plan. Sidelight and overhead windows brighten a foyer that opens to the family and living rooms. A plant shelf spans the entry into the living room, which is united with the dining room under a high ceiling. A vaulted ceiling also augments the family room. Notice the two-way fireplace and access to a covered patio here. The kitchen is convenient to the dining room and to a bayed breakfast nook. The master bedroom also has a bay window plus a full bath with oversized shower. Two additional bedrooms share a full bath. Plans include two different elevation choices!

Design by
Home Design
Services, Inc.

© HOME DESIGN SERVICES, INC.

Design S8605

Square Footage: 2,171

● This four-bedroom, three-bath home is designed to minimize wasted space, such as hallways. There are loads of living options especially in the placement of the secondary bedrooms. Bedroom 2 can be a much needed mother-in-law room, with semi-private bath that doubles as a pool bath for outdoor living. The classic family room/nook area and kitchen work well together for convenient living. The secluded living room and bay-windowed dining room are a special bonus for formal entertaining. The master suite provides the best of everything from twin vanities to handy linen storage. There's also a huge walk-in closet and private commode. The interior architecture of this home boasts soaring vaulted ceilings throughout.

Design by
Home Design
Services, Inc.

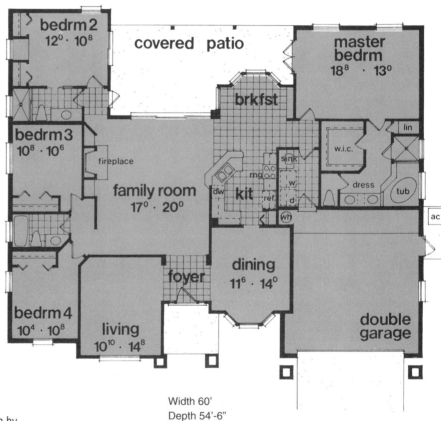

Width 60'
Depth 54'-6"

Design S8667

Square Footage: 2,258

● Columns add the finishing touches to a home with a choice of facades. The double-door entry opens to the foyer with a front-to-back view. The adjacent vaulted living room has sliding glass doors to the covered patio. The kitchen is open to the living room, the formal dining room and the bayed nook. A bow window and a fireplace define the rear of the family room. The tray-ceilinged master bedroom features covered patio access, dual walk-in closets and a spa tub with spectacular window treatment. Two additional bedrooms share a full bath with a bumped-out window. A study adjacent to the master bedroom, with a full bath nearby, can be turned into a fourth bedroom if needed. This plan includes both elevations.

Width 66'
Depth 73'-4"

Design by
Home Design
Services, Inc.

23

Design S8606

Square Footage: 2,253

● Brick detailing makes an elegant statement in this one-story contemporary; large multi-paned windows add a touch of distinction. Past the front-facing living room and tiled foyer, the large family room is provided extra dimension by its high volume ceiling and corner fireplace. A tiled breakfast nook and kitchen are separated by a convenient eating bar; nearby is the formal dining room. The master bedroom features a walk-in closet, U-shaped dressing area with double vanity and a full bath. Two additional large bedrooms, each with a walk-in closet, share a full bath with double vanity. This plan includes a concrete slab foundation.

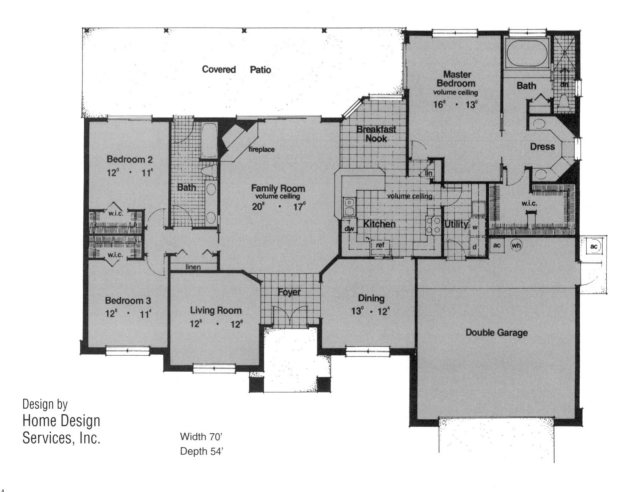

Design by
Home Design
Services, Inc.

Width 70'
Depth 54'

Width 58'-6"
Depth 74'

**Design by
Home Design
Services, Inc.**

Design S8645
Square Footage: 2,224

● Arches crowned by gentle, hipped rooflines provide an Italianate charm in this bright, spacious, family-oriented plan. A covered entry leads to the foyer that presents the angular, vaulted living and dining rooms. A wet bar in the living room enhances livability. A kitchen with V-shape counter includes a walk-in pantry and looks out over the breakfast nook and family room with a fireplace. The master suite features a sitting area, two walk-in closets and a full bath with garden tub. Two additional bedrooms share a full bath located between them. A fourth bedroom, with its own bath, opens off the family room and works perfectly as a guest room.

Design S9256

Square Footage: 1,347

● Though it may appear oversized, this plan is really quite compact and economical. From the ten-foot ceiling in the entry to the spacious great room with fireplace, it has an open feeling. A snack bar and pantry in the kitchen complement the work area. Bright windows light up the entire breakfast area. To the left side of the plan are three bedrooms, two of which share a full bath. The master suite has a boxed window, built-in bookcase and tiered ceiling. The skylit dressing area features a double vanity and there's a whirlpool in the bath.

Design by
**Design
Basics,
Inc.**

© 1990 design basics inc.

Design by
Design
Basics,
Inc.

Design S9328
Square Footage: 1,496

● Sleek roof lines, lap siding and brick accents highlight the exterior of this three-bedroom ranch home. A tiled entry views the spacious great room featuring a sloping cathedral ceiling and window-framed fireplace. Note the strategic location of the dining room (with nine-foot boxed ceiling and wet bar/servery) which accommodates formal entertaining and family gatherings. Natural light and warmth add comfort to the bayed breakfast area with pantry, handy planning desk and the peninsula kitchen. Well-segregated sleeping quarters add to the flexibility of this modern floor plan. Both secondary bedrooms share a full bath and linen closet. Bedroom 3 is easily converted to a den or home office. With the nine-foot-high boxed ceiling, walk-in closet, sunlit whirlpool tub and double vanities, the master suite is soothing and luxurious.

w/p

Bfst.
10⁰ x 12⁰
snack bar

Kit.
9³ x 10⁰

DESK

Grt. rm.
14⁴ x 19⁰

Mbr.
13⁰ x 13⁰
9'-0"
CEILING

LIN.

R.   P.
WET BAR

Din.
13⁰ x 10⁰
9'-0" CLG.

CATHEDRAL CEILING

W
D

52'-0"

DN

LIN.

Gar.
19³ x 22⁸

Br.3
10⁰ x 10²
OPTIONAL DEN
9'-0" CLG.

Br.2
10⁴ x 10⁰

COVERED
STOOP

48'-0"

© design basics inc. 1991

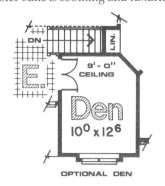

DN   LIN.
9'-0"
CEILING

Den
10⁰ x 12⁶

OPTIONAL DEN

27

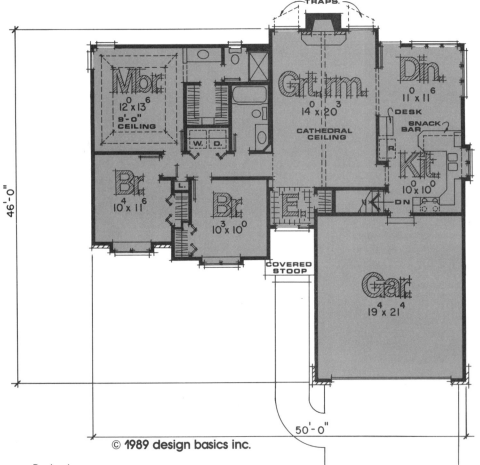

Design S9236
Square Footage: 1,271

● This charmingly snug three-bedroom home offers all the many features you've been looking for in a family home. The great room has a lovely cathedral ceiling and a fireplace surrounded by windows. Nearby is the dining area and efficient kitchen with window box, planning desk, lazy Susan and snack bar counter. Intriguing ceiling treatment dominates the master bedroom where you'll also find corner windows, a dressing area with large vanity, a walk-in closet and a compartmented stool and shower. Two family bedrooms share a full bath and are located near the laundry room.

Design by
Design Basics, Inc.

Quote One®

Cost to build? See page 216 to order complete cost estimate to build this house in your area!

Design S9200
Square Footage: 1,604

● Thoughtful arrangement makes this uncomplicated three-bedroom plan comfortable. The living and working areas are grouped together for convenience — a great room with cathedral ceiling, dining room with wet bar pass-through and kitchen with breakfast room. The sleeping area features a spacious master suite with skylit bath and whirlpool and large walk-in closet. Two secondary bedrooms accommodate the rest of the family. An alternate elevation is available at no extra cost.

8'-8" CEILING

Mbr
13⁰ x 14⁰

Grt. rm.
15⁰ x 20⁰

Bfst.
9¹⁰x12⁷

WET BAR

DESK

Kit.
9⁶x10⁷

SKYLIGHT

W/P

CATHEDRAL CEILING

9'-0" CEILING

Dn.
13⁰ x 11⁰

L.

DN

HUTCH

W.

D.

Br.
10⁸ x 10³

Br.
11⁰ x 10⁰

Gar
19⁴ x 23⁰

COVERED STOOP

48'-0"

48'-8"

© 1989 design basics inc.

Design by
Design Basics, Inc.

29

Quote One®

Cost to build? See page 216 to order complete cost estimate to build this house in your area!

Design by
Design Basics, Inc.

Design S9204

Square Footage: 1,911

● This sophisticated three-bedroom, ranch with Palladian entry is a welcome addition to any neighborhood. Off the entry are the dining room with twelve-foot detailed ceiling and arched window and the enormous great room which shares a through-fireplace with the hearth room. The well-planned kitchen features a spacious work area, with snack bar pass-through to the breakfast area. The private master suite features a detailed ceiling, corner windows, whirlpool bath and giant walk-in closet. Two family bedrooms are placed on the other side of the plan to ensure peace and quiet. An alternate elevation is available at no extra cost.

© 1989 design basics inc.

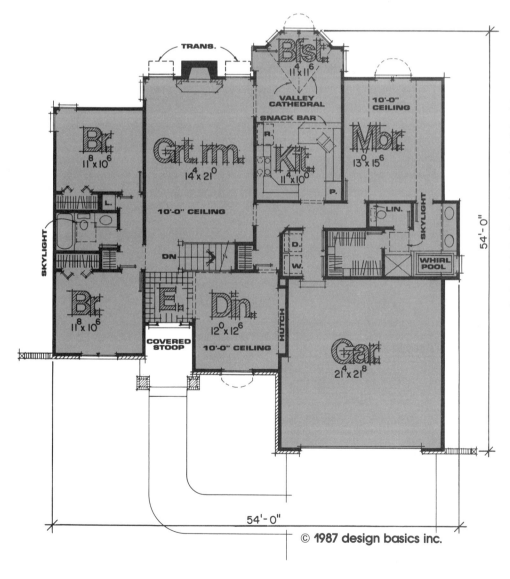

Design S9237

Square Footage: 1,697

● This volume-look home gives the impression of size and scope in just under 1,700 square feet. The large great room with fireplace is perfect for entertaining. Its proximity to the kitchen, with breakfast room, and to the formal dining room ensures easy serving and clean-ups. Besides a large walk-in closet, other features in the master bedroom include a whirlpool tub, double vanity, skylit dressing area, and convenient linen storage. Two family bedrooms share a full bath with skylight and offer ample closet space.

Design by
Design Basics, Inc.

31

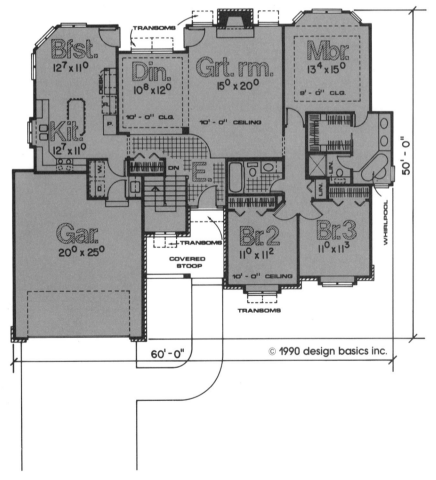

Bfst.
12⁷ x 11⁰

Din.
10⁸ x 12⁰

Grt. rm.
15⁰ x 20⁰

Mbr.
13⁴ x 15⁰
9' - 0" CLG.

Kit.
12⁷ x 11⁰

DESK

P.

10' - 0" CLG.

10' - 0" CEILING

TRANSOMS

D. W.

DN

WHIRLPOOL

LIN.

LIN.

LIN.

Gar.
20⁰ x 25⁰

Br. 2
11⁰ x 11²

Br. 3
11⁰ x 11³

COVERED
STOOP

TRANSOMS

10' - 0" CEILING

TRANSOMS

50' - 0"

60' - 0"

© 1990 design basics inc.

Design S9257
Square Footage: 1,735

● A covered porch at the entry to this home welcomes family and guests alike. Ten-foot ceilings at the entry foyer, great room and dining room give a feeling of open spaciousness to living areas. The formal dining room sits between the kitchen area and great room—a perfect spot for entertaining. Note service entrance with laundry just off the kitchen en route to the garage. Three bedrooms include two secondary bedrooms with shared bath and a master suite with elegant bayed window and bath with angled whirlpool, double vanity and walk-in closet. An open staircase in the entry allows for the possibility of a finished basement area in the future.

Design by
Design
Basics,
Inc.

Design S9202

Square Footage: 1,808

● Discriminating buyers will love the refined yet inviting look of this three-bedroom ranch plan. A tiled entry with ten-foot ceilings leads into the spacious great room with large bay window. An open-hearth fireplace warms both the great room and kitchen. The sleeping area features a large master suite with dramatic arched window and bath with whirlpool, His and Hers vanities and walk-in closet. Don't miss the storage space in the oversized garage.

Design by
**Design
Basics,
Inc.**

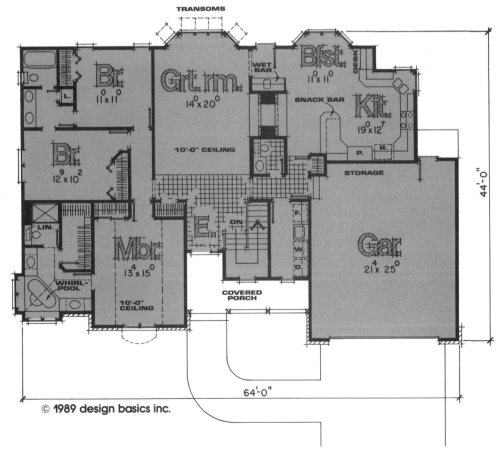

TRANSOMS

Br.
11 x 11

Grt. rm.
14⁰ x 20⁰

Bfst.
11⁰ x 11⁰

WET BAR

DESK

SNACK BAR

Kit.
19⁰ x 12⁷

10'-0" CEILING

Br.
12 x 10

STORAGE

R.

P.

LIN.

Mbr.
13⁴ x 15⁰

DN

F.

W.
D.

Gar.
21⁴ x 25⁰

WHIRL-POOL

10'-0"
CEILING

COVERED PORCH

44'-0"

64'-0"

© 1989 design basics inc.

33

Design S9431
Square Footage: 1,316

● An exceptional use of cedar shingles, horizontal cedar siding and brick highlights the exterior of this one-story home. And the floor plan is bursting with amenities found normally on much larger homes. Note, for example, the dramatically vaulted great room with the plant shelf floating across the entry. The master bedroom is also vaulted. The covered patio lends itself to great outdoor living even in inclement weather. Opening off the entry with a pair of French doors is a den which could be used as a third bedroom.

◀ 46' ▶

▲
50'
▼

COVERED PATIO

DINING
10/0 X 10/4

VAULTED
GREAT RM.
15/0 X 15/0

VAULTED
MASTER
12/0 X 15/0

PLANT SHELF

9/6 X 11/8

LIN.

P.

VAULTED
DEN/ BR. 3
11/0 X 11/0 +/-

BR. 2
12/8 X 10/0

GARAGE
19/4 X 21/8

Design by
Alan Mascord
Design Associates, Inc.

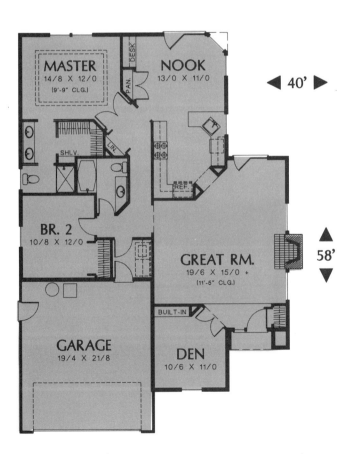

MASTER
14/8 X 12/0
(9'-9" CLG.)

NOOK
13/0 X 11/0

◄ 40' ►

BR. 2
10/8 X 12/0

GREAT RM.
19/6 X 15/0 +
(11'-5" CLG.)

▲
58'
▼

BUILT-IN

GARAGE
19/4 X 21/8

DEN
10/6 X 11/0

Design S9508
Square Footage: 1,523

● The repeated roof treatments and varying exterior materials add interest to this darling home. Inside, the great room commands attention with its fireplace, high ceiling and overall spaciousness. Double doors lead to a den where built-ins enhance an already attractive room—perfect for quiet getaways. A built-in desk adds to the inviting character of the kitchen and breakfast nook. The great room could easily support a formal dining area serviced by the angular kitchen passageway. The sleeping quarters consist of a master suite with a private bath and a walk-in closet, and a secondary bedroom for family or guests. A utility area ties the house and garage together well.

Design by
Alan Mascord
Design Associates, Inc.

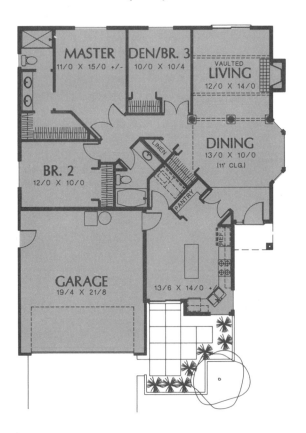

◀ 42' ▶

MASTER
11/0 X 15/0 +/-

DEN/BR. 3
10/0 X 10/4

VAULTED
LIVING
12/0 X 14/0

BR. 2
12/0 X 10/0

LINEN

DINING
13/0 X 10/0
[11' CLG.]

PANTRY

GARAGE
19/4 X 21/8

REF.

13/6 X 14/0 +/-

▲
50'
▼

Design S9429
Square Footage: 1,367

● Featuring a combination of cedar shingles and vertical cedar siding, this ranch home has a compact, convenient floor plan. Both kitchen and nook face the front where a courtyard wall provides privacy for outdoor relaxation. The entry and dining room both have eleven-foot ceilings, allowing for attractive transom windows. This area is also enhanced by a series of columns separating the vaulted living room from the dining room. Opening off the hallway with a pair of French doors is a den which could be used as a third bedroom.

Design by
Alan Mascord
Design Associates, Inc.

36

Width 50'
Depth 52'-10"

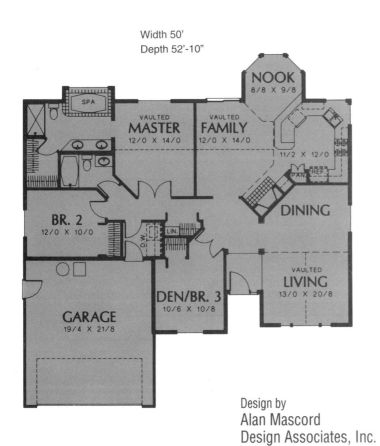

NOOK
8/8 X 9/8

VAULTED
MASTER
12/0 X 14/0

VAULTED
FAMILY
12/0 X 14/0

SPA

11/2 X 12/0

PAN REF.

DINING

BR. 2
12/0 X 10/0

LIN.

D.W.

GARAGE
19/4 X 21/8

DEN/BR. 3
10/6 X 10/8

VAULTED
LIVING
13/0 X 20/8

Design by
Alan Mascord
Design Associates, Inc.

Design S9403

Square Footage: 1,565

● If you're looking for a traditional-styled ranch, this one with front-facing gables and a combination of cedar shingles and vertical cedar siding may be just right for you. The vaulted living room faces the street and is set off with a gorgeous Palladian window. The family room (note angled fireplace here) and master bedroom also have vaulted ceilings. Look for a spa tub, large shower and walk-in closet in the master bedroom. Through French doors in the entry is a den that could be used as a third bedroom.

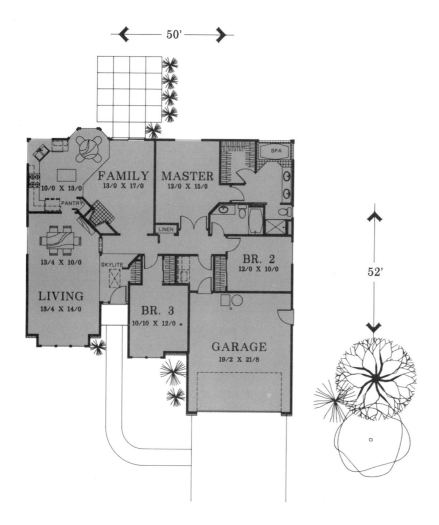

50'

FAMILY
13/0 X 17/0

MASTER
12/0 X 15/0

SPA

10/0 X 13/0

PANTRY

13/4 X 10/0

LINEN

SKYLITE

BR. 2
12/0 X 10/0

LIVING
13/4 X 14/0

BR. 3
10/10 X 12/0

GARAGE
19/2 X 21/8

52'

Design S9427
Square Footage: 1,687

● Intriguing roof lines create a dynamic exterior for this home. It is even further enhanced by a tasteful accenting of brick. The interior floor plan is equally attractive. Towards the rear a wide archway forms the entrance to the spacious family living area with its centrally placed fireplace and bay-windowed nook area. An island and a walk-in pantry complete the efficient kitchen (note the corner window treatment overlooking the yard). This home also boasts a terrific master suite complete with walk-in wardrobe, spa tub with corner windows and a compartmentalized shower and toilet area.

Design by
**Alan Mascord
Design Associates, Inc.**

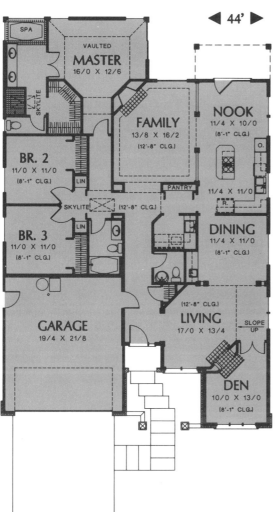

44'

66'

SPA

VAULTED
MASTER
16/0 X 12/6

FAMILY
13/8 X 16/2
(12'-8" CLG.)

NOOK
11/4 X 10/0
(8'-1" CLG.)

SKYLITE

BR. 2
11/0 X 11/0
(8'-1" CLG.)

LIN

PANTRY

11/4 X 11/0

SKYLITE   (12'-8" CLG.)

BR. 3
11/0 X 11/0
(8'-1" CLG.)

LIN

DINING
11/4 X 11/0
(8'-1" CLG.)

R.

(12'-8" CLG.)

GARAGE
19/4 X 21/8

LIVING
17/0 X 13/4

SLOPE
UP

DEN
10/0 X 13/0
(8'-1" CLG.)

Design S9451
Square Footage: 2,089

● This one-story design gives a
sense of space with dramatic raised
ceilings in the entry, master suite,
living room and family room.
Formal living dominates the front of
the plan but flows gracefully to
more casual family living at the rear.
Corner fireplaces in both areas add
warmth and coziness. The bedrooms
are to the left of the plan and include
family sleeping quarters in addition
to the luxurious master suite.

Design by
Alan Mascord
Design Associates, Inc.

Design by
Design Traditions

Design S9839 Square Footage: 1,800 (without basement)

● This European-inspired cottage contains one of the most efficient floor plans available. From the formal dining room at the front of the plan to the commodious great room at the rear, it accommodates various lifestyles in less than 2,000 square feet. An opulent master suite with deck access and grand bath dominates the right wing of the house. Two family bedrooms and a full bath are found to the left. There's even a powder room for guests. The gourmet-style kitchen has an attached breakfast area with glassed bay for sunny brunches. Bonus space in the basement allows for future development.

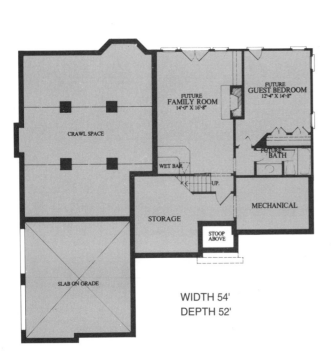

DECK

BREAKFAST
11'-4" X 8'-6"

BEDROOM NO. 3
11'-6" X 11'-0"

GREAT ROOM
14'-0" X 17'-6"

KITCHEN
11'-4" X 10'-0"

MASTER
BEDROOM
12'-4" X 15'-6"

BATH

HIS

FOYER
6'-6" X 5'-0"

DN

BEDROOM NO. 2
11'-0" X 12'-2"

STOOP

DINING ROOM
11'-4" X 10'-6"

PWDR.

MASTER
BATH

LAUNDRY

HERS

TWO-CAR GARAGE
20'-4" X 19'-4"

WORKSHOP/
STORAGE

FUTURE
FAMILY ROOM
14'-0" X 17'-6"

FUTURE
GAME ROOM
11'-4" X 18'-6"

FUTURE
GUEST BEDROOM
11'-10" X 14'-6"

MECHANICAL

STOOP
ABOVE

UP.

FUTURE
BATH

STORAGE

SLAB ON GRADE

Design S9840
Square Footage: 1,684

Quote One®
Cost to build? See page 216
to order complete cost estimate
to build this house in your area!

Width 55'-6"
Depth 57'-6"

● Charmingly compact, this one-story home is as beautiful as it is practical. The impressive arch over the double front door is repeated with an arched window in the formal dining room. This room opens to a spacious great room with fireplace and is nearby the kitchen and bayed breakfast area. Split sleeping arrangements put the master suite with His and Hers walk-in closets at the right of the plan and two family bedrooms at the left. Additional space in the basement can later be developed as the family grows.

Design by
Design Traditions

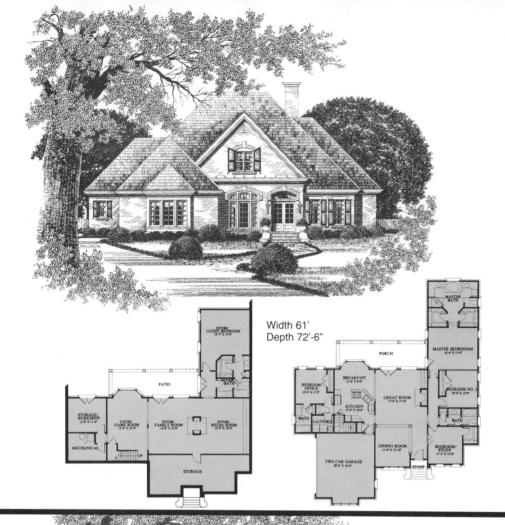

Design S9844

Square Footage: 2,090
(without basement)

● Grace and elegance in one-story living abound in this Traditional English Country home. It contains all the necessary elements of a convenient floor plan as well: great room with fireplace, formal dining room, kitchen with attached breakfast nook, guest room/office, three bedrooms including a master suite. A large unfinished basement area allows for future expansion.

Design by
Design Traditions

Cost to build? See page 216 to order complete cost estimate to build this house in your area!

Width 61'
Depth 72'-6"

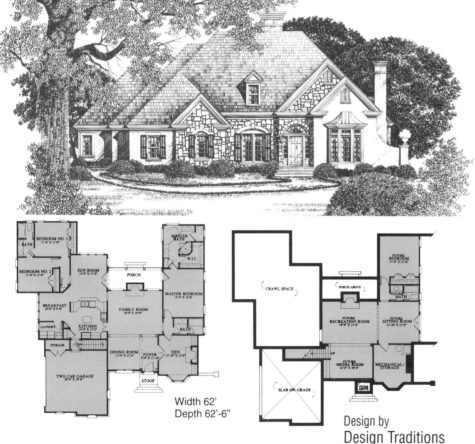

Design S9843

Square Footage: 2,120
(without basement)

● As quaint as the European countryside, this charming cottage boasts a unique interior. Living patterns revolve around the central family room—notice the placement of the formal dining room, kitchen with attached breakfast nook and sun room. Family bedrooms are tucked quietly away to the rear, while the master suite maintains privacy at the opposite end of the plan. A den with fireplace attaches to the master bedroom or can be accessed from the entry foyer. Bonus space in the basement can be developed later.

Width 62'
Depth 62'-6"

Design by
Design Traditions

Copyright 1992 Stephen S. Fuller, Inc.

PORCH

BREAKFAST
10'-0" X 10'-0"

GREAT ROOM
16'-0" X 18'-0"

MASTER BEDROOM
15'-0" X 14'-0"

W.I.C.

MASTER BATH

POWDER

KITCHEN
14'-0" X 11'-4"

BEDROOM NO. 2
11'-2" X 11'-0"

FOYER
5'-0" X 9'-0"

BEDROOM
NO. 3
10'-6" X 10'-0"

DINING ROOM
10'-6" X 13'-0"

BATH

LAUND
5'-2" X
10'-6"

DN.

TWO CAR GARAGE
20'-4" X 19'-4"

WIDTH 60'
DEPTH 58'-6"

Design by
Design Traditions

QUOTE ONE®

Cost to build? See page 216
to order complete cost estimate
to build this house in your area!

Design S9872

Square Footage: 1,815

● The approach to this European home has an inviting quality about it. The stucco exterior with arched detail on the windows furthers the feel of style and grace while the front door adds a majestic touch to an already stately presence. Inside, the foyer opens into the great room with a vaulted ceiling and a dining room defined by an asymmetrical column arrangement. Kitchen tasks are made easy with this home's step-saving kitchen and breakfast bar. Nestled away at the opposite end of the home, the master suite combines perfect solitude with elegant luxury. Features include a double door entry, tray ceiling, niche detail and private rear deck. Additional bedrooms and bath are provided for children and guests.

WIDTH 64'
DEPTH 64'-4"

Quote One®

Cost to build? See page 216
to order complete cost estimate
to build this house in your area!

Design by
Design Traditions

Design S9831
Square Footage: 2,150

● This home draws its inspiration from both French and English country homes. From the arched covered entry to the jack-arch window, it has the distinction of a much larger home. Beginning at the dramatic entrance, this home has an openness that flows gracefully from room to room. From the foyer and across the spacious great room, French doors and a large side window give a generous view of the covered rear porch. The adjoining dining room is subtly defined by the use of columns and a large triple window. The accommodating kitchen, with its generous work island, adjoins the breakfast area and keeping room with a fireplace, a vaulted ceiling and an abundant use of windows. A bedroom to the front of the first floor may act as guest quarters. Another bedroom shares a bath with this one. The home is completed by a quiet master suite located at the rear. It contains a bay window, a garden tub and His and Hers vanities. Space on the lower level can be developed later into recreation space and additional bedrooms. This home is designed with a basement foundation.

Quote One®

Cost to build? See page 216 to order complete cost estimate to build this house in your area!

Design by
Design Traditions

Design S9874

Square Footage: 2,095

● The interesting shape of the flared eaves creates a natural cover for the front entry, establishing the focal point of this one-level brick traditional home. Inside, the foyer opens to the living room defined through the use of columns and the large dining room accented by dramatic window detail. A butler pantry is strategically located just off the kitchen to provide ease of access when entertaining. The open family room displays a fireplace and built-in cabinetry for added storage. A wall of windows in the family room leads to the octagon-shaped breakfast area and deck outside. The right wing of this home features the master bedroom with bright window arrangement and tray ceiling detail. The large master bath with dual vanities, jacuzzi tub and shower is complete with a spacious walk-in closet. On the opposite side of the home are two additional bedrooms, each having their own vanity while sharing a tub area.

DECK

BREAKFAST
11'-4" X 9'-4"

BATH

BEDROOM NO. 2
11'-0" X 12'-0"

KITCHEN
10'-8" X 12'-2"

FAMILY ROOM
17'-8" X 15'-4"

MASTER BEDROOM
13'-8" X 15'-4"

DN.

BEDROOM NO. 3
11'-0" X 12'-0"

LAUNDRY

POWDER

MASTER BATH

FOYER
6'-0" X 12'-0"

LIVING ROOM
11'-4" X 14'-0"

W.I.C.

DINING ROOM
11'-8" X 15'-0"

STOOP

TWO CAR GARAGE
20'-4" X 19'-10"

Width 65'
Depth 55'-11"

Design S9862

Square Footage: 2,170

● This classic cottage features a stone and wooden exterior with an arch-detailed porch and box-bay window. From the foyer, double doors open to the den with built-in bookcases and a fireplace. A full bath is situated next to the den, allowing for an optional guest room. The family room is centrally located, just beyond the foyer. Its hearth is framed by windows overlooking the porch at the rear of the home. The master bedroom opens onto the rear porch. The master bath, with a large walk-in closet, double vanities, a corner tub and a separate shower and water closet completes this relaxing retreat. Left of the family room awaits a sun room with access to the covered porch. A breakfast area complements the attractive and efficiently designed kitchen. A short hallway from the sun room leads to two bedrooms with large closets and a shared full bath featuring double vanities. This home is designed with a basement foundation.

Design by
Design Traditions

QUOTE ONE®
Cost to build? See page 216 to order complete cost estimate to build this house in your area!

BEDROOM NO. 3
11'-6" X 11'-0"

BATH

BEDROOM NO. 2
11'-4" X 11'-0"

SUN ROOM
12'-0" X 13'-8"

PORCH

MASTER
BATH

W.I.C.

PORCH

BREAKFAST
10'-0" X 9'-0"

FAMILY ROOM
18'-0" X 14'-0"

MASTER BEDROOM
13'-4" X 15'-6"

LAUNDRY

KITCHEN
12'-0" X 13'-2"

BATH

STORAGE

DN

DINING ROOM
11'-4" X 11'-4"

FOYER
6'-8" X 11'-10"

TWO CAR GARAGE
20'-4" X 19'-8"

PORCH

DEN/GUEST
BEDROOM
11'-4" X 14'-0"

Width 62'-4"
Depth 62'-2"

Design by
Design Traditions

Design S9853
Square Footage: 2,090

● This traditional home features board and batten and cedar shingles in an attractively proportioned exterior. Finishing touches include a covered entrance and porch with column detailing and arched transom, flower boxes and shuttered windows. The foyer opens to both the dining room and great room beyond with French doors opening onto the porch. Through the double doors to the right of the foyer is the combination bedroom/study. A short hallway leads to a full bath and a secondary bedroom with ample closet space. The master bedroom is spacious, with walk-in closets on both sides of the entrance to the master bath. With separate vanities, shower and toilet, the master bath is of symmetrical design, and forms a private retreat at the rear of the home. Convenient to both the great room and dining room, the kitchen opens to an attractive breakfast area featuring a bay window. An additional room is remotely located off the kitchen, providing a retreat for today's at-home office or guest.

MASTER BATH

MASTER BEDRDOOM
16'-4" X 13'-6"

BEDROOM NO. 2
10'-4" X 12'-0"

BATH

PORCH

BREAKFAST
13'-4" X 9'-0"

BEDROOM/
OFFICE
10'-4" X 11'-0"

GREAT ROOM
17'-0" X 17'-8"

KITCHEN
13'-4" X 10'-6"

BATH

LAUNDRY

DN

DINING ROOM
11'-4" X 12'-10"

FOYER
5'-4" X
12'-10"

BEDROOM/
STUDY
11'-2" X 12'-0"

TWO CAR GARAGE
20'-6" X 19'-6"

PORCH

Width 61'
Depth 70'-6"

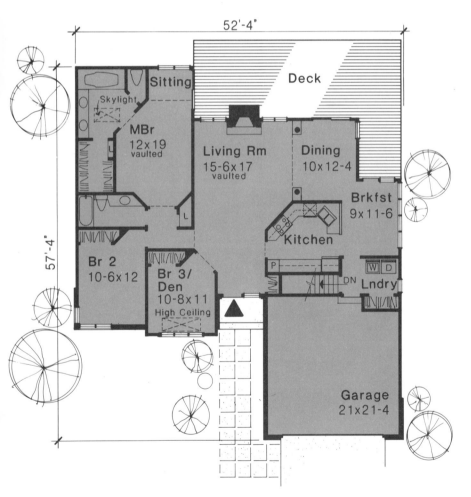

Deck

Sitting

Skylight

MBr
12 x 19
vaulted

Living Rm
15-6 x 17
vaulted

Dining
10 x 12-4

Brkfst
9 x 11-6

Kitchen

Br 2
10-6 x 12

Br 3/
Den
10-8 x 11
High Ceiling

P

W D

DN Lndry

Garage
21 x 21-4

52'-4"

57'-4"

Design S8890
Square Footage: 1,630

● This home design effectively separates living and sleeping zones for added comfort. A vaulted living room offers a fireplace flanked by bright windows. Columns define the dining room which accesses a rear wraparound deck. The well-designed kitchen easily serves the airy breakfast room. A nearby laundry room makes chores a breeze. In the sleeping wing, the master bedroom suite impresses with its vaulted ceiling, sitting room and skylit bathroom with dual vanities, compartmented toilet and walk-in closet. Bedroom 3 could also be a den, perfect for home computing.

Design by
LifeStyle
HomeDesigns

Design S3600/S3601

Square Footage: 2,258/2,424

● This unique one-story plan seems tailor-made for a small family or for empty-nesters. Formal areas are situated well for entertaining—living room to the right and formal dining room to the left. A large family room is found to the rear. It has access to a rear wood deck and is warmed in the cold months by a welcoming hearth. The U-shaped kitchen features an attached morning room for casual meals. It is near the laundry and powder rooms. Bedrooms are split. The master suite sits to the right of the plan and has a walk-in closet and a fine bath. A nearby office has a private porch. One family bedroom is on the other side of the home and also has a private bath. If needed, the plan can also be built with a third bedroom sharing the bath.

Design S3600

Design by
Home Planners

QUOTE ONE™

Cost to build? See page 216
to order complete cost estimate
to build this house in your area!

Design S3601

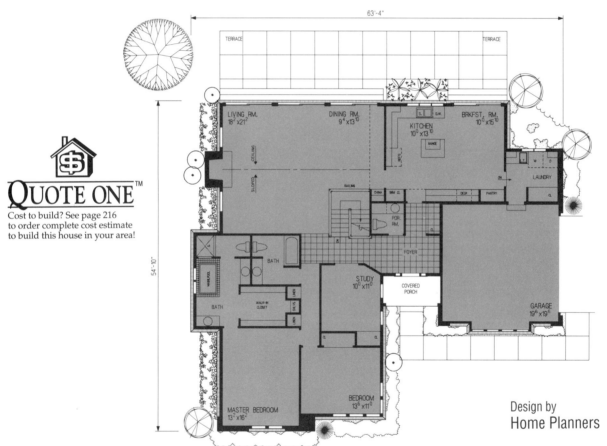

QUOTE ONE™

Cost to build? See page 216
to order complete cost estimate
to build this house in your area!

Design by
Home Planners

Design S2962

Square Footage: 2,112

● In this Tudor design, each of the three main living zones—the sleeping zone, living zone and working zone—are but a couple of steps from the foyer. This spells out easy, efficient traffic patterns. Open planning, sloping ceilings and plenty of glass create a nice environment for the living and dining area. Its appeal is further enhanced by the open staircase to the lower-level recreation/hobby area. The L-shaped kitchen, with an island range and work surface, is delightfully open to the large breakfast room. Nearby is the step-saving first-floor laundry. The sleeping zone has the flexibility of functioning as a two- or a three-bedroom area.

Design by
Home Planners

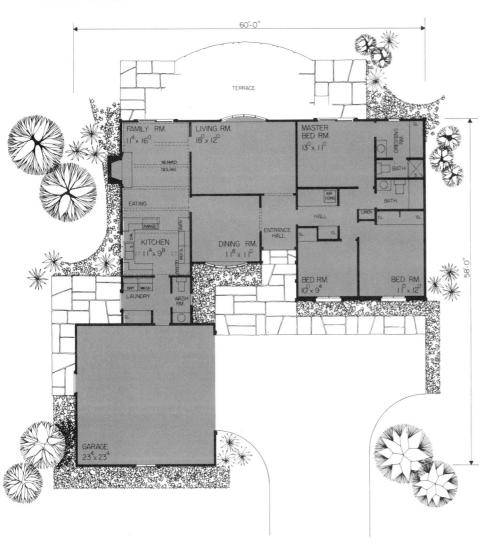

60'-0"

TERRACE

FAMILY RM.
11⁴ x 16⁰

LIVING RM.
18⁰ x 12⁰

MASTER
BED RM.
13⁰ x 11⁰

DRESSING
RM.

BEAMED
CEILING

BATH.

EATING

AIR
COND.

BATH.

RANGE

OVEN

HALL

LINEN

CL.

KITCHEN
11⁴ x 9⁸

ENTRANCE
HALL

DINING RM.
11⁸ x 11⁰

REF'G.

CL.

CL.

DRY. WASH.

WASH
RM.

BED RM.
10⁰ x 9⁴

BED RM.
11⁰ x 12⁰

LAUNDRY

58'-0"

GARAGE
23⁴ x 23⁴

Design S2606
Square Footage: 1,499

MASTER BED RM.

LINEN

BATH

ENT.
HALL

DN.

HALL

CL.

BED RM.

BED RM.

OPTIONAL BASEMENT

● This modest-sized house with its 1,499 square feet could hardly offer more in the way of exterior charm and interior livability. Measuring only sixty feet in width means it will not require a huge, expensive piece of property. The orientation of the garage and the front drive court are features which promote an economical use of property. In addition to the formal, separate living and dining rooms, there is the informal kitchen/family room area. Note the beamed ceiling, the fireplace, the sliding glass doors and the eating area of the family room.

QUOTE ONE™
Cost to build? See page 216
to order complete cost estimate
to build this house in your area!

Design by
Home Planners

Design S3314

First Floor: 1,959 square feet

● Formal living areas in this plan are joined by a sleeping wing that holds three bedrooms. Two verandas and a screened porch enlarge the plan and enhance indoor/outdoor livability. Notice the abundant storage space.

Quote One™

Cost to build? See page 216 to order complete cost estimate to build this house in your area!

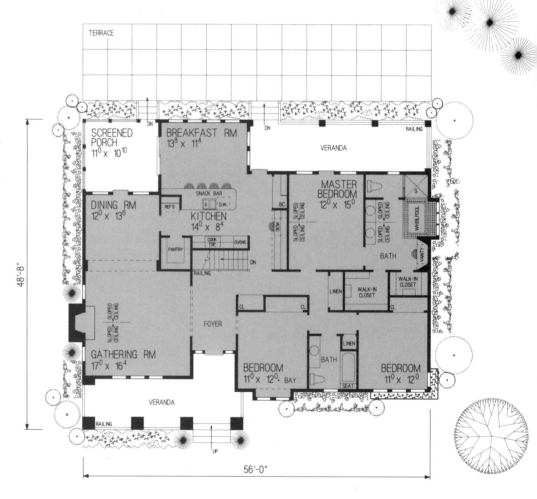

Design S3569

Square Footage: 1,981

● A graceful entry opens
this impressive one-story
design; the foyer introduces
an open gathering room/din-
ing room combination. A
front-facing study could easily convert into a bedroom for
guests—a full bath is directly
accessible from the rear of
the room. In the kitchen,
such features as an island
cooktop and a built-in desk
add to livability. A corner
bedroom takes advantage of
front and side views. The
master bedroom accesses the
rear terrace and also sports a
bath with dual lavatories and
a whirlpool. Other special
features of the house include
multi-pane windows, a
warming fireplace, a cozy
covered dining porch and a
two-car garage. Note the
handy storage closet in the
laundry area.

Design by
Home Planners

Design S9123
Square Footage: 1,184

● Build small, then add on as the family grows or as needs increase. The economical Phase 1 project of this home allows for all the livability of much larger plans: an ample living area, hexagonal dining area, U-shaped kitchen and large bedroom with full bath and huge closet. When you outgrow the Basic Plan, you can add the two additional bedrooms with walk-in closets. The utility room provides adequate space for a washer and dryer. The covered front porch is not only charming, but adds a welcome indoor/outdoor relationship.

PHASE 2
Bedrooms 2 and 3
Adds 355 square feet
to Basic Plan

Design by
Larry W.
Garnett &
Associates, Inc.

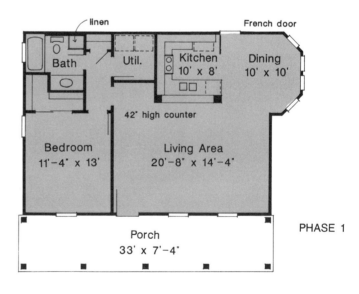

Width 37'-4"
Depth 31'-4"

Design S9045

Square Footage: 902 (Plus Optional Loft: 127 additional square feet)

Design by
Larry W. Garnett & Associates, Inc.

● This adorable European-style doll-house embodies the very essence of charm. For the single home owner, empty-nesters, or as a cozy country retreat, it could not be any more perfect. Simple floor planning includes an open living area with cathedral ceiling and exposed wood trusses, a kitchen/dining area, two bedrooms and a full bath with compartmented stool and tub. For added space —possibly for use as a studio or additional sleeping — there's an optional loft available with sloped ceiling. The two-car garage offers an ample storage area.

4' wall →

Loft
10' x 11'
sloped ceiling

Optional Loft

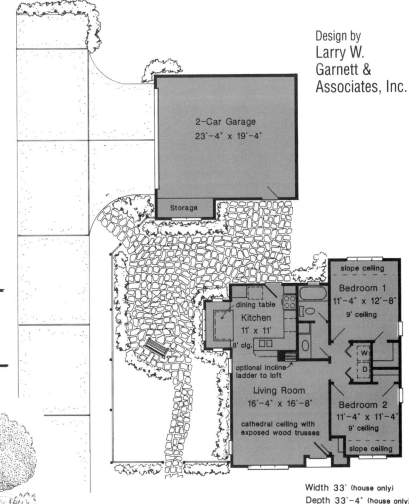

2-Car Garage
23'-4" x 19'-4"

Storage

dining table

Kitchen
11' x 11'
8' clg.

Bedroom 1
11'-4" x 12'-8"
9' ceiling

slope ceiling

W
D

optional incline
ladder to loft

Living Room
16'-4" x 16'-8"

Bedroom 2
11'-4" x 11'-4"
9' ceiling

cathedral ceiling with
exposed wood trusses

slope ceiling

Width 33' (house only)
Depth 33'-4" (house only)

Design S9034
Square Footage: 1,078

● Here's a cozy home that provides abundant livability in just over 1000 square feet. The covered front porch gives way to a floor plan that is open and inviting. Notice the sloped ceiling in the living room with fireplace and sliding glass doors to the rear yard. The dining area is adjacent to a U-shaped kitchen and features a cathedral ceiling. Besides the master bedroom with full, private bath, there are two family bedrooms which share a bath. The two-car garage offers space for storage and laundry facilities.

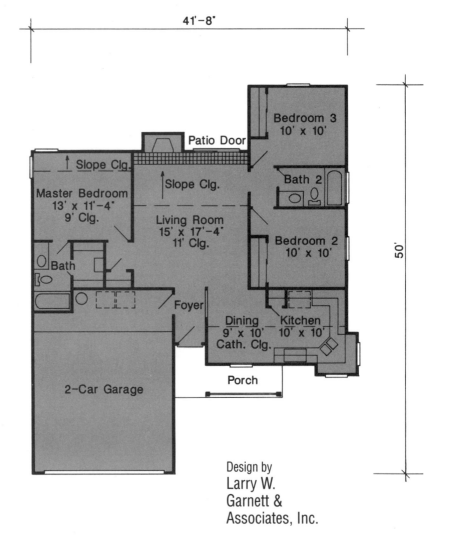

41'-8"

50'

Bedroom 3
10' x 10'

Patio Door

Slope Clg.

Bath 2

Slope Clg.

Master Bedroom
13' x 11'-4"
9' Clg.

Living Room
15' x 17'-4"
11' Clg.

Bedroom 2
10' x 10'

Bath

Foyer

Dining
9' x 10'
Cath. Clg.

Kitchen
10' x 10'

2-Car Garage

Porch

Design by
Larry W.
Garnett &
Associates, Inc.

Design S9144

Square Footage: 1,198

● The elegant bay window and porch detailing combine to create a cozy home that is actually economical to construct. A 42"-high wall separates the dining area from the living room with its 9' sloped ceiling and expansive corner windows. The efficient kitchen has plenty of cabinets, along with a pantry and a corner sink. The master bedroom has a 9' sloped ceiling and a bath with a large walk-in closet.

QUOTE ONE®

Cost to build? See page 216 to order complete cost estimate to build this house in your area!

Design by
Larry W. Garnett & Associates, Inc.

Width 43'-4"
Depth 50'

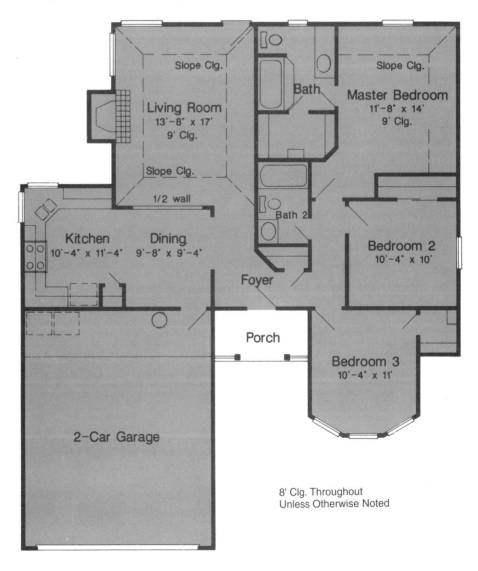

57

Quote One®

Cost to build? See page 216 to order complete cost estimate to build this house in your area!

Cost to build? See page 216

Design by
Larry W.
Garnett &
Associates, Inc.

Design S9006

Square Footage: 1,772

● Designed for casual living inside and out, this one-story farmhouse is an ideal family home. The family room features a ten-foot ceiling and a corner fireplace. An enormous dining area can handle even the largest family dinners. The large rear porch is perfect for outdoor entertaining. The laundry room is conveniently located near the three bedrooms. His and Hers walk-in closets and twin lavatories are part of the luxurious master bath. Plans for a 24' x 24' detached garage are included with this design.

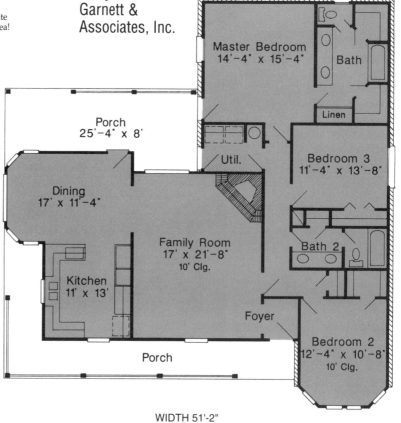

Master Bedroom
14'-4" x 15'-4"

Bath

Linen

Porch
25'-4" x 8'

Util.

Bedroom 3
11'-4" x 13'-8"

Dining
17' x 11'-4"

Family Room
17' x 21'-8"
10' Clg.

Bath 2

Kitchen
11' x 13'

Foyer

Porch

Bedroom 2
12'-4" x 10'-8"
10' Clg.

WIDTH 51'-2"
DEPTH 52'-10"

Design S9038
Square Footage: 1,659

● Here's a three-bedroom home with style and comfort that meets family living requirements with less than 2,000 square feet! Gathering areas are accommodated in the living room with built-in bookshelves and fireplace, and the well-planned kitchen/dining area combination. Besides two family bedrooms, there is a lovely master with cathedral ceiling and bath with double vanity. The bay windows, covered front porch and other special design details make this a house to remember.

Bath

Linen

Bedroom 3
10'-4" x 10'

Kitchen
15' x 10'

Dining
15' x 10'

Bath 2

Util.

Books

Master Bedroom
15'-4" x 13'
Cathedral Clg.

Books

Living Room
20' x 15'-4"
10' Clg.

Bedroom 2
11'-4" x 13'-8"

Porch

Width 63'-4"
Depth 37'-10"

Design by
Larry W.
Garnett &
Associates, Inc.

Design S9639
Square Footage: 1,541

● This traditional three-bedroom home projects the appearance of a much larger home. The great room features a cathedral ceiling, a fireplace and an arched window above the sliding glass door to the expansive rear deck. The master suite contains a pampering master bath and a walk-in closet. Two other bedrooms share a full bath with a double-bowl vanity. Please specify basement or crawlspace foundation when ordering.

Design by
Donald A.
Gardner,
Architects, Inc.

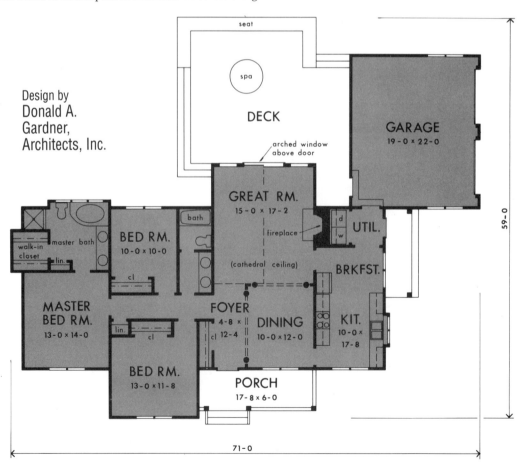

● This economical plan offers an impressive visual statement with its comfortable and well-proportioned appearance. The entrance foyer leads to all areas of the house. The great room, dining area and kitchen are all open to one another allowing visual interaction. The great room and dining area both have a cathedral ceiling. The fireplace is flanked by book shelves and cabinets. The master suite has a cathedral ceiling, walk-in closet and master bath with double-bowl vanity, whirlpool tub and shower. The plan is available with a crawl-space foundation.

Design by
Donald A.
Gardner,
Architects, Inc.

Cost to build? See page 216
to order complete cost estimate
to build this house in your area!

Design S9664
Square Footage: 1,287

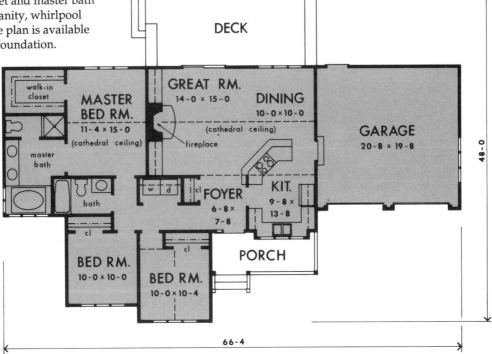

DECK

spa

MASTER BED RM.
13-4 x 13-8

master bath

skylights

storage

w
d

walk-in closet

fireplace

BRKFST.
11-4 x 7-4

BED RM.
11-4 x 11-4

GREAT RM.
15-4 x 16-10
(cathedral ceiling)

cl

bath

cl

KITCHEN
11-4 x 10-0

GARAGE
20-0 x 19-8

FOYER
8-2 x 6-6

cl

BED RM./STUDY
11-4 x 10-4

PORCH

DINING RM.
11-4 x 11-4

50-8

59-8

Design by
Donald A.
Gardner,
Architects, Inc.

Design S9726

Square Footage: 1,498

● This charming one-story home utilizes multi-pane windows, columns, dormers and a covered porch to offer a welcoming front exterior. Inside, the great room with a dramatic cathedral ceiling commands attention; the kitchen and breakfast room are just beyond a set of columns. The tiered ceilinged dining room presents a delightfully formal atmosphere for dinner parties or family gatherings. A tray ceiling in the master bedroom will please, as will a large walk-in closet and a gracious master bath with dual lavatories, a garden tub, and a separate shower. The secondary bedrooms are located at the opposite end of the house for privacy. This plan is available with a crawlspace foundation.

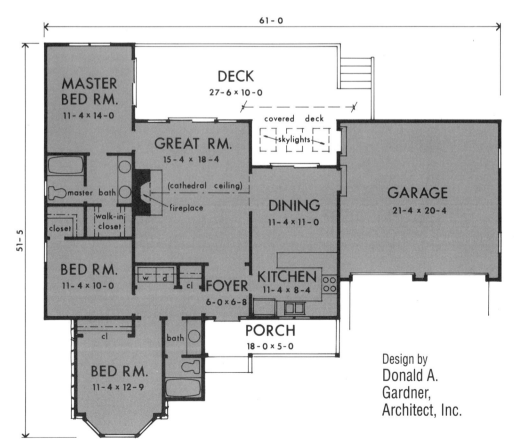

MASTER BED RM.
11-4 x 14-0

master bath

closet

BED RM.
11-4 x 10-0

w d cl

closet

BED RM.
11-4 x 12-9

DECK
27-6 x 10-0

covered deck

skylights

GREAT RM.
15-4 x 18-4

(cathedral ceiling)

fireplace

walk-in closet

FOYER
6-0 x 6-8

bath

DINING
11-4 x 11-0

KITCHEN
11-4 x 8-4

GARAGE
21-4 x 20-4

PORCH
18-0 x 5-0

61-0

51-5

Design by
Donald A.
Gardner,
Architect, Inc.

Design S9620
Square Footage: 1,310

● A multi-paned bay window, dormers, a cupola, a covered porch and a variety of building materials dress up this one-story cottage. The entrance foyer leads to an impressive great room with cathedral ceiling and fireplace. The U-shaped kitchen, adjacent to the dining room, provides an ideal layout for food preparation. An expansive deck offers shelter while admitting cheery sunlight through skylights. A luxurious master bedroom located to the rear of the house takes advantage of the deck area and is assured privacy from two other bedrooms at the front of the house. These family bedrooms share a full bath.

Design S9604

Square Footage: 1,506

● This unusual compact house maximizes its use of living areas and offers features found mostly only in larger house plans. A lovely facade, adorned with multi-paned windows, shutters, dormers, bay windows and a covered porch, gives way to a truly livable floor plan. The great room with cathedral ceiling, fireplace, paddle fan, built-in cabinets and bookshelves has direct access to the sun room through two sliding glass doors. Decorative columns between the foyer and great room create a dramatic entrance. Sleeping accommodations include a master with ample closet space and two family bedrooms. Note the split-bedroom plan configuration — providing utmost privacy.

DECK
28-6 × 10-0

seal

SUN RM.
16-0 × 8-0

DINING
11-4 × 11-10

wash dry

storage

GARAGE
21-0 × 21-0

BED RM.
11-4 × 10-0

fireplace

GREAT RM.
18-0 × 14-0
(cathedral ceiling)

KIT.
11-4 × 8-0

cl

bath

cl

bath

FOYER
7-4 × 5-8

lin.

cl

cl

cl

cl

MASTER
BED RM.
11-4 × 14-0

PORCH
16-0 × 5-4

BED RM.
11-4 × 11-0

42-4

71-0

Design by
Donald A.
Gardner,
Architect, Inc.

64

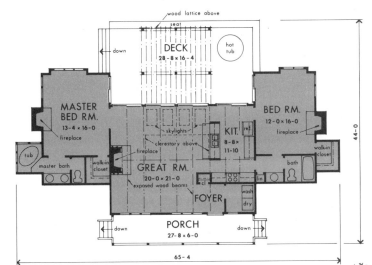

Design S9607
Square Footage: 1,299

● Though rustic in appearance, this two-bedroom plan provides all the features sought after in today's well-planned home. A large central area includes a great room, entrance foyer and kitchen with serving and eating counter. Note the use of cathedral ceilings with exposed wood beams, skylights, clerestory windows and fireplace in this area. The master suite has an optional fireplace, walk-in closet, and whirlpool tub. The second bedroom also has an optional fireplace and a full bath. All rooms open to the rear deck, which supplies space for a hot tub.

REAR

Design by
**Donald A.
Gardner,
Architect, Inc.**

FRONT

FRONT

REAR

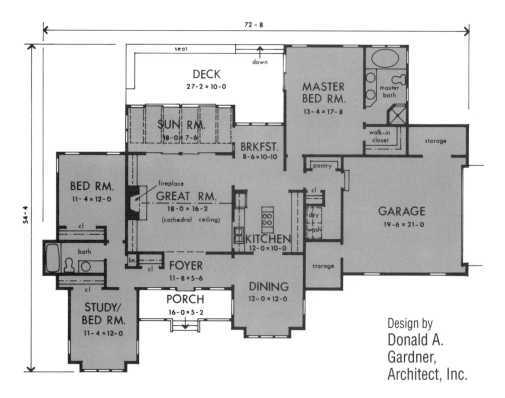

Design S9602
Square Footage: 1,899

● Multi-paned windows, dormers, a covered porch and two projected windows with shed roofs at the dining room and study offer a welcoming front exterior to this home. The great room has a cathedral ceiling, paddle fan, built-in cabinets and book shelves, and has direct access to the sunroom through two sliding glass doors. The convenient kitchen features a center island cook top and provides service to both the formal dining room and breakfast area. It is connected to the great room by a pass-through. Overlooking the private rear deck is the sumptuous master suite with double-bowl vanity, shower and garden tub. Two other bedrooms are located at the other end of the house for privacy (the front bedroom could double as a study). The two-car garage has ample storage space.

Design by
Donald A.
Gardner,
Architect, Inc.

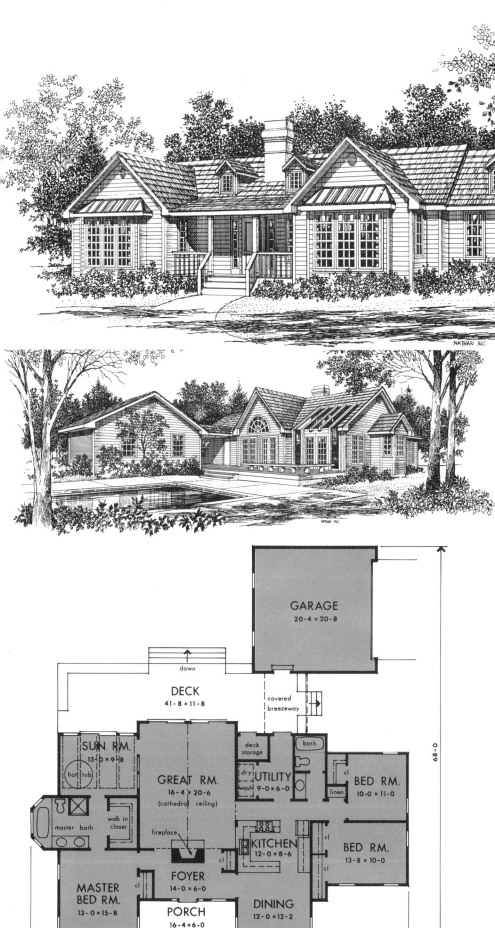

Design S9682

Square Footage: 1,826

● Multi-paned windows, dormers, a covered porch, round gable vents and two projected windows at the dining area and the master bedroom add to the flavor of this country-style home. A sun room with a hot tub sits adjacent to the master bath and accesses the large rear deck. The great room has a fireplace, a cathedral ceiling and sliding glass doors to the deck with an arched window above to allow for natural light. The kitchen is centrally located between the dining area and the great room for maximum flexibility in layout. The generous master bedroom has a walk-in closet and a spacious master bath with a double-bowl vanity, a shower and a garden tub. Two additional bedrooms are located at the other end of the house for privacy.

Design by
**Donald A.
Gardner,
Architects, Inc.**

67

Design S9651

Square Footage: 2,128

● This three-bedroom traditional home with bay windows displays a well-balanced exterior with emphasis on the front entrance and the casual living area at the back. A generous foyer reinforces the great room entry with round columns. The great room has many features including a cathedral ceiling, paddle fan, fireplace, built-in cabinets and a pass-through from the kitchen. A sun room boasts a cathedral ceiling and paddle fan as well and also has arched windows over doors leading to the deck and great room.

Design by
Donald A.
Gardner,
Architect, Inc.

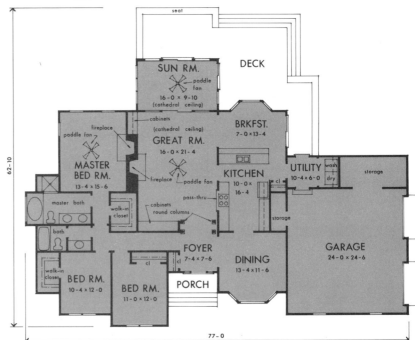

REAR

Design S9670
Square Footage: 2,046

● This three-bedroom country cottage projects an intriguing appearance with its bay windows, dormers and L-shaped layout. The great room has a cathedral ceiling along with an arched window above the exterior door leading to the deck. The sun room with operable skylights is accessible from the great room, kitchen and deck for maximum exposure. The centrally located kitchen allows direct access to eating and living areas. Three bedrooms include a master suite and a bedroom that might also be useful as a study.

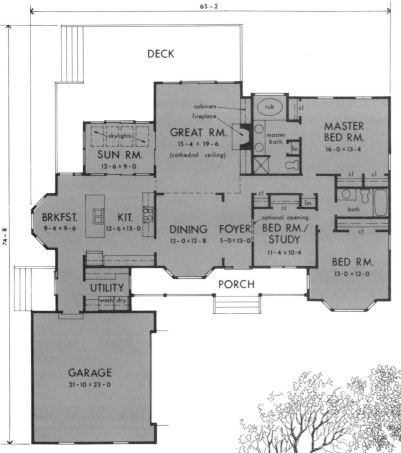

DECK

65–2

74–8

skylights

SUN RM.
12-6 × 9-0

GREAT RM.
15-4 × 19-6
(cathedral ceiling)

cabinets
fireplace

tub

cl

MASTER
BED RM.
16-0 × 13-4

master
bath

lin.

BRKFST.
9-4 × 9-6

KIT.
12-6 13-0

DINING
12-0 × 12-8

FOYER
5-0 × 13-0

cl

lin.

cl cl

bath

optional opening

BED RM./
STUDY
11-4 × 10-4

cl

UTILITY

wash dry

PORCH

BED RM.
13-0 × 12-0

GARAGE
21-10 × 23-0

Design by
Donald A.
Gardner,
Architect, Inc.

This home, as shown in the photograph, may differ from the actual blueprints. For more detailed information, please check the floor plans carefully.

Photo by Andrew D. Lautman

Design by
Home Planners

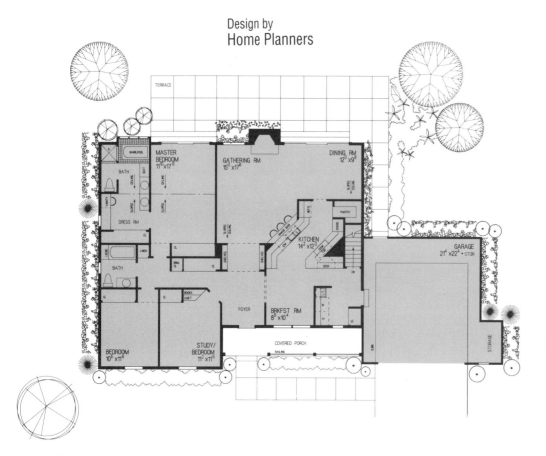

Width 75'
Depth 43'-5"

Design S2947
Square Footage: 1,830

● This charming one-story traditional home greets visitors with a covered porch. A galley-style kitchen shares a snack bar with the spacious gathering room where a fireplace is the focal point. An ample master suite includes a luxury bath with a whirlpool tub and a separate dressing room. Two additional bedrooms, with one that could double as a study, are located at the front of the home.

QUOTE ONE™

Cost to build? See page 216
to order complete cost estimate
to build this house in your area!

Design S1920
Square Footage: 1,600

● This home offers a charming exterior with a truly great floor plan. The covered front porch at the entrance heralds outstanding features inside. The sleeping zone has three bedrooms and two full baths. Each of the bedrooms has its own walk-in closet. Note the efficient U-shaped kitchen with the family room and dining room to each side. There is also a laundry with wash room just off the garage. Blueprints for this design include details for both basement and non-basement construction.

QUOTE ONE™

Cost to build? See page 216 to order complete cost estimate to build this house in your area!

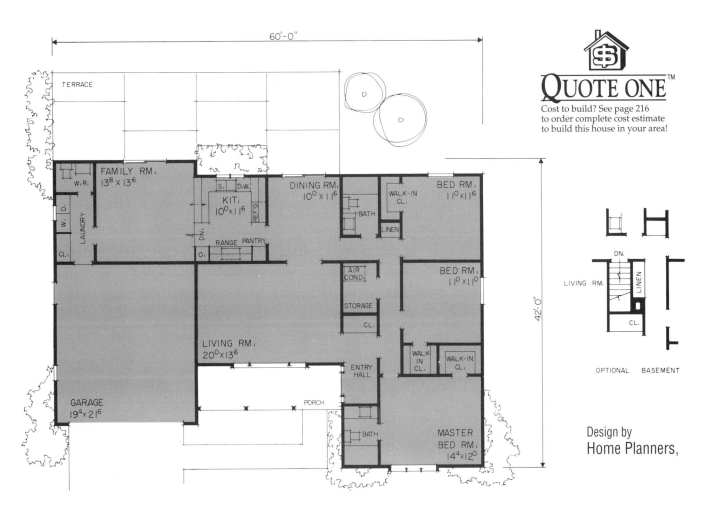

Design by
Home Planners,

Design S3332

First Floor: 2,203 square feet

● Nothing completes a traditional-style home quite as well as a country kitchen with fireplace. Notice also the sloped-ceiling living room and well-appointed master suite. A handy washroom is near the laundry, just off the garage.

Design by
Home Planners

Width 77'-2"
Depth 46'-6"

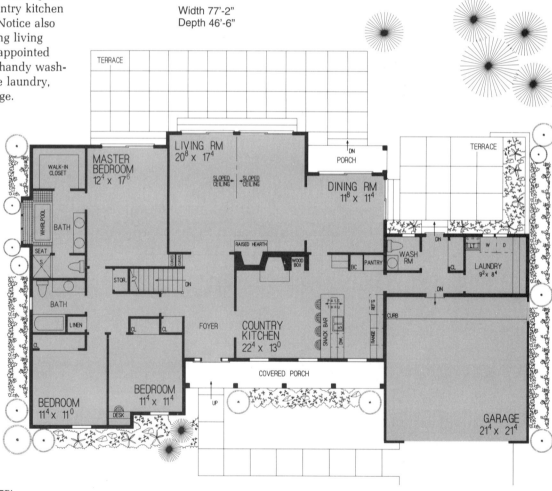

Design by
Home Planners

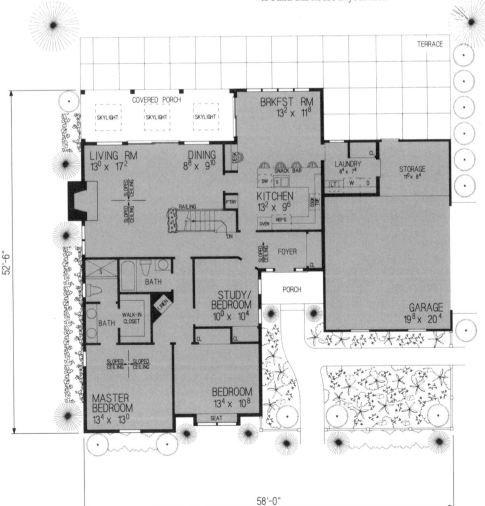

TERRACE

COVERED PORCH

SKYLIGHT   SKYLIGHT   SKYLIGHT

BRKFST RM
13² x 11⁸

LIVING RM
13⁰ x 17²

DINING
8⁸ x 9¹⁰

LAUNDRY
8⁴ x 7⁸

STORAGE
11⁰ x 8⁴

SLOPED CEILING   SLOPED CEILING

RAILING

P'TRY

SNACK BAR

DW   S

KITCHEN
13² x 9⁶

OVEN   REF'G

DN

FOYER

SLOPED CEILING

52'-6"

BATH

BATH

WALK-IN CLOSET

LINEN

STUDY/
BEDROOM
10⁰ x 10⁴

PORCH

GARAGE
19⁸ x 20⁴

SLOPED CEILING   SLOPED CEILING

MASTER
BEDROOM
13⁴ x 13⁰

BEDROOM
13⁴ x 10⁸

SEAT

58'-0"

Design S3340

First Floor: 1,689 square feet

● You may not decide to
build this design simply because of its delightful covered porch. But it certainly
will provide its share of
enjoyment if this plan is
your choice. Notice also how
effectively the bedrooms are
arranged out of the traffic
flow of the house. One bedroom could double nicely as
a TV room or study. The living room/dining area is
highlighted by a fireplace,
sliding glass doors to the
porch, and an open staircase
with built-in planter to the
basement.

Design by
Home Planners

Width 54'
Depth 52'

Design S3355

Square Footage: 1,387

● Though it's only just under 1,400 total square feet, this plan offers three bedrooms (or two with a study) and a sizable gathering room with a fireplace and a sloped ceiling. The galley kitchen provides a pass-through snack bar and has a planning desk and an attached breakfast room. Besides two smaller bedrooms with a full bath, there's an extravagant master suite with a large dressing area, a double vanity and a raised whirlpool tub. The full-length terrace to the rear of the house extends the living potential to the outdoors. For information on customizing this design, call 1-800-521-6797, ext. 800.

QUOTE ONE®

Cost to build? See page 216
to order complete cost estimate
to build this house in your area!

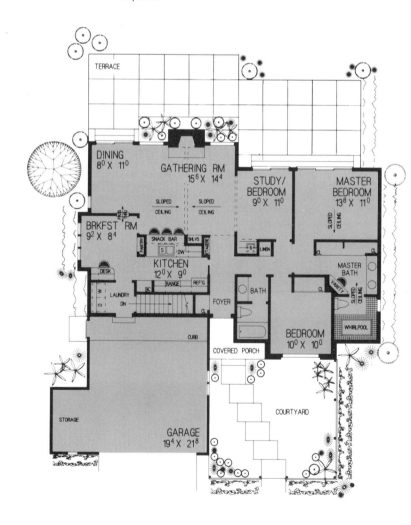

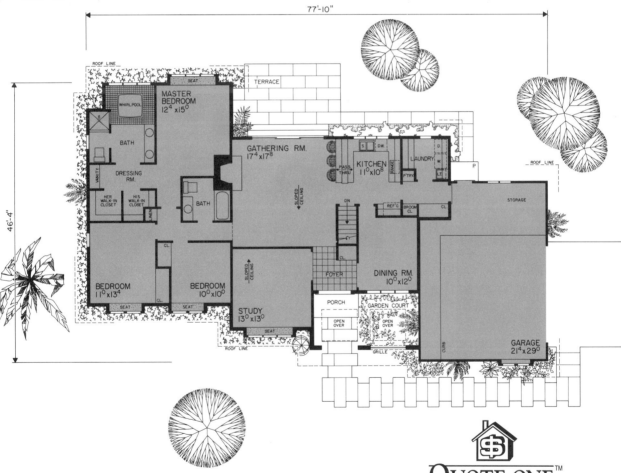

Design S2875

Square Footage: 1,913

● This elegant Spanish design incorporates excellent indoor-outdoor living relationships for families who enjoy the sun and the comforts of a well-planned home. Note the overhead openings for the rain and sun to fall upon the front garden, while a twin arched entry leads to the front porch and the foyer. Inside, the floor plan features a U-shaped kitchen with a pass-through to the large gathering room with its comfortable fireplace. Other features include a formal dining room, a large laundry room, a study off the foyer plus three bedrooms, including a master bedroom with its own whirlpool.

Design by
Home Planners

This home, as shown in the photograph, may differ from the actual blueprints.
For more detailed information, please check the floor plans carefully.

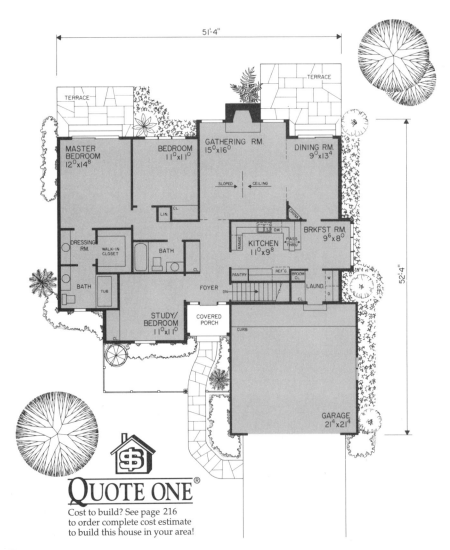

51'-4"

TERRACE

TERRACE

MASTER
BEDROOM
12⁰x14⁸

BEDROOM
11⁰x11⁰

GATHERING RM.
15⁰x16⁰

DINING RM.
9⁰x13⁴

SLOPED ← → CEILING

LIN.

CL.

BRKFST RM.
9⁶x8⁰

DRESSING
RM.

WALK-IN
CLOSET

BATH

KITCHEN
11⁰x9⁸

PASS
THRU

RANGE

BATH

TUB

PANTRY

REF'G.

BROOM
CL.

52'-4"

FOYER

DN

LAUND.

W

D

CL.

STUDY/
BEDROOM
11⁰x11⁰

COVERED
PORCH

CURB

CL.

GARAGE
21⁴x21⁴

Design S2878
Square Footage: 1,521

● This charming one-story traditional design offers plenty of livability in a compact size.
Thoughtful zoning puts all sleeping areas to one side of the house
apart from household activity in
the living and service areas. The
home includes a spacious gathering room with a sloped ceiling, in
addition to a formal dining room
and a separate breakfast room.
There's also a handy pass-through
between the breakfast room and
the large efficient kitchen. The
laundry is strategically located
adjacent to the garage and the
breakfast/kitchen areas for handy
access. A master bedroom enjoys a
private bath and a walk-in closet. A
third bedroom can double as a sizable study just off the central foyer.

Design by
Home Planners

QUOTE ONE®
Cost to build? See page 216
to order complete cost estimate
to build this house in your area!

Design S3460
Square Footage: 1,389

Design by
Home Planners

● This special farmhouse offers two elevations in its blueprint package. Though rooflines and porch options are different, the floor plan is basically the same and very livable. A formal living room/dining room combination has a warming fireplace and a delightful bay window. The kitchen, with its efficient snack bar and pantry, separates this formal area from the more casual family room. Three bedrooms include two family bedrooms served by a full bath and a lovely master suite with its own private bath. Notice the convenient location of the washer and dryer.

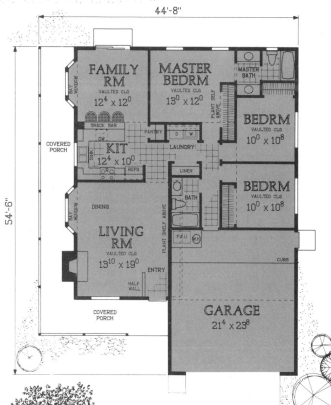

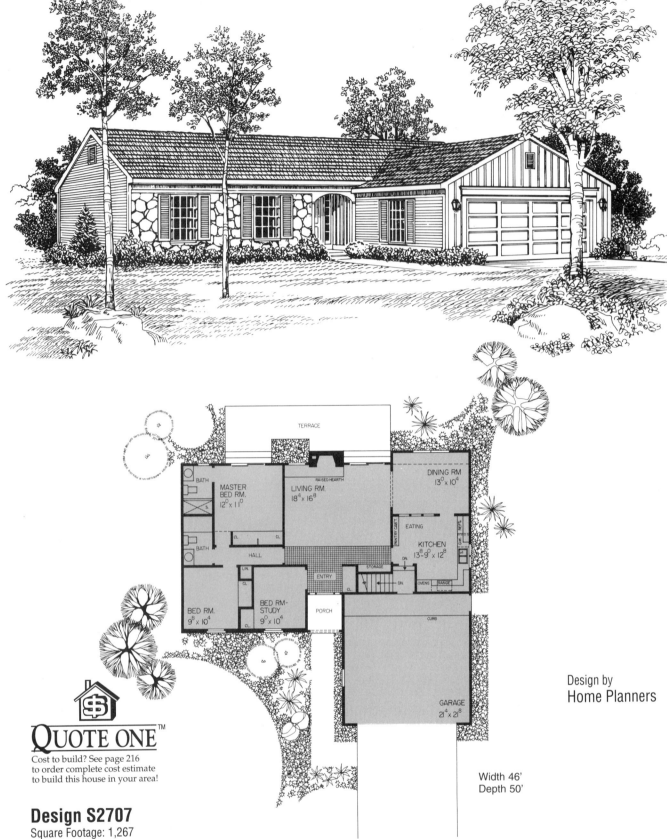

TERRACE

BATH

MASTER
BED RM.
12⁰ x 11⁰

LIVING RM.
18⁴ x 16⁸

RAISED HEARTH

DINING RM.
13⁰ x 10⁴

PANTRY CAB'T.

EATING

BATH

KITCHEN
13'-9⁸ x 12⁸

REFR.

HALL

CL.

CL.

LIN.

CL.

STORAGE

DN.

DN.

OVENS

RANGE

BED RM.
9⁸ x 10⁴

BED RM.-
STUDY
9⁰ x 10⁴

ENTRY

CL.

PORCH

CL.

GARAGE
21⁴ x 21⁸

CURB

Design by
Home Planners

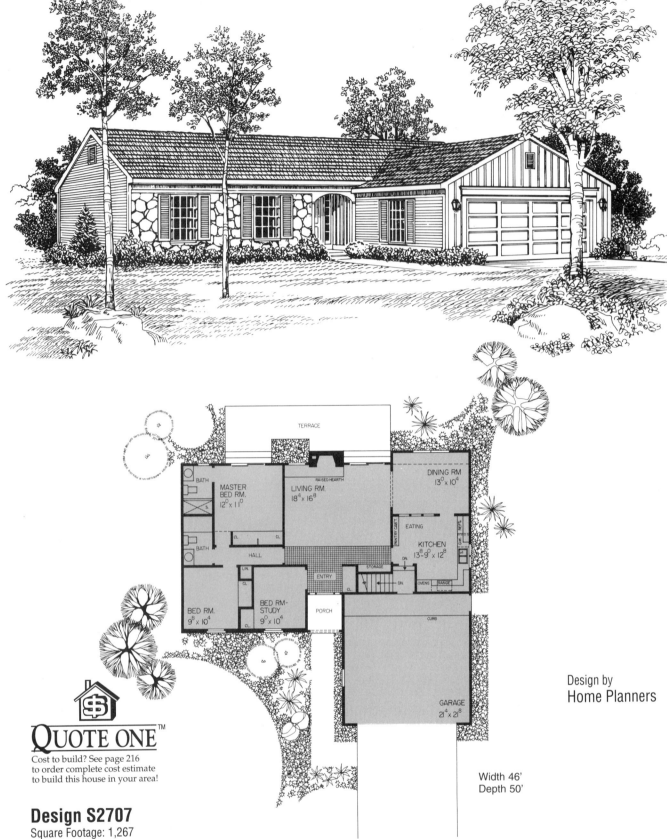

Width 46'
Depth 50'

Design S2707

Square Footage: 1,267

● Here is a charming Early American adaptation that will serve as a picturesque and practical retirement home. Also, it will serve admirably those with a small family in search of an efficient, economically built home. The living area is spacious.

The kitchen features eating space and easy access to the garage and basement. The dining room is adjacent to the kitchen and views the rear yard. Then, there is the basement for recreation and hobby pursuits. The bedroom wing offers three bedrooms and two

full baths. Don't miss the sliding doors to the terrace from the living room and the master bedroom. Storage units are plentiful including a pantry cabinet in the eating area of the kitchen.

QUOTE ONE™
Cost to build? See page 216 to order complete cost estimate to build this house in your area!

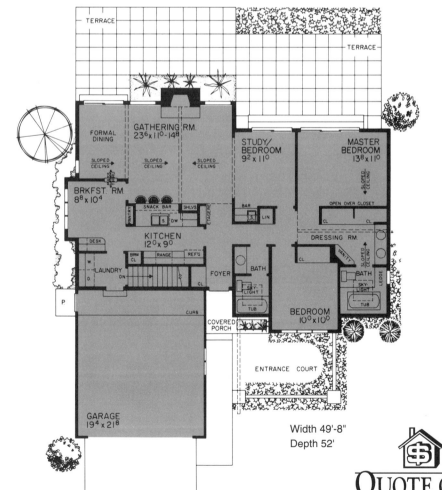

Design by
Home Planners

Design S2864
Square Footage: 1,387

● Projecting the garage to the front of this house is very economical. It reduces the required lot size for building and it protects the interior from street noise. Many other characteristics about this design deserve mention, too. The interior kitchen has an adjacent breakfast room and a snack bar on the gathering room side. A study with a wet bar is near by. Sliding glass doors here and in the master bedroom open to the terrace.

Width 49'-8"
Depth 52'

QUOTE ONE™
Cost to build? See page 216
to order complete cost estimate
to build this house in your area!

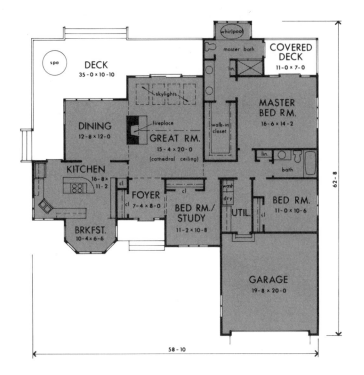

Design S9611
Square Footage: 1,817

● This inviting ranch offers many special features uncommon to the typical house this size. A large entrance foyer leads to the spacious great room with cathedral ceiling, fireplace, and operable skylights that allow for natural ventilation. A bedroom just off the foyer doubles nicely as a study. The large master suite contains a walk-in closet and a pampering master bath with double-bowl vanity, shower and whirlpool tub. For outdoor living, look to the open deck with spa at the great room and kitchen, as well as the covered deck at the master suite.

Design by
Donald A.
Gardner,
Architect, Inc.

FRONT

REAR

Design by
Donald A.
Gardner,
Architect, Inc.

Design S9612

Square Footage: 1,874

● An arched window adds beauty to this modest traditional ranch. The generous entrance foyer opens to the great room and optional study. The great room provides a cathedral ceiling with exposed wood beams and skylights allowing natural ventilation. The large kitchen has an attached breakfast area and an island. The master suite has a large walk-in closet and master bath with double-bowl vanity, shower and whirlpool tub.

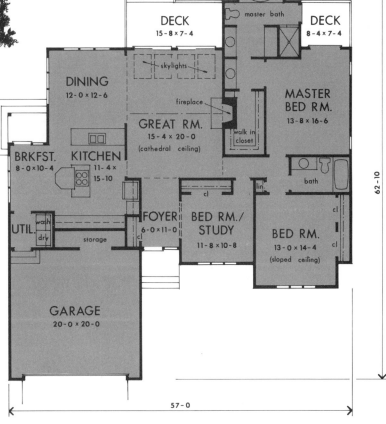

whirlpool

master bath

DECK
15-8 x 7-4

DECK
8-4 x 7-4

DINING
12-0 x 12-6

skylights

fireplace

GREAT RM.
15-4 x 20-0
(cathedral ceiling)

walk in closet

MASTER
BED RM.
13-8 x 16-6

BRKFST.
8-0 x 10-4

KITCHEN
11-4 x
15-10

cl

lin.

bath

UTIL

wash

dry

storage

FOYER
6-0 x 11-0

BED RM./
STUDY
11-8 x 10-8

cl

BED RM.
13-0 x 14-4
(sloped ceiling)

cl

GARAGE
20-0 x 20-0

62-10

57-0

Design S9655
Square Footage: 2,032

● Simplicity embraces elegance in this three-bedroom home. It features stucco siding, round columns, arched windows and copper dormer roofs. An added special feature of this plan is the sun room with hot tub accessed from the master bath and the great room. Details in the great room include a fireplace, cathedral ceiling and sliding glass door with arched window above. The spacious master bedroom has a walk-in closet and master bath with double-bowl vanity, shower and garden tub. Two family bedrooms are located at the other end of the house for privacy. The master bedroom and breakfast area have vaulted ceilings at the arched windows to allow maximum natural light.

Design by
Donald A.
Gardner,
Architect, Inc.

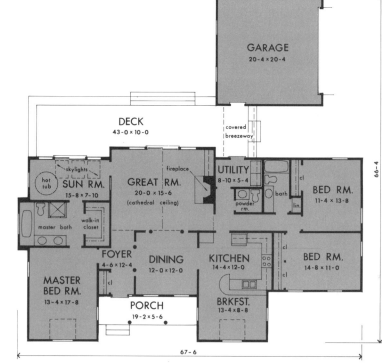

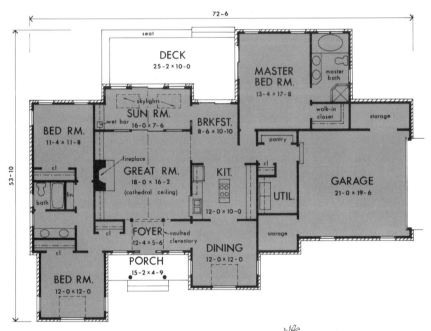

DECK
25-2 x 10-0

seat

SUN RM.
16-0 x 7-6

skylights

wet bar

BED RM.
11-4 x 11-8

cl

fireplace

GREAT RM.
18-0 x 16-2
(cathedral ceiling)

bath

lin

cl

BRKFST.
8-6 x 10-10

MASTER
BED RM.
13-4 x 17-8

master
bath

walk-in
closet

storage

pantry

KIT.

cl

12-0 x 10-0

UTIL.

GARAGE
21-0 x 19-6

FOYER
12-4 x 5-6

vaulted
clerestory

cl

DINING
12-0 x 12-0

storage

PORCH
15-2 x 4-9

BED RM.
12-0 x 12-0

72-6

53-10

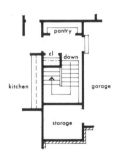

pantry

cl

down

kitchen

garage

storage

ALTERNATE PLAN
FOR BASEMENT

Design S9634
Square Footage: 2,099

● This enchanting design incorporates
the best in floor planning all in one level.
The central great room is the hub of the
plan from which all other rooms radiate.
The master suite is split from the family
bedrooms and has access to the rear
deck. Notice the skylit sun room and the
convenient work area in the kitchen.
Extra storage space is available in the
garage. Please specify basement or crawl-
space foundation when ordering.

Design by
Donald A.
Gardner,
Architects, Inc.

Design S3488

Square Footage: 1,944

● The tudor facade of this comfortable home is just the beginning to a truly unique design. As you enter the foyer via a quaint covered porch, you are greeted by the sleeping zone on the right and the living zone on the left, beginning with the breakfast area which faces the front. A large kitchen connects to this room and includes a desk, a walk-in pantry, a spacious counter area with a snack bar that connects to the gathering room and entry to the for-mal dining room. The massive gathering room features a fireplace, a sloped ceiling and access to the back-yard ter-race. The master bedroom also accesses the terrace and revels in a master bath with a whirlpool tub, a separate shower, dual lavs and an individual vanity. A study at the front of the home could be converted into an addi-tional bedroom.

QUOTE ONE™

Cost to build? See page 216 to order complete cost estimate to build this house in your area!

Width 72'-8"
Depth 47'-4"

Design by
Home Planners

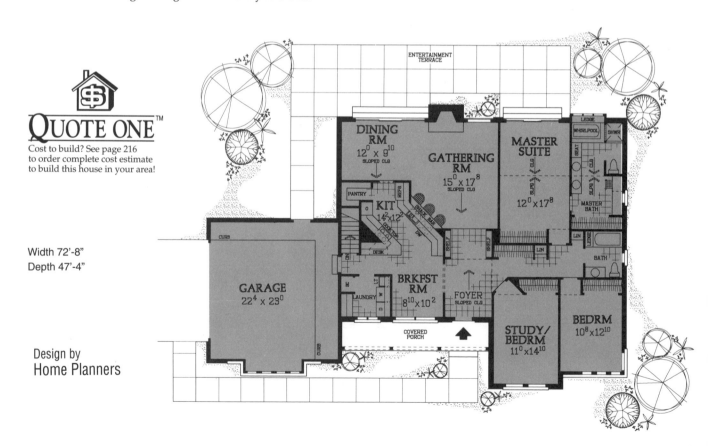

Design S8614
Square Footage: 2,100

● Gingerbread trim crowns the roof of this spreading plan, enhanced by an intricate facade with high-ceilinged spaces. The covered porch gives way to a tiled foyer. Double doors on the right open to a den or study with a twelve-foot ceiling. The splendid great room sports a tray ceiling, corner fireplace and French doors to a covered patio. The pass-through kitchen serves the front-facing dining room and bayed breakfast room with equal ease. Bedrooms include a master suite with patio access and a sunken shower, and two secondary bedrooms which share a bath.

WIDTH 102'
DEPTH 59'-4"

Covered Patio

Double Garage

Porch

Utility

Breakfast Rm.
12' flat clg.

Great Rm.
15⁰ 18⁰
12' flat clg.

Master Suite
13⁴ 17⁰
12' flat clg.

Kitchen

Stg.

Bath

tray ceiling

fireplace

Master Ba.

W.I.C.

Bed Room 2
11⁰ 14⁴
10' flat clg.

Bed Room 3
11⁰ 12⁰
10' flat clg.

Dining Rm.
10⁹ 12⁸
12' flat clg.

Foyer

Den/Study
13⁰ 13⁰
12' flat clg.

Entry

Covered Porch

Design by
**Home Design
Services, Inc.**

Design S8601
Square Footage: 2,125

● A luxurious master suite is yours with this lovely plan—and it comes with two different options. Family bedrooms are on the opposite end of the home, separated from the master by the great room and kitchen/breakfast area. A formal dining room and den or study are to the front.

Design by
Home Design Services, Inc.

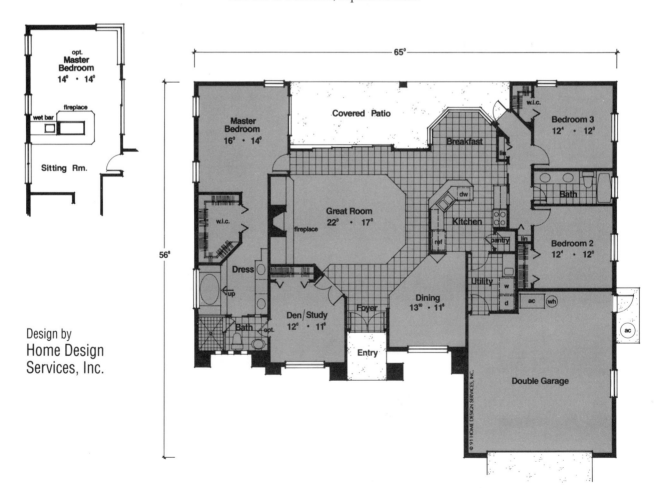

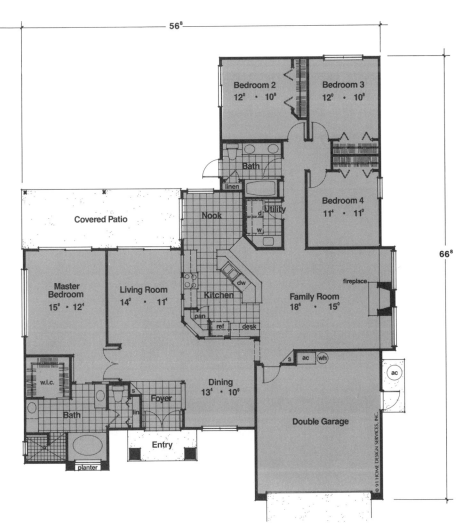

Covered Patio

Master Bedroom
15⁹ · 12⁴

Living Room
14⁰ · 11⁴

Nook

Bath

linen

Utility

Kitchen

Bedroom 2
12⁰ · 10⁸

Bedroom 3
12⁰ · 10⁸

Bedroom 4
11⁴ · 11⁰

fireplace

Family Room
18⁶ · 15⁰

ref   desk

pan

w.i.c.

Bath

Foyer

lin

Dining
13⁴ · 10⁸

Double Garage

Entry

planter

ac wh

ac

56⁸

66⁸

© 911 HOME DESIGN SERVICES, INC.

Design S8638
Square Footage: 2,144

● This is the ultimate family house! This unique arrangement of rooms creates spaces which are functional and individual. The entry opens to the formal living and dining room areas with a magnificent view of the outdoor living space and yard. Double doors lead to the master suite located in its very own private wing of the home for perfect privacy and quiet. The His and Hers sinks, soaking tub and step-down shower add luxury. The private toilet room and huge walk-in closet add practicality. Beyond the formal and master wing is the family space with the kitchen at its hub. The bedroom wing has great amenities for the kids— outdoor access in the shared bath and a nearby laundry room.

Design by
Home Design Services, Inc.

Design S3486

Square Footage: 2,000

● This classic stucco design provides a cool retreat in any climate. From the covered porch, enter the skylit foyer to find an arched ceiling leading to the central gathering room with its raised-hearth fireplace and terrace access. A connecting corner dining room is conveniently located near the amenity-filled kitchen that features an abundant pantry, a snack bar and a separate breakfast area. The large master bedroom includes terrace access and a master bath with a whirlpool tub, a separate shower and plenty of closet space. A second bedroom and a study that can be converted to a bedroom complete this wonderful plan.

Design by
Home Planners

Quote One™

Cost to build? See page 216 to order complete cost estimate to build this house in your area!

Width 75'
Depth 55'

Width 61'-6"
Depth 67'-4"

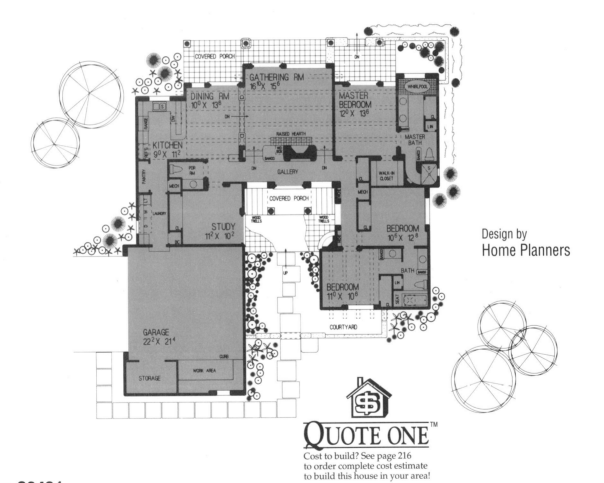

Design by
Home Planners

QUOTE ONE™
Cost to build? See page 216
to order complete cost estimate
to build this house in your area!

Design S3431
Square Footage: 1,907

● Graceful curves welcome you into the courtyard of this Santa Fe home. Inside, a gallery directs traffic to the work zone on the left or the sleeping zone on the right. Straight ahead lies a sunken gathering room with a beamed ceiling and a raised-hearth fireplace. A large pantry offers extra storage space for kitchen items. The covered rear porch is accessible from the dining room, the gathering room and the secluded master bedroom. Luxury describes the feeling in the master bath. Two family bedrooms share a compartmented bath. The study could serve as a guest room, media room or home office.

Design S8604
Square Footage: 2,153

Design by
**Home Design
Services, Inc.**

● Sophistication and elegance are the bywords of this four-bedroom, 2½-bath home. Among the many special features are a dramatic foyer, column-encircled dining room, and 12-foot ceilings. The kitchen is a true gourmet's delight and opens to a light-filled breakfast nook. The family room is enhanced by a barrel ceiling and a fireplace. Secondary bedrooms are separated from the master suite. Each contains a spacious closet; two contain corner windows. The master suite is luxurious with a walk-in closet, sliding glass doors to the rear porch, and bath with double sink and step-up tub.

Bedroom 3
volume ceiling
10⁴ · 10⁴

Bedroom 4
volume ceiling
11⁴ · 10⁴

Bedroom 2
volume ceiling
12⁴ · 10⁴

Bath

w d
Utility
lin

Breakfast
volume ceiling

Porch

fireplace

Family Room
volume ceiling
21⁰ · 14⁰

dw

Kitchen

ref

Living Room
volume ceiling
17⁴ · 13⁰

Master
Bedroom
volume ceiling
17⁰ · 13⁴

lin

ac wh l.t.

Dining
16⁶ · 12⁰

Foyer

w.i.c.

Bath

up

Double Garage

Entry

Width 61'
Depth 67'-8"

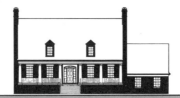

1½-STORY HOMES

Budget-Wise With a Bonus

Historically, the American home has been associated with a one- or two-room structure which changed significantly in appearance and living area as the family grew. Sometimes the first addition to a home was horizontal with construction of a bedroom or keeping room. Frequently, the expansion was vertical for the development of upstairs sleeping rooms.

Present-day 1½-story houses are as divergent as they are functional and affordable. Some contain all sleeping areas on the second floor, providing a cozy separation from living areas; others have bedrooms on both floors, allowing for a more private first-floor master bedroom or guest room. Frequently, such plans are essentially one-story houses with bonus second-floor bedroom space, providing perfect quarters for empty-nesters with visiting children and other guests. Because of the added half story, this design is more dramatic and spacious feeling, adding height to the typical one-story plan. Whatever the arrangement, the 1½-story house delivers expanded sleeping capabilities to meet growing needs with only a modest investment.

Perhaps the most affordable aspect of the 1½-story house is that it provides a completed first-floor bedroom or two and an unfinished "attic" upon occupancy. Later, the second floor can be converted as needed and as budget permits.

Examples abound of "starter" houses that began as somewhat minimal housing units then blossomed to accommodate increased needs. The popular and highly identifiable rambling Cape Cod house is a case in point. Its symmetrical styling and distinctive detailing (such as multi-paned windows and central entrance foyer) usually complement the half-story bedrooms or a study/studio. The expansion capability of the 1½-story house recommends it for prime consideration as an affordable house type. Neither one-story, two-story nor multi-level houses lend themselves to expansion as ideally as 1½-stories.

The homes in this section represent varying sizes and styles of 1½-story designs. Among the examples are small starter houses that grow to family-handling four-bedroom plans, rambling Cape Cods and contemporary and Tudor adaptations. Special features are found in these plans that make them great places to call home.

Design S9666 First Floor: 1,027 square feet

Second Floor: 580 square feet; Total: 1,607 square feet

● This economical, rustic three-bedroom plan sports a relaxing country image with both front and back covered porches. The openness of the expansive great room to kitchen/dining areas and loft/study areas is reinforced with a shared cathedral ceiling for impressive space. The first level allows for two bedrooms, a full bath and a utility area. The master suite on the second level has a walk-in closet and a master bath with whirlpool tub, shower and double-bowl vanity. The plan is available with a crawl-space foundation.

Design by
Donald A.
Gardner,
Architect, Inc.

QUOTE ONE®

Cost to build? See page 216
to order complete cost estimate
to build this house in your area!

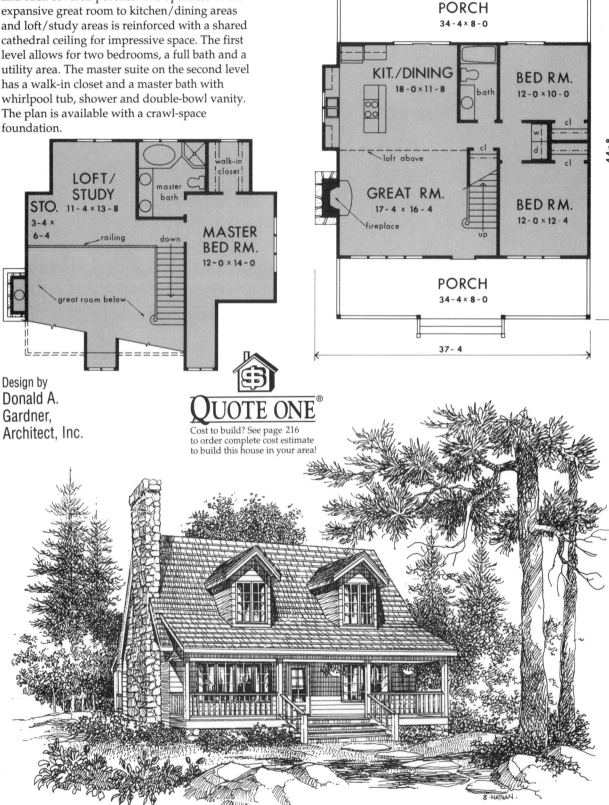

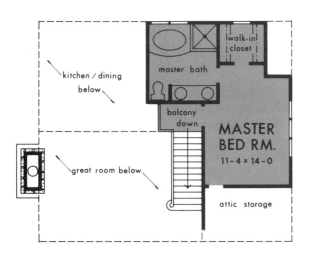

kitchen / dining below

great room below

walk-in closet

master bath

balcony down

MASTER BED RM.
11-4 × 14-0

attic storage

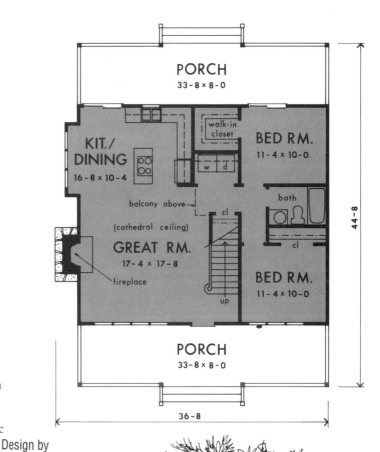

PORCH
33-8 × 8-0

walk-in closet

BED RM.
11-4 × 10-0

w | d

KIT./ DINING
16-8 × 10-4

bath

cl

cl

balcony above

(cathedral ceiling)

GREAT RM.
17-4 × 17-8

fireplace

up

BED RM.
11-4 × 10-0

44-8

36-8

PORCH
33-8 × 8-0

Design S9663 First Floor: 1,002 square feet
Second Floor: 336 square feet; Total: 1,338 square feet

● A mountain retreat, this rustic version features covered porches front and rear. Open living is enjoyed in the great room and the kitchen/dining room combination. The cathedral ceiling gives an open inviting sense of space. Two bedrooms and a full bath on the first level are complemented by a master suite on the second level which includes a walk-in closet and a deluxe bath. There is also attic storage available on the second level. Please specify basement or crawlspace foundation when ordering.

Design by
Donald A.
Gardner,
Architects, Inc.

Design S9608

First Floor: 1,228 square feet
Second Floor: 492 square feet
Total: 1,720 square feet

● An open and spacious interior with the best in up-to-date floor planning offers new excitement in this delightful compact country-style home. Besides the oversized great room with fireplace, there is a wonderful country kitchen incorporating dining space and having access to the sun room for alternate dining and entertaining. The generous master bedroom has its own fireplace and access to the sun room. A walk-in closet assures plenty of storage space. Upstairs, in addition to two bedrooms sharing a full bath, there is a charming balcony and ample attic storage. A covered porch and a deck — front and rear — add to outdoor lifestyles.

Design by
Donald A. Gardner, Architect, Inc.

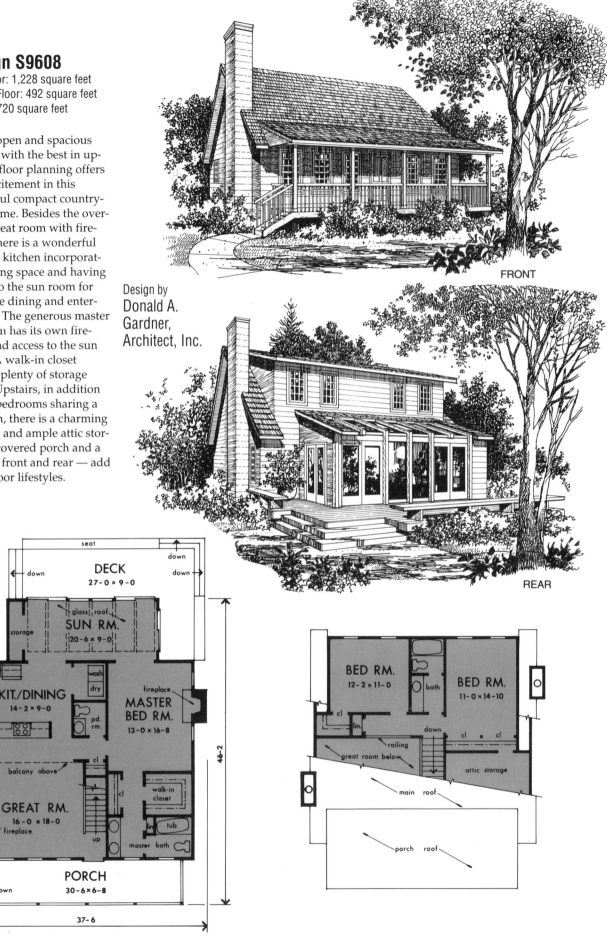

FRONT

REAR

DECK
27-0 × 9-0

SUN RM.
20-6 × 9-0

seat

down

down

down

storage

glass roof

KIT./DINING
14-2 × 9-0

wash
dry

fireplace

MASTER
BED RM.
13-0 × 16-8

pd.
rm.

balcony above

cl

walk-in
closet

GREAT RM.
16-0 × 18-0
fireplace

up

lin.

tub

master bath

46-2

PORCH
30-6 × 6-8

down

37-6

BED RM.
12-2 × 11-0

bath

BED RM.
11-0 × 14-10

cl

lin.

down

cl

cl

railing

great room below

attic storage

main roof

porch roof

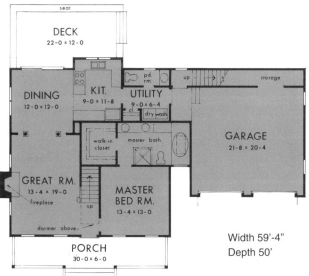

DECK
22-0 × 12-0

DINING
12-0 × 12-0

KIT.
9-0 × 11-8

UTILITY
9-0 × 6-4

dry wash

pd rm

storage

up

GARAGE
21-8 × 20-4

walk-in closet

master bath

GREAT RM.
13-4 × 19-0
fireplace

MASTER BED RM.
13-4 × 13-0

dormer above

PORCH
30-0 × 6-0

Width 59'-4"
Depth 50'

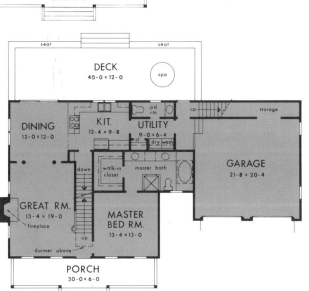

DECK
40-0 × 12-0

spa

DINING
12-0 × 12-0

KIT.
12-4 × 9-8

UTILITY
9-0 × 6-4

dry wash

pd rm

storage

up

down

GARAGE
21-8 × 20-4

walk-in closet

master bath

GREAT RM.
13-4 × 19-0
fireplace

MASTER BED RM.
13-4 × 13-0

dormer above

PORCH
30-0 × 6-0

BASEMENT PLAN

Design by
Donald A. Gardner, Architects, Inc.

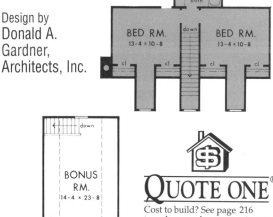

attic storage

bath

BED RM.
13-4 × 10-8

down

BED RM.
13-4 × 10-8

cl cl cl cl

down

BONUS RM.
14-4 × 23-8

QUOTE ONE®

Cost to build? See page 216
to order complete cost estimate
to build this house in your area!

Design S9626

First Floor (crawlspace foundation): 1,057 square feet
First Floor (basement foundation): 1,110 square feet
Second Floor (crawlspace or basement): 500 square feet
Total (crawlspace foundation): 1,557 square feet
Total (basement foundation): 1,610 square feet
Bonus Room: 342 square feet

● This compact, two-story, cozy country cottage is perfect for the economically conscious family. Its entrance foyer is highlighted by a clerestory dormer above for natural light. The master suite is conveniently located on the first level for privacy and accessibility. Its attached master bath boasts a whirlpool tub with a skylight above, a separate shower and a double-bowl vanity. Second-level bedrooms share a full bath and there's a wealth of storage on this level. An added advantage to this house is the bonus room above the garage. Please specify basement or crawlspace foundation when ordering.

Quote One™

Cost to build? See page 216
to order complete cost estimate
to build this house in your area!

Design by
Home Planners

Design S3497

First Floor: 1,581 square feet
Second Floor: 592 square feet
Total: 2,173 square feet

● For the best in traditional styling, this 1½-story bungalow design takes the cake. A shingled exterior complements raised roof lines and a front porch. Inside, the entry gives way to a living room with a fireplace and a dining room serviced by a U-shaped kitchen and a wet bar. An airy breakfast room is situated nearby. In the family room, a back porch acts as a pleasant enhancement. The first-floor master bedroom suite leaves room for a sitting area. Upstairs, two secondary bedrooms share a full bath with dual lavatories. No matter what your family's style, this home will provide all the desired livability.

Design S9430

First Floor: 1,150 square feet
Second Floor: 543 square feet
Total: 1,693 square feet

● While fitting on some of the smallest lots imaginable, this great 1½-story still encompasses some dynamic features. Check out the dramatic, two-story hearth room that serves as the main living area in the home. Tall windows flank the fireplace and a glass door leads to the outdoor living area. A section of the upper hallway overlooks the hearth room integrating the upper floor with the lower floor. The master bedroom is conveniently located on the main floor overlooking the back yard, with direct access to the full bath serving the lower floor. Two large bedrooms and a bath round out the upper floor.

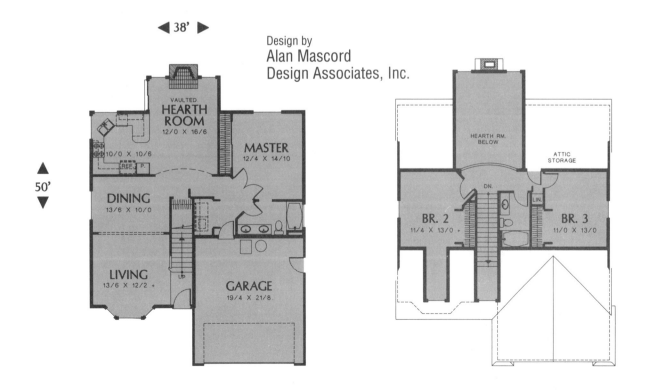

Design by
Alan Mascord
Design Associates, Inc.

Design S9464 First Floor: 1,166 square feet; Second Floor: 1,019 square feet; Total: 2,185 square feet

● This home, designed to fit on a 50' lot, provides an abundance of features due to its efficient use of space. The two-story foyer forms a central core providing convenient access to any part of the home. The comfortable master suite includes a walk-in closet and double vanity as well as a shower and spa tub. The informal area of the home stretches across the rear and features a bayed-out nook with a sliding patio door providing convenient access to the outdoor living spaces. A more attractive four-bedroom home with these features and compact footprint would be hard to find!

Design by
Alan Mascord
Design Associates, Inc.

Design S9487

First Floor: 1,175 square feet
Second Floor: 891 square feet
Total: 2,066 square feet

● Volume ceilings are the choice in this fine two-story home. Note that the den features a vaulted ceiling to complement its half-round window, the living and dining rooms have 11'4" ceilings to complement transom windows and the master suite has a 9' tray ceiling. Other special features include fireplaces in both living and family rooms, columns and plant shelves between the living room and dining room and a whirlpool spa in the master bath. Because it is only 38' wide, this home will work well on a narrow lot.

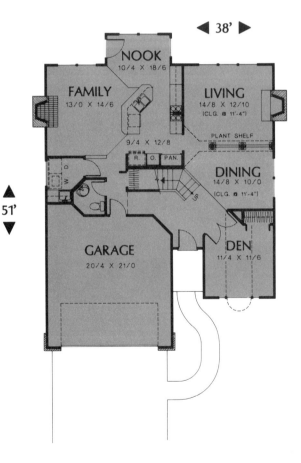

38'

51'

NOOK
10/4 X 18/6

FAMILY
13/0 X 14/6

LIVING
14/8 X 12/10
(CLG. @ 11'-4")

9/4 X 12/8

PLANT SHELF

R. O. PAN.

W D

DINING
14/8 X 10/0
(CLG. @ 11'-4")

GARAGE
20/4 X 21/0

DEN
11/4 X 11/6

Design by
Alan Mascord
Design Associates, Inc.

SPA

MASTER
13/0 X 16/4
CLG. @ 9'-0"

DN

OPEN TO FOYER

LINEN

BR. 3
10/0 X 11/4

BR. 2
10/0 X 11/8+

99

Design S2661

First Floor: 1,020 square feet
Second Floor: 777 square feet
Total: 1,797 square feet

● Any other starter house or retirement home couldn't have more charm than this design. Its compact frame houses a very livable plan. A outstanding feature of the first floor is the large country kitchen. Its fine attractions include a beam ceiling, a raised-hearth fireplace, a built-in window seat and a door leading to the outdoors. A living room is in the front of the plan and has another fireplace which shares the single chimney. The rear dormered second floor houses the sleeping and bath facilities.

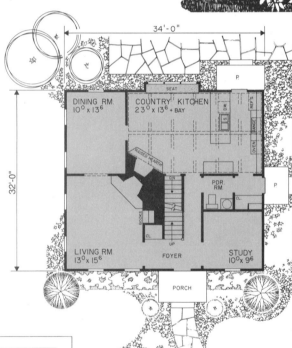

Cost to build? See page 216
to order complete cost estimate
to build this house in your area!

Design by
Home Planners

This home, as shown in the photograph, may differ from the actual blueprints. For more detailed information, please check the floor plans carefully.

Photo by Laszlo Regos

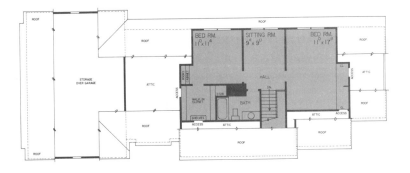

Design S2563

First Floor: 1,500 square feet
Second Floor: 690 square feet
Total: 2,190 square feet

● This charming Cape Cod definitely will capture your heart with its warm appeal. This home offers you and your family a lot of livability. Upon entering this home, to your left, is a nice-sized living room with a fireplace. Adjacent is a dining room. An efficient kitchen and a large, farm kitchen eating area with a fireplace will be enjoyed by all. A unique feature on this floor is the master bedroom with a full bath and a walk-in closet. Also take notice of the first-floor laundry, the pantry and a study for all of your favorite books. Note the sliding glass doors in the farm kitchen and master bedroom. Upstairs you'll find two bedrooms, one with a walk-in closet. Also here, a sitting room and a full bath are available. Lastly, this design accommodates a three-car garage.

Design by
Home Planners

QUOTE ONE™
Cost to build? See page 216 to order complete cost estimate to build this house in your area!

Design S2657

First Floor: 1,217 square feet
Second Floor: 868 square feet
Total: 2,085 square feet

QUOTE ONE™

Cost to build? See page 216
to order complete cost estimate
to build this house in your area!

● Deriving its design from the traditional Cape Cod style, this facade features clapboard siding, small-paned windows and a transom-lit entrance flanked by carriage lamps. A central chimney services two fireplaces, one in the country-kitchen and the other in the formal living room which is removed from the disturbing flow of traffic. The master suite is located to the left of the upstairs landing. A full bathroom services two additional bedrooms on the second floor.

Design by
Home Planners

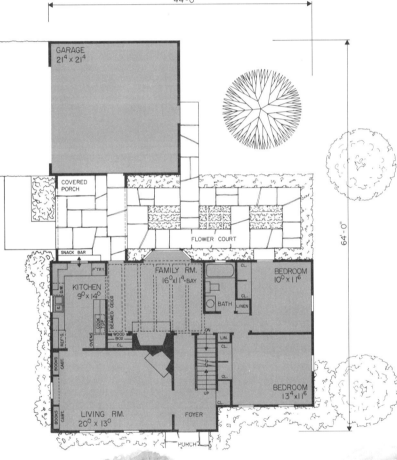

Design S2145

First Floor: 1,182 square feet
Second Floor: 708 square feet
Total: 1,890 square feet

Cost to build? See page 216
to order complete cost estimate
to build this house in your area!

● Historically referred to as a "half house", this authentic adaptation has its roots in the heritage of New England. With completion of the second floor, the growing family doubles their sleeping capacity. Notice that the overall width of the house is only 44 feet. Take note of the covered porch leading to the garage and the flower court.

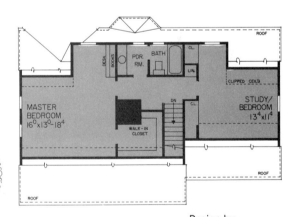

Design by
Home Planners

Photos by Andrew D. Lautman

This home, as shown in the photograph, may differ from the actual blueprints. For more detailed information, please check the floor plans carefully.

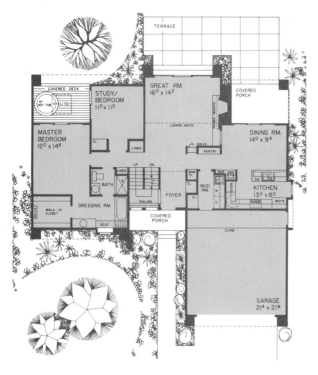

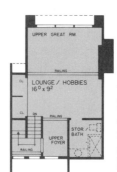

Design S2822

First Floor: 1,363 square feet
Second Floor: 351 square feet
Total: 1,714 square feet

● Here is a truly unique design. While functioning as a one-story home, the second floor provides an extra measure of livability when required. In addition, this two-story section adds to the dramatic appeal of both the exterior and the interior. With 1,363 square feet on the first floor, this contemporary delivers refreshing and outstanding living patterns for those who are buying their first home, those who have raised their family and are looking for a smaller home and those in search of a retirement home.

Width 54'-8"
Depth 54'

Design by
Home Planners

QUOTE ONE®
Cost to build? See page 216 to order complete cost estimate to build this house in your area!

104

Design by
Home Planners

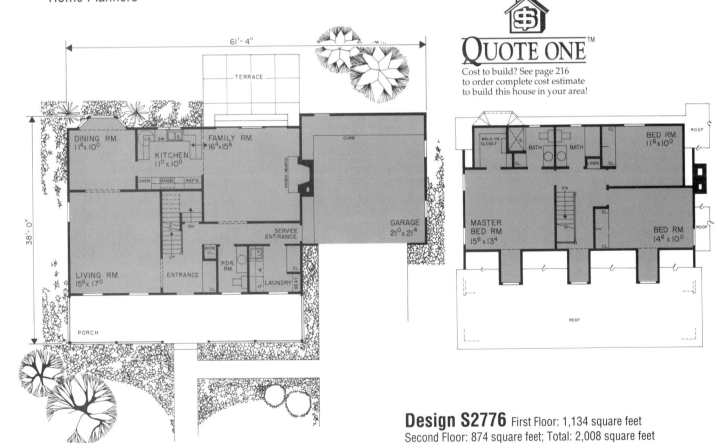

Design S2776 First Floor: 1,134 square feet
Second Floor: 874 square feet; Total: 2,008 square feet

● This board-and-batten farmhouse design has all of the country charm of New England. The large front covered porch surely will be appreciated during the beautiful warm weather months. Immediately off the front entrance is the delightful corner living room. The dining room with a bay window will be easily served by the U-shaped kitchen. Informal family living enjoyment will be obtained in the family room which features a raised-hearth fireplace, sliding glass doors to the rear terrace and easy access to the work center. The second floor houses all of the sleeping facilities. There is a master bedroom with a private bath and walk-in closet. Two other bedrooms share a bath.

Design S9044

First Floor: 814 square feet
Second Floor: 467 square feet
Total: 1,281 square feet

● Here's an adorable shingled cottage that offers more that just another charming face. Because the living room opens directly to the dining room, an appearance of space is created. Abundant windows further enhance the roomy feeling. The kitchen overlooks a garden side yard. The pampering master bedroom includes a huge walk-in closet and a bath with separate tub and shower. Upstairs are two more bedrooms and an alcove loft that can be used as a study area. Note the two-story foyer and linen storage in the upstairs bath. A guest half-bath is thoughtfully placed at entry.

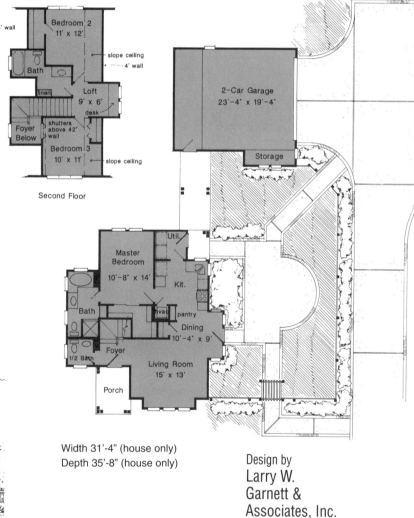

Second Floor

Width 31'-4" (house only)
Depth 35'-8" (house only)

Design by
Larry W.
Garnett &
Associates, Inc.

Design S9117

First Floor: 693 square feet
Second Floor: 342 square feet
Total: 1,035 square feet

● This quaint, cozy cottage serves a variety of needs. It could be used as a second home or leisure get-away; it could be the perfect guest house or mother-in-law cottage; or it may even make a great primary residence for a single person or a couple. It's fine detailing and traditional features make it a favorite with everyone.

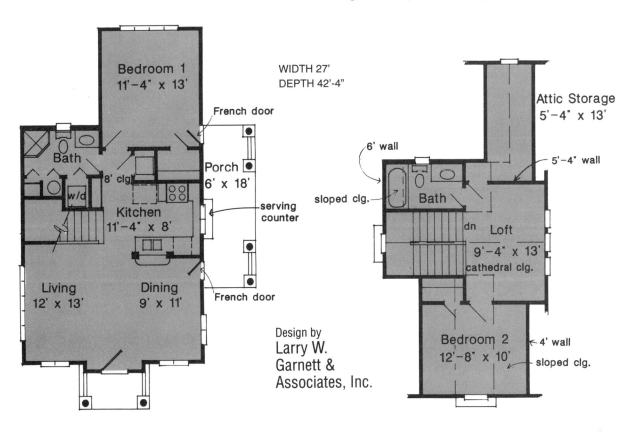

WIDTH 27'
DEPTH 42'-4"

Bedroom 1
11'-4" x 13'

French door

Bath

8' clg.

Porch
6' x 18'

serving counter

Kitchen
11'-4" x 8'

w/d

Living
12' x 13'

Dining
9' x 11'

French door

Design by
Larry W.
Garnett &
Associates, Inc.

Attic Storage
5'-4" x 13'

6' wall

5'-4" wall

sloped clg.

Bath

dn   Loft
9'-4" x 13'
cathedral clg.

Bedroom 2
12'-8" x 10'

4' wall

sloped clg.

Design S9041

First Floor: 945 square feet
Second Floor: 528 square feet
Total: 1,473 square feet

● Because of the compact nature of this shingle cottage, you might never guess that it contains three bedrooms and two full baths. And that's not all! The living room is appointed with built-in bookshelves, a fireplace and French doors to the rear yard. This room connects to the kitchen and dining area for a wonderfully open plan. The master bedroom is found on the first floor and has a compartmented bath with linen storage and a window seat. Upstairs are two more bedrooms sharing a full bath. Each of these has ample closet space. Note the second-floor balcony area with built-in cabinets and bookshelves.

Design by
Larry W.
Garnett &
Associates, Inc.

6' wall   cabinets and books
slope ceiling
Bedroom 2
11'-4" x 10'-8"
Bath
Balcony
8' x 6'
linen
slope ceiling
Bedroom 3
12' x 11'-8"

2-Car Garage
19'-4" x 24'-4"

Util.
Dining
10'-8" x 10'
French Doors
pantry
Kitchen
10' x 10'
42" bar
Living Room
17'-4" x 14'
books
Foyer
Master Bedroom
12' x 14'
linen
Bath
seat
Porch

Width 51'-10"
Depth 46'-8"

Design S9131

First Floor: 978 square feet
Second Floor: 464 square feet
Total: 1,442 square feet

● From the covered front veranda to the second-story Palladian window, this home exudes warmth and grace. Though smaller in square footage, the floor plan offers plenty of room. The living area is complemented by a cozy corner fireplace and is attached to a dining area with French doors to a screened porch and the front veranda. The galley-style kitchen is the central hub of the first floor. A large bedroom on this floor has an attached full bath and serves equally well as guest bedroom or master bedroom. The second floor holds two bedrooms and another full bath. An open balcony area here overlooks the foyer below.

Width 35'-8"
Depth 44'-8"

QUOTE ONE®

Cost to build? See page 216 to order complete cost estimate to build this house in your area!

Design by
Larry W. Garnett & Associates, Inc.

Design S9119

First Floor: 1,554 square feet
Second Floor: 592 square feet
Total: 2,146 square feet

● One-and-a-half story living means bonus space on a second floor. This design utilizes that space for split-bedroom planning with the master suite on the main level and family or guest rooms on the second level. Living and working areas are open and nicely appointed: a living room with window seat and fireplace, and a formal dining room with pass-through bar to the kitchen. The breakfast room features a bay window and French door to a side porch. A half bath in the hall serves the needs of guests handily.

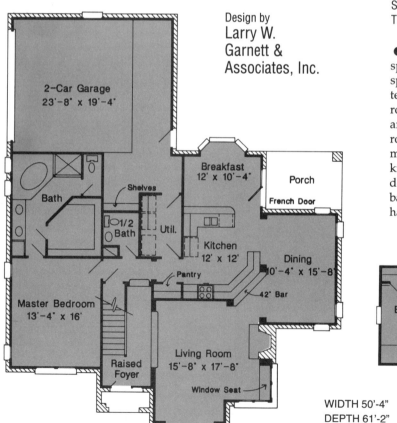

Design by
Larry W.
Garnett &
Associates, Inc.

2-Car Garage
23'-8" x 19'-4"

Breakfast
12' x 10'-4"

Porch

French Door

Bath

Shelves

1/2 Bath

Util.

Kitchen
12' x 12'

Dining
10'-4" x 15'-8"

Pantry

42" Bar

Master Bedroom
13'-4" x 16'

Raised Foyer

Living Room
15'-8" x 17'-8"

Window Seat

WIDTH 50'-4"
DEPTH 61'-2"

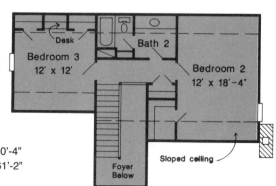

Desk

Bedroom 3
12' x 12'

Bath 2

Bedroom 2
12' x 18'-4"

Foyer Below

Sloped ceiling

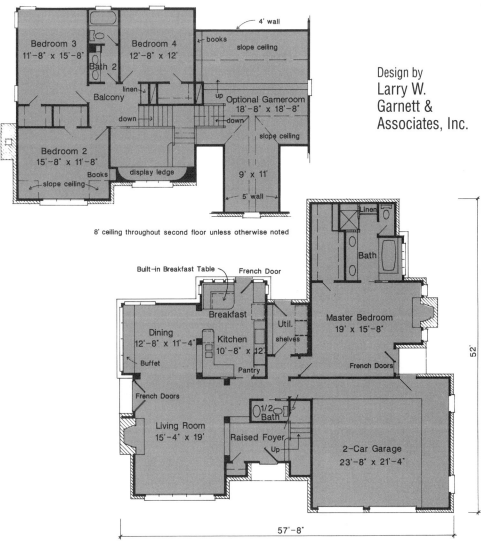

Bedroom 3
11'-8" x 15'-8"

Bath 2

Bedroom 4
12'-8" x 12'

books

slope ceiling

4' wall

linen

Balcony

up

Optional Gameroom
18'-8" x 18'-8"

down

down

slope ceiling

Bedroom 2
15'-8" x 11'-8"

Books

display ledge

9' x 11'

slope ceiling

5' wall

8' ceiling throughout second floor unless otherwise noted

Design by
Larry W.
Garnett &
Associates, Inc.

Built-in Breakfast Table

French Door

Linen

Bath

Breakfast

Master Bedroom
19' x 15'-8"

Dining
12'-8" x 11'-4"

Kitchen
10'-8" x 12'

Util.

shelves

Buffet

Pantry

French Doors

French Doors

1/2
Bath

Living Room
15'-4" x 19'

Raised Foyer

Up

2-Car Garage
23'-8" x 21'-4"

52'

57'-8"

9' ceilings throughout first floor

Design S8927

First Floor: 1,579 square feet
Second Floor: 764 square feet
Total: 2,343 square feet
Optional Gameroom: 468 square feet

● This stately two-story home is highlighted by interesting multi-pane windows, an arched entry way and a brick exterior. Open floor planning makes this design appear larger than it is. The formal living and dining area combine to create a spacious formal living area. A cheery fireplace and a built-in buffet flank French doors that open onto the side yard. Casual dining is a delight with the built-in breakfast table lit by surrounding windows, perfect for lingering over the morning paper. The master bedroom provides a welcome retreat with its cozy fireplace, huge walk-in closet and pampering bath. Upstairs, Bedrooms 2, 3 and 4 (all with walk-in closets) share a full bath. An optional gameroom provides additional space for indoor recreation and a bookcase to hold books for more quiet times.

Design S9621

First Floor: 1,325 square feet
Second Floor: 453 square feet
Total: 1,778 square feet

● For the economy-minded family desiring a wraparound covered porch, this compact design has all the amenities available in larger plans with little wasted space. In addition, a front Palladian window, dormer and rear arched windows provide exciting visual elements to the exterior. The spacious great room has a fireplace, cathedral ceiling and clerestory arched windows. A second-level balcony overlooks this gathering area. The kitchen is centrally located for maximum flexibility in layout and features a pass-through to the great room. Besides the generous master suite with well-appointed full bath, there are two family bedrooms located on the second level sharing a full bath with double vanity. Note the ample attic storage space. For a crawl-space foundation, order Design S9621; for a basement foundation, order Design S9621-A.

FRONT

REAR

Design by
Donald A. Gardner,
Architect, Inc.

QUOTE ONE®

Cost to build? See page 216 to order complete cost estimate to build this house in your area!

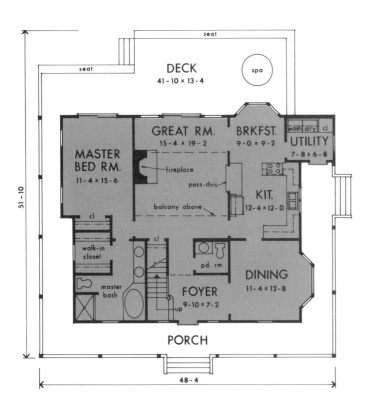

DECK
41 - 10 x 13 - 4

spa

seat

GREAT RM.
15 - 4 x 19 - 2

BRKFST.
9 - 0 x 9 - 2

wash dry cl
UTILITY
7 - 8 x 6 - 8

MASTER BED RM.
11 - 4 x 15 - 6

fireplace

pass-thru

KIT.
12 - 4 x 12 - 0

balcony above

cl

walk-in closet

cl

pd. rm.

DINING
11 - 4 x 12 - 8

master bath

FOYER
9 - 10 x 7 - 2

up

PORCH

51 - 10

48 - 4

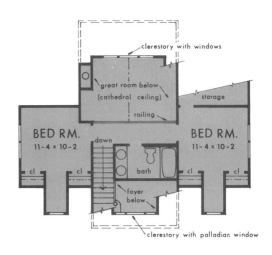

clerestory with windows

great room below
(cathedral ceiling)

storage

railing

BED RM.
11 - 4 x 10 - 2

down

BED RM.
11 - 4 x 10 - 2

cl   cl

bath

cl   cl

foyer below

clerestory with palladian window

112

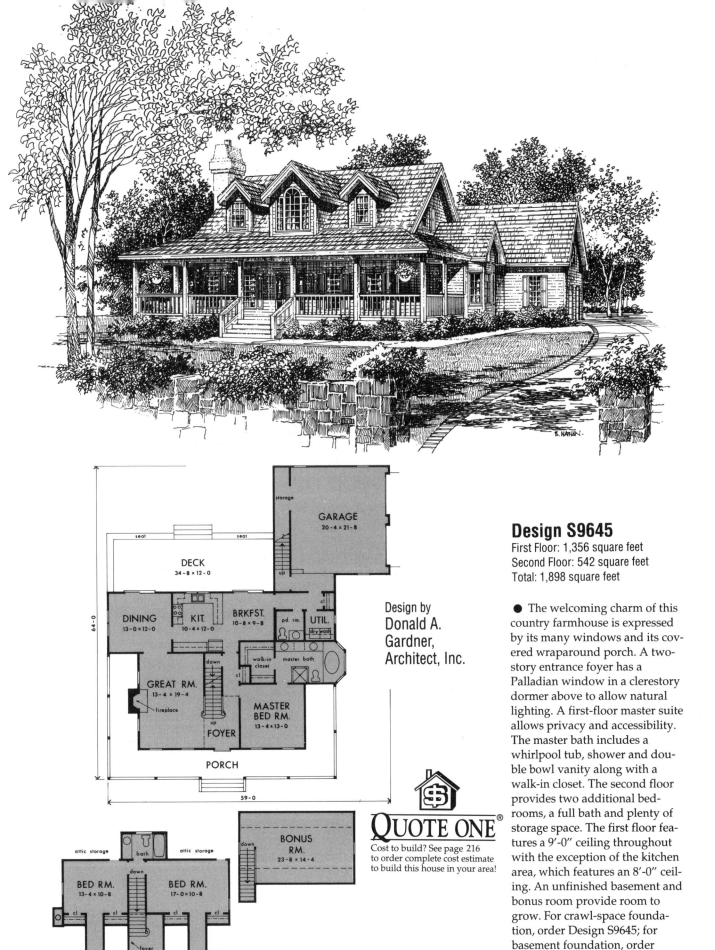

DECK
34-8 x 12-0

GARAGE
20-4 x 21-8

storage

seat   seat

DINING
13-0 x 12-0

KIT.
10-4 x 12-0

BRKFST.
10-8 x 9-8

pd. rm.

UTIL.

dry wash

walk-in closet

master bath

cl

down

GREAT RM.
13-4 x 19-4

fireplace

up

FOYER

MASTER BED RM.
13-4 x 13-0

PORCH

64-0

59-0

Design by
Donald A. Gardner, Architect, Inc.

attic storage   bath   attic storage

BED RM.
13-4 x 10-8

down

BED RM.
17-0 x 10-8

cl   cl   cl   cl

foyer below

clerestory with palladian window

down

BONUS RM.
23-8 x 14-4

QUOTE ONE®

Cost to build? See page 216
to order complete cost estimate
to build this house in your area!

Design S9645

First Floor: 1,356 square feet
Second Floor: 542 square feet
Total: 1,898 square feet

● The welcoming charm of this country farmhouse is expressed by its many windows and its covered wraparound porch. A two-story entrance foyer has a Palladian window in a clerestory dormer above to allow natural lighting. A first-floor master suite allows privacy and accessibility. The master bath includes a whirlpool tub, shower and double bowl vanity along with a walk-in closet. The second floor provides two additional bedrooms, a full bath and plenty of storage space. The first floor features a 9'-0" ceiling throughout with the exception of the kitchen area, which features an 8'-0" ceiling. An unfinished basement and bonus room provide room to grow. For crawl-space foundation, order Design S9645; for basement foundation, order Design S9645-A.

Design S9625

First Floor: 1,581 square feet
Second Floor: 549 square feet
Total: 2,130 square feet
Bonus Room: 334 square feet

● Great flexibility is available in this plan—the great room/dining room can be reworked into one large great room with the dining room relocated to the family room. A sun room with cathedral ceiling and sliding glass door to the deck is accessible from both the breakfast and dining rooms. A large kitchen boasts a convenient cooking island. The master bedroom has a fireplace, walk-in closet and spa-cious master bath. Two second-level bedrooms are equal in size and share a full bath with double-bowl vanity. Both bedrooms have a dormer window and a walk-in closet. A large bonus room over the garage is accessible from the utility room below. For a crawl-space foundation order Plan S9625; for a basement foundation order Plan S9625-A.

Design by
Donald A.
Gardner,
Architect, Inc.

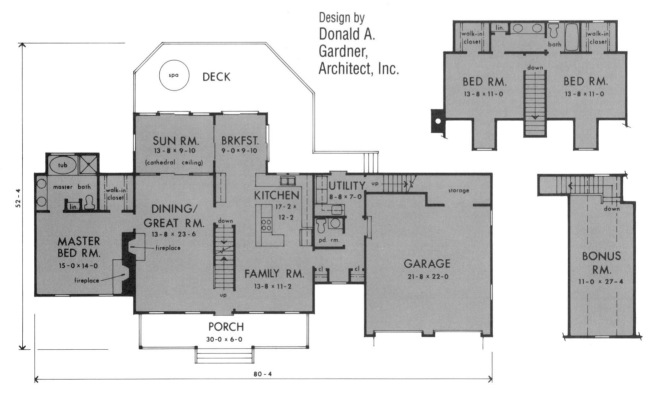

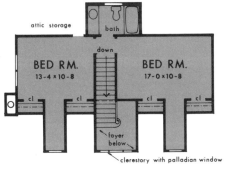

attic storage

bath

BED RM.
13-4 × 10-8

down

BED RM.
17-0 × 10-8

cl · cl · cl · cl

foyer below

clerestory with palladian window

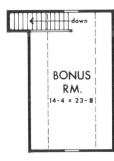

down

BONUS RM.
14-4 × 23-8

Design by
Donald A. Gardner, Architect, Inc.

Design S9606

First Floor: 1,289 square feet
Second Floor: 542 square feet
Total: 1,831 square feet

● This cozy country cottage is perfect for the growing family — offering both an unfinished basement option and a bonus room. Enter through the two-story foyer with a Palladian window in a clerestory dormer above. The master suite is on the first floor for privacy and accessibility. Its accompanying bath boasts a whirlpool tub with skylight above and double-bowl vanity. The second floor has two bedrooms, a full bath and plenty of storage. Note that all first-floor rooms except the kitchen and utility room have nine-foot ceilings. For crawl-space foundation, order Plan S9606; for basement foundation, order S9606-A.

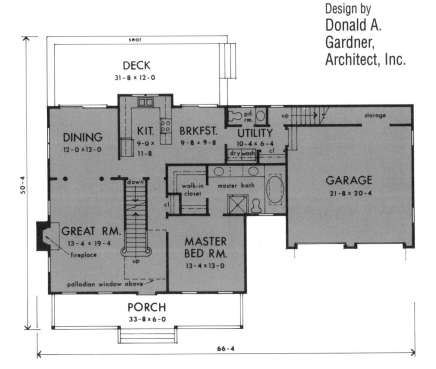

seat

DECK
31-8 × 12-0

DINING
12-0 × 12-0

KIT.
9-0 × 11-8

BRKFST.
9-8 × 9-8

UTILITY
10-4 × 6-4

pd. rm.

up

storage

dry wash · cl

down

walk-in closet

master bath

GARAGE
21-8 × 20-4

GREAT RM.
13-4 × 19-4

fireplace

up

MASTER BED RM.
13-4 × 13-0

palladian window above

50-4

PORCH
33-8 × 6-0

66-4

QUOTE ONE®

Cost to build? See page 216
to order complete cost estimate
to build this house in your area!

115

Design S9605

First Floor: 1,562 square feet
Second Floor: 537 square feet
Total: 2,099 square feet

● Outdoor living is realized in a wraparound covered porch at the front and sides of this house, as well as the open deck with storage to the rear. Also notice how the country feel is updated with arched rear windows and a sun room. Inside find the spacious great room with fireplace, cathedral ceiling and clerestory with arched windows. The kitchen occupies a central location between the dining room and the great room for equally convenient formal and informal occasions. A generous master suite has a fireplace and access to the sun room and covered porch. On the second level are two more bedrooms, a full bath and storage space.

Design by
Donald A.
Gardner,
Architect, Inc.

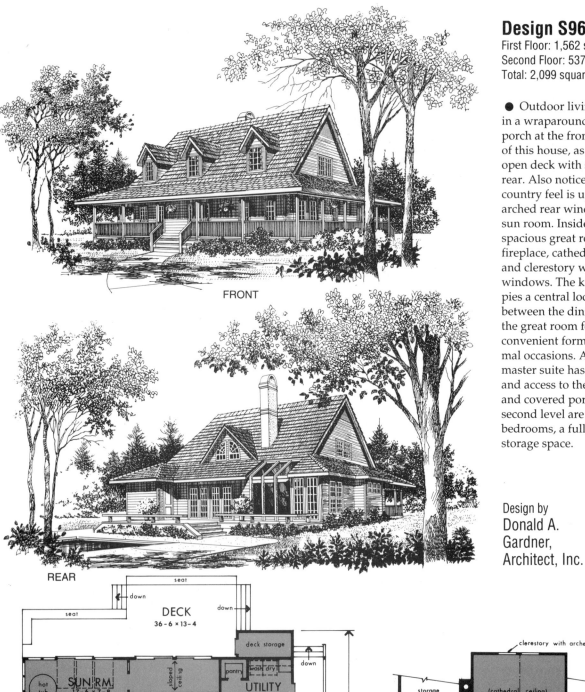

FRONT

REAR

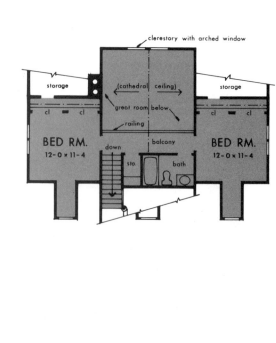

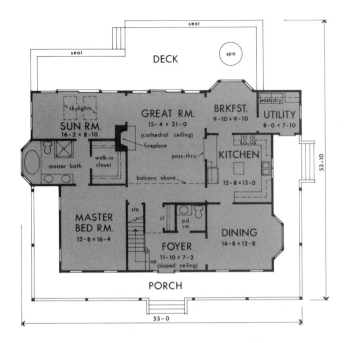

Design S9623

First Floor: 1,651 square feet
Second Floor: 567 square feet
Total: 2,218 square feet

● A wonderful wraparound covered porch at the front and sides of this house and the open deck with spa at the back provide plenty of outside living area. Inside, the spacious great room has a fireplace, cathedral ceiling and clerestory with arched window. The kitchen is centrally located for maximum flexibility in layout and has a food preparation island for convenience. Besides the master bedroom with access to the sun room, there are two second-level bedrooms that share a full bath. For a crawl-space foundation, order Design S9623; for a basement foundation, order Design S9623-A.

QUOTE ONE®

Cost to build? See page 216 to order complete cost estimate to build this house in your area!

Design by
Donald A. Gardner, Architect, Inc.

Design by
Donald A.
Gardner,
Architect, Inc.

● Enjoy outdoor living with a covered front porch at the front of this home and an expansive deck to the rear. The floor plan allows for great livability and features split-bedroom styling with the master suite on the first floor. Upstairs bedrooms share a full bath. There is also bonus space above the garage for a studio, study or play room. For a crawl-space foundation, order Plan S9654; for a basement foundation, order S9654-A.

Design S9654

First Floor: 1,578 square feet
Second Floor: 554 square feet
Total: 2,132 square feet

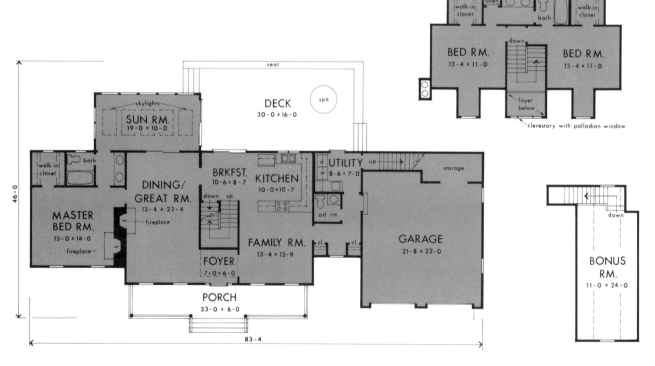

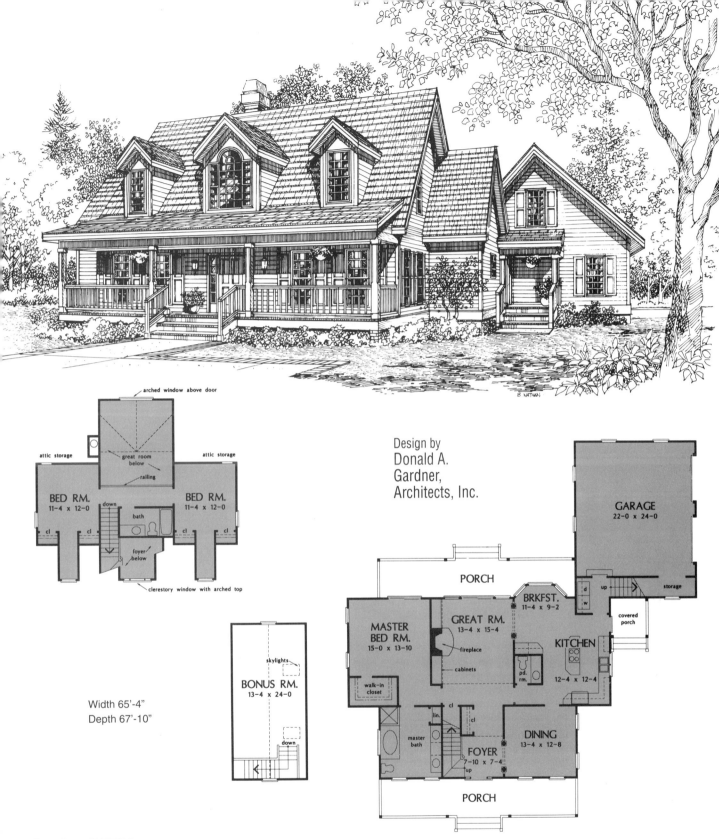

arched window above door

attic storage

attic storage

great room below

railing

BED RM.
11-4 x 12-0

BED RM.
11-4 x 12-0

down

bath

cl

cl

cl

cl

foyer below

clerestory window with arched top

Design by
Donald A.
Gardner,
Architects, Inc.

GARAGE
22-0 x 24-0

up

storage

PORCH

BRKFST.
11-4 x 9-2

d

w

covered porch

skylights

BONUS RM.
13-4 x 24-0

down

MASTER
BED RM.
15-0 x 13-10

GREAT RM.
13-4 x 15-4

fireplace

cabinets

pd. rm.

KITCHEN
12-4 x 12-4

Width 65'-4"
Depth 67'-10"

walk-in closet

master bath

cl

lin.

cl

FOYER
7-10 x 7-4

up

DINING
13-4 x 12-8

PORCH

Design S9732

First Floor: 1,506 square feet; Second Floor: 513 square feet
Total: 2,019 square feet; Bonus Room: 397 square feet

● This three-bedroom, country home with front and rear porches offers an open plan layout with minimal wasted space. A front Palladian window dormer and a rear arched window along with the overall massing of the home adds to its exterior visual intrigue. The entrance foyer rises with a sloped ceiling and enjoys an abundance of light from a Palladian window clerestory. In the spacious great room, a fireplace, a cathedral ceiling and a clerestory with an arched window all add to appeal. A second-level balcony overlooks the great room. The master suite features all of the amenities while two secondary bedrooms reside on the second level. A bonus room offers room to grow.

Design S3443

First Floor: 1,211 square feet
Second Floor: 614 square feet
Total: 1,825 square feet

● What a pampering retreat! The master suite in this house is on a level all its own. The twenty-one-foot bedroom includes a sitting area. The master bath features a walk-in closet, dual vanities, a separate tub and shower and a compartmented toilet. A second bedroom or optional den, with a full bath nearby, is located on the first floor. The formal living and dining rooms have sloped ceilings separated by a plant shelf and bay windows. The family room features a snack bar to the kitchen and patio access. Tiled floors throughout add a special touch. Note the hobby shop in the garage.

Design by
Home Planners

QUOTE ONE®

Cost to build? See page 216 to order complete cost estimate to build this house in your area!

Design S3444

First Floor: 1,453 square feet
Second Floor: 520 square feet
Total: 1,973 square feet

Design by
Home Planners

● This compact plan offers full-scale livability on two floors. The first floor begins with an elegant living room—a bay window here allows for an infiltration of natural light. The dining room remains open to this room and will delight with its spaciousness. The kitchen is just beyond and extends room enough for a dinette set. Comfortable gatherings are the name of the game in the family room which enjoys shared space with the kitchen area. A warming fireplace gains attention here as do a pair of graceful windows that flank it. Also on the first floor, the master bedroom expands into a spacious and luxurious bathroom. A garden tub set below a window is sure to satisfy as is a large walk-in closet. For family and guests, two upstairs bedrooms are situated around a Hollywood bath.

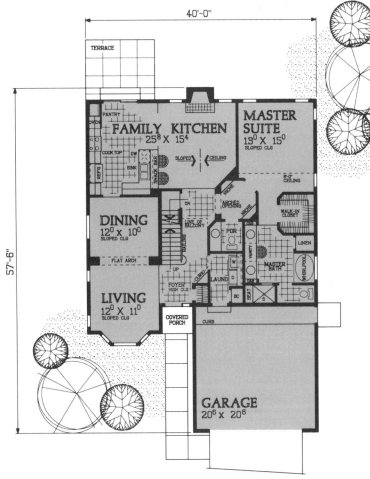

Cost to build? See page 216
to order complete cost estimate
to build this house in your area!

Quote One™

Cost to build? See page 216 to order complete cost estimate to build this house in your area!

Design S3438

First Floor: 1,489 square feet
Second Floor: 741 square feet
Total: 2,230 square feet

● A unique farmhouse plan which provides a grand floor plan, this home is comfortable in country or suburban settings. Formal entertaining areas share first-floor space with family gathering rooms and work and service areas. The master suite is also on this floor for convenience and privacy. Upstairs is a guest bedroom, private bath and loft area that makes a perfect studio. Special features make this a great place to come home to.

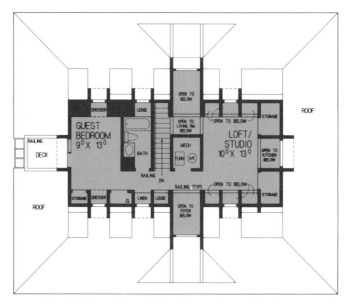

Design by
Home Planners

Photo by Bob Greenspan

This home, as shown in the photograph, may differ from the actual blueprints.
For more detailed information, please check the floor plans carefully.

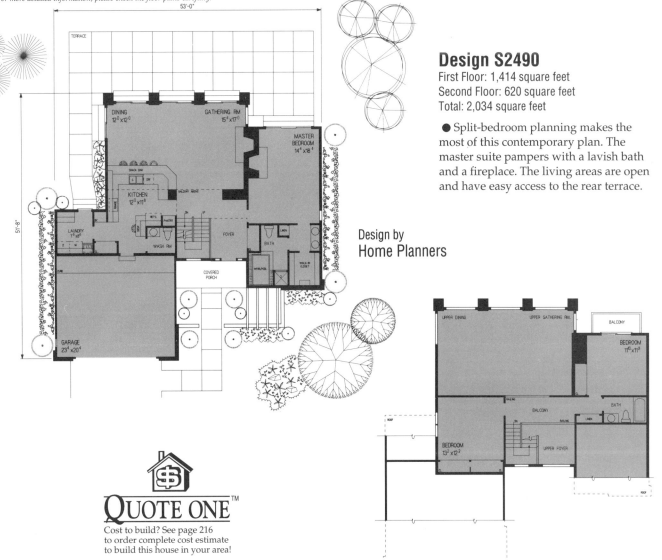

Design S2490

First Floor: 1,414 square feet
Second Floor: 620 square feet
Total: 2,034 square feet

● Split-bedroom planning makes the most of this contemporary plan. The master suite pampers with a lavish bath and a fireplace. The living areas are open and have easy access to the rear terrace.

Design by
Home Planners

QUOTE ONE™

Cost to build? See page 216 to order complete cost estimate to build this house in your area!

Copyright Stephen S. Fuller, Inc.

Design S9875

First Floor: 1,475 square feet
Second Floor: 545 square feet
Total: 2,020 square feet

● This quaint country manor combines stucco and stone to create unrivaled warmth and charm. The two-story foyer is highlighted by the beautiful open-railed staircase and view of the living and dining rooms. The kitchen, equipped with ample space and work island, makes preparations a breeze. The breakfast area opens to a keeping room with corner fireplace and French doors, bringing the out of doors comfortably inside. Privately located on the opposite side of the home is the luxurious master suite with sitting area and master bath complete with dual vanities, garden tub, enclosed shower and large walk-in closet. Upstairs, the gallery overlooks the living and dining rooms below. Down the hallway two bedrooms and a bonus room share access to a centrally located hall bath.

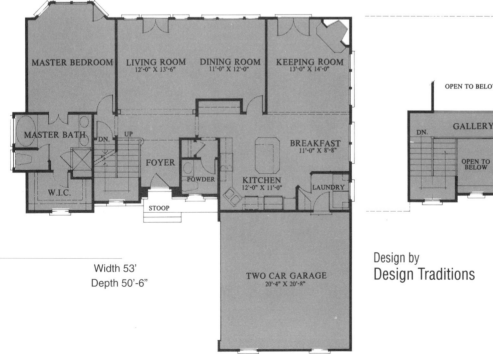

Width 53'
Depth 50'-6"

MASTER BEDROOM

LIVING ROOM
12'-0" X 13'-6"

DINING ROOM
11'-0" X 12'-0"

KEEPING ROOM
13'-0" X 14'-0"

MASTER BATH

DN. UP

FOYER

POWDER

BREAKFAST
11'-0" X 8'-8"

KITCHEN
12'-0" X 11'-0"

LAUNDRY

W.I.C.

STOOP

TWO CAR GARAGE
20'-4" X 20'-8"

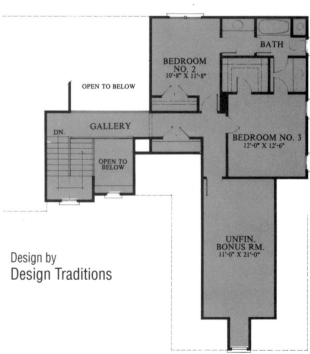

Design by
Design Traditions

BATH

BEDROOM
NO. 2
10'-8" X 11'-8"

OPEN TO BELOW

DN. GALLERY

OPEN TO BELOW

BEDROOM NO. 3
12'-0" X 12'-6"

UNFIN.
BONUS RM.
11'-0" X 21'-0"

124

Copyright 1992 Stephen S. Fuller, Inc.

Design S9876

First Floor: 1,720 square feet
Second Floor: 545 square feet
Total: 2,265 square feet

● The foyer opens to the living and dining areas, providing a spectacular entrance to this English country cottage. Just beyond the dining room is a gourmet kitchen with work island and food bar opening onto the breakfast room. Accented by a fireplace and built-in bookcase, the family room with a ribbon of windows is an excellent setting for family gatherings. Remotely located off the central hallway, the master suite includes a rectangular ceiling detail and access to the rear deck, while the master bath features His and Hers vanities, garden tub, and spacious walk-in closet. The central staircase leads to the balcony overlook and three bedrooms with spacious closets and baths.

BEDROOM NO. 3
11'-10" X 12'-0"

OPEN TO BELOW

BATH

BALCONY

FUTURE
BEDROOM NO. 4
13'-6" X 12'-0"

DN

BEDROOM
NO. 2
13'-0" X 12'-0"

FUTURE
BATH

OPEN TO
BELOW

FUTURE
STORAGE

Design by
Design Traditions

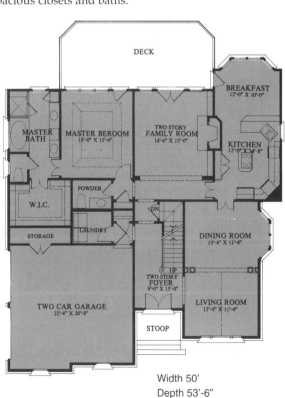

DECK

BREAKFAST
12'-0" X 10'-0"

MASTER
BATH

MASTER BEDROOM
13'-0" X 15'-4"

TWO STORY
FAMILY ROOM
14'-6" X 15'-0"

KITCHEN
12'-0" X 14'-8"

POWDER

W.I.C.

LAUNDRY

STORAGE

DN

DINING ROOM
13'-4" X 11'-8"

UP

TWO CAR GARAGE
22'-4" X 20'-8"

TWO STORY
FOYER
9'-0" X 15'-0"

LIVING ROOM
13'-4" X 11'-4"

STOOP

Width 50'
Depth 53'-6"

Design S9265

First Floor: 1,297 square feet
Second Floor: 388 square feet
Total: 1,685 square feet

● A lovely covered porch welcomes family and guests to this delightful 1½-story home. From the entry, the formal dining room with boxed windows and the great room with fireplace are visible. A powder room for guests is located just beyond the dining room. An open kitchen/dinette features a pantry, planning desk and a snack-bar counter. The elegant master suite is appointed with formal ceiling detail and a window seat. The skylight above the whirlpool, the decorator plant shelf and the double lavatories all dress up the master bath. Secondary bedrooms on the second floor share a centrally located bath.

QUOTE ONE®

Cost to build? See page 216
to order complete cost estimate
to build this house in your area!

Design by
Design Basics, Inc.

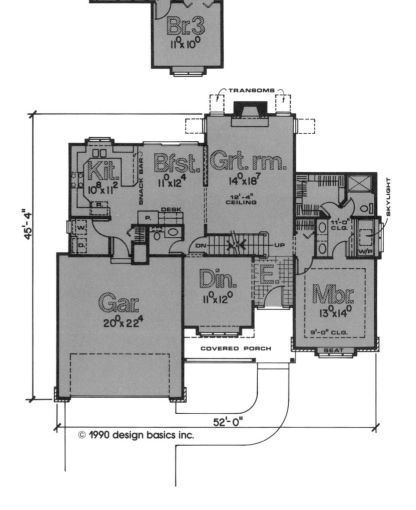

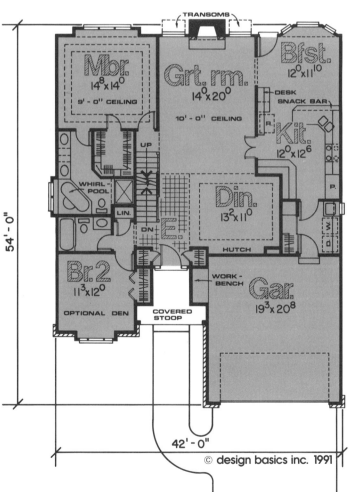

Design S9339

First Floor: 1,517 square feet
Second Floor: 234 square feet
Total: 1,751 square feet

● Attractive brick and wood siding and a covered front porch make this a beautiful design—even for narrower lots. The entry gives way to a dining room with hutch space and then further opens to a bright, airy great room. The kitchen is highlighted by a French door entry, ample counters, and a roomy pantry. The first floor holds two bedrooms—a secondary bedroom with bath and the master suite with roomy walk-in closet, corner whirlpool, and dual lavs. On the second floor is a totally private third bedroom with its own bath.

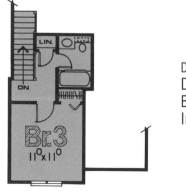

Design by
Design
Basics,
Inc.

© design basics inc. 1991

Design S9206

First Floor: 1,421 square feet
Second Floor: 578 square feet
Total: 1,999 square feet

● Growing families will love this unique plan which combines all the essentials with an abundance of stylish touches. Start with the living areas — a spacious great room with high ceilings, windows overlooking the back yard, a through-fireplace to the kitchen and access to the rear yard. A dining room with hutch space accommodates formal occasions. The hearth kitchen features a well-planned work area and a bay-windowed breakfast area. The master suite with whirlpool and walk-in closet is found downstairs while three family bedrooms are upstairs.

Quote One®

Cost to build? See page 216 to order complete cost estimate to build this house in your area!

Design by
Design Basics, Inc.

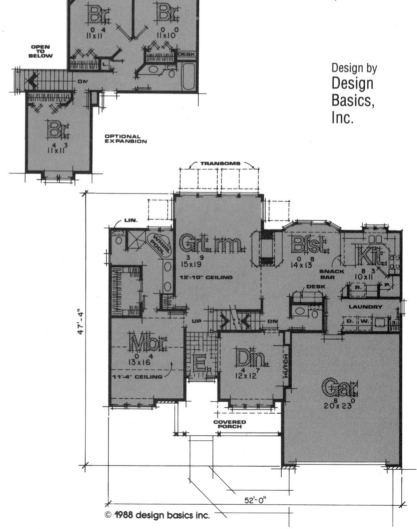

© 1988 design basics inc.

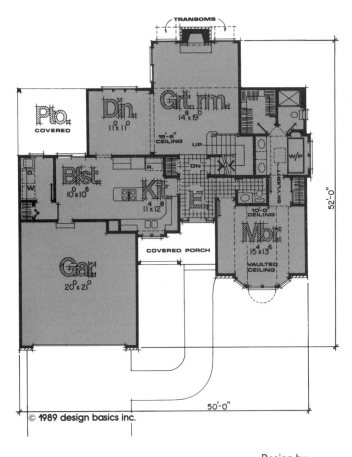

© 1989 design basics inc.

Design by
Design
Basics,
Inc.

Design S9315

First Floor: 1,306 square feet
Second Floor: 599 square feet
Total: 1,905 square feet

● Note the hard surface entry with coat closet as you pass through to the volume great room with cozy fireplace. Open to the great room is a formal dining room served by the adjoining island kitchen. A vaulted ceiling and arched bayed window grace the master bedroom. The accommodating skylit dressing/bath area with sloped ceiling features a whirlpool and decorator plant shelf. Overlooking the great room and entry for a sensational view is the upstairs landing. Each secondary bedroom shares a generous compartmented bath. This home will be your dream come true.

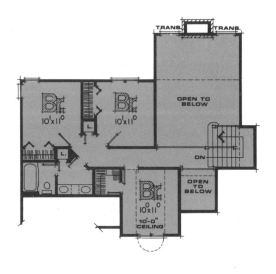

Design S9324

First Floor: 1,519 square feet
Second Floor: 594 square feet
Total: 2,113 square feet

● Sophisticated styling and comfortable living define this 1½-story home both inside and out. To the right of the volume entry is a formal living room with a 10-foot ceiling. Boxed windows brighten the formal dining room. In the kitchen/breakfast area, practical features include two Lazy Susans, a snack bar and planning desk. Nearby, the casual family room offers a sloped ceiling and cozy fireplace. The secluded main-floor master bedroom sports a 10-foot ceiling. Study the dressing area with dual lavs, a pampering whirlpool and large walk-in closet. Each secondary bedroom has convenient access to a hall bath complete with a linen closet. A loft area, open to the family room, easily converts to an optional bedroom.

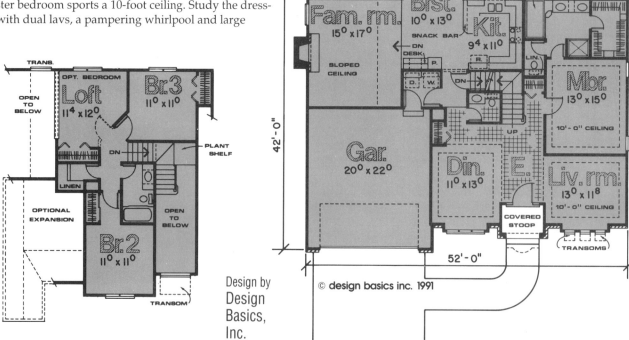

Design by
Design
Basics,
Inc.

© design basics inc. 1991

Design S7282

First Floor: 1,015 square feet
Second Floor: 675 square feet
Total: 1,690 square feet

● This home's comfortable living room with bayed window and vaulted ceiling opens to the formal dining room. The efficient kitchen overlooks the sunken family room with its raised-hearth fireplace. The bayed breakfast area has a planning desk. On the upper level, the secondary bedrooms share a functional hall bath. The master bedroom's vaulted ceiling, window seat, walk-in closet and private bath are fine features. Storage space in the garage and a full basement assure room for everything.

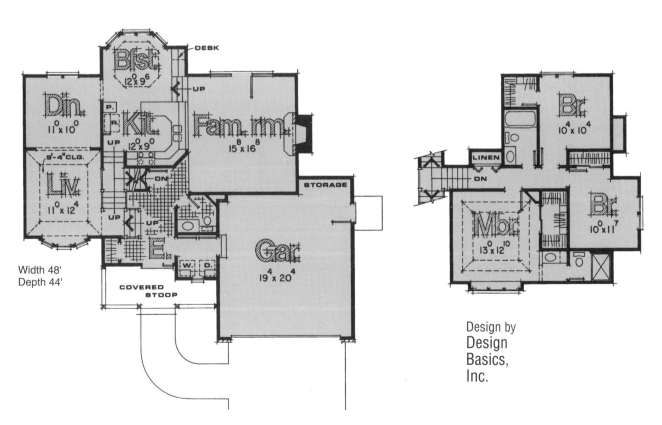

Width 48'
Depth 44'

Design by
Design Basics, Inc.

Design S9281
First Floor: 1,697 square feet
Second Floor: 694 square feet; Total: 2,391 square feet

● Arched transom windows plus the combination of siding and brick create the magic of this four-bedroom, 1½-story home. French doors lead into the volume living room with arched window. To the right, a hutch space adds to the versatility of the dining room. Casual traffic patterns start with the large great room with a two-sided fireplace and windows out the back. A walk-in pantry, desk and island in the kitchen opens to a semi-gazebo dinette. Don't miss the luxurious master dressing/bath area featuring His and Hers vanities, a walk-in closet and a corner whirlpool. Each secondary bedroom upstairs benefits from a built-in desk and a shared, compartmented bath.

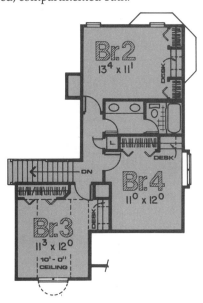

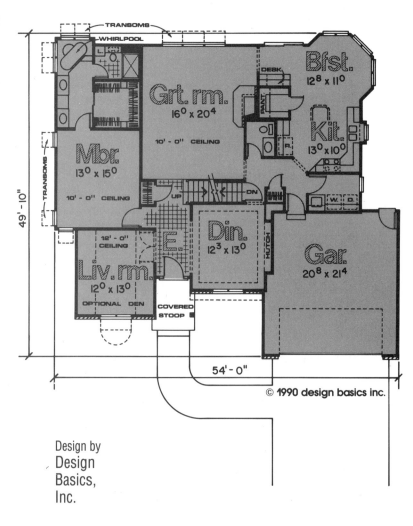

Design by
Design Basics, Inc.

© 1990 design basics inc.

Design S9340

First Floor: 1,595 square feet
Second Floor: 641 square feet
Total: 2,236 square feet

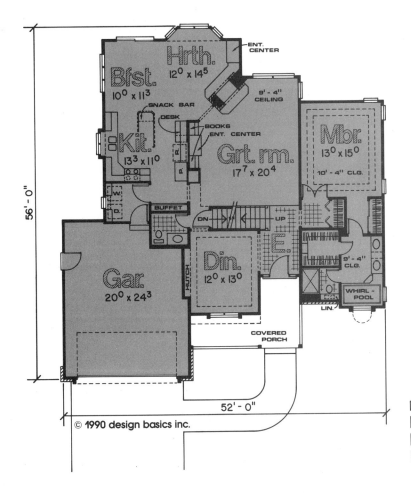

© 1990 design basics inc.

● Distinctive and livable are two words which describe this 1½-story home. Gracing the exterior is a generous covered porch. To the left of the entry is a formal dining room with a hutch space and interesting ceiling details. An angled through-fireplace warms the great room which features a bookcase and volume ceiling. The hearth room, which includes a bayed window and entertainment center, adjoins the breakfast area with snack bar. Special amenities in the island kitchen are a snack bar, pantry and built-in buffet serving counter. Double doors lead into the luxurious main-floor master bedroom accented by a tiered ceiling. The master dressing area features a roomy walk-in closet and dual vanities plus a volume ceiling and whirlpool. Upstairs, each secondary bedroom is special in its own way. Especially noteworthy is the front secondary bedroom which features a volume ceiling and an arched window.

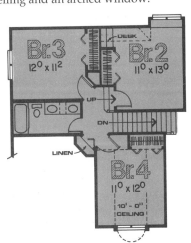

Design by
Design
Basics,
Inc.

133

Design S9332

First Floor: 1,302 square feet
Second Floor: 599 square feet
Total: 1,901 square feet

● Sleek lines coupled with impressive detailing enhance the elevation of this modern Victorian design. From the covered veranda, the entry opens to a volume great room with a fireplace flanked by cheerful windows. Off this informal living space is a bright dining room perfect for entertaining. In the kitchen/breakfast area, an island cooktop and access to a covered patio merit special attention. The secluded main-floor master sleeping quarters include a decorative ceiling and bright boxed window. A luxurious master bath boasts two wardrobes, a decorator plant shelf and separate wet and dry areas. A scenic view is available from a bridge overlook on the second level. Three generous secondary sleeping quarters share a compartmented bath with dual lavs.

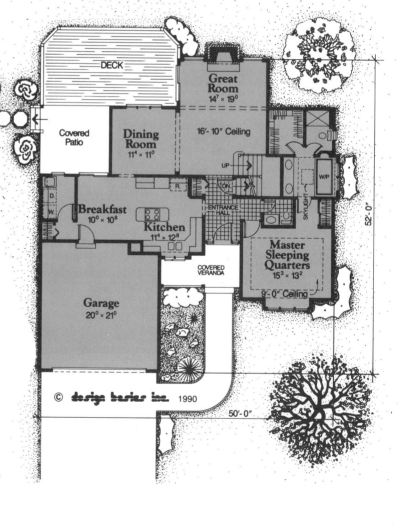

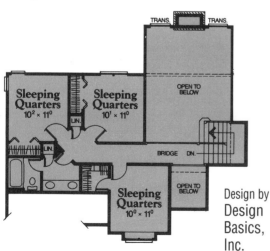

Design by
Design
Basics,
Inc.

Design S9251

First Floor: 1,653 square feet
Second Floor: 700 square feet
Total: 2,353 square feet

● Beautiful arches and elaborate detail give the elevation of this four-bedroom, 1½-story home an unmistakable elegance. Inside the floor plan is equally appealing. Note the formal dining room with bay window, visible from the entrance hall. The large great room has a fireplace and a wall of windows out the back. A hearth room, with bookcase, adjoins the kitchen area with walk-in pantry. The master suite on the first floor features His and Hers wardrobes, a large whirlpool and double lavatories. Upstairs quarters share a full bath with compartmented sinks.

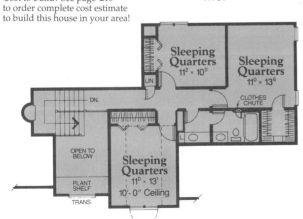

QUOTE ONE®

Cost to build? See page 216 to order complete cost estimate to build this house in your area!

Design by
Design Basics, Inc.

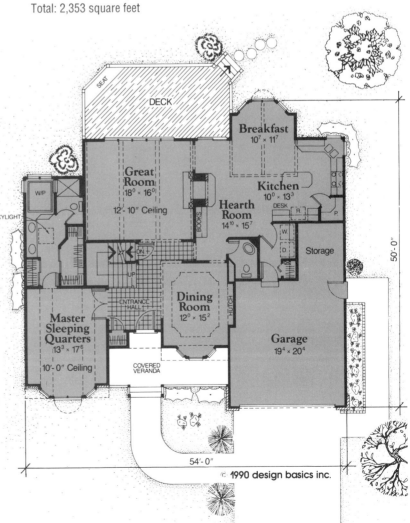

Design S9341

First Floor: 1,401 square feet
Second Floor: 891 square feet
Total: 2,292 square feet

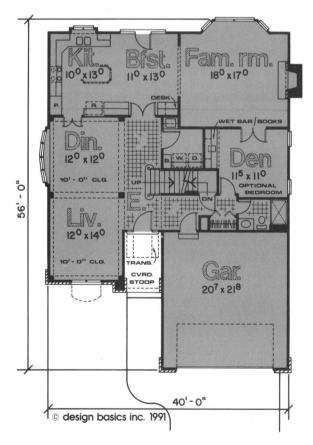

● At 40 feet wide, this 1½-story home is perfect for a narrow lot line. Inside, elegant window details highlight the dining and family rooms where French doors access an optional den with a wet bar. A gourmet island kitchen has wrapping counters, a pantry and a planning desk to serve the sunny breakfast area. Homeowners will appreciate the second level configuration, designed to offer privacy. Each secondary bedroom enjoys handy access to a pampering compartmented bath with dual lavs. Bedroom 2 includes a built-in bookcase. Attractions in the master suite include an arched transom window, two walk-in closets and French doors to a balcony overlook. Special touches in the master bath are dual vanities, corner windows and a sparkling glass block wall between the shower stall and whirlpool tub.

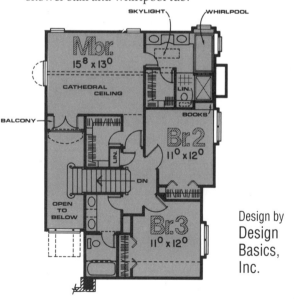

Design by
Design
Basics,
Inc.

TWO-STORY HOMES

Construction Efficiency In Stacked Livability

For generations Americans have "gone upstairs to bed." This comfortable living pattern, which emanated from the early Colonial period, continues today in economical and thoroughly livable designs. The popular two-story represents not only the best return per construction dollar spent, but also a budget-smart residence option in the long-run.

The "stacked livability" features of the two-story house rival other designs in allowing frugality of construction and operating costs. The full two-story creates a doubling of livable square footage without incurring the additional roof or foundation costs required for a similar size one-story.

Another construction advantage is the ease with which plumbing and heating/cooling systems can be installed. Having two stories means shorter wiring and ductwork runs. Also, single-stack plumbing for toilet facilities is possible when upstairs bathrooms are located above those on the first floor.

Before the days of central heating, the two-story chimney often served two or more fireplaces. The rooms on each floor relied upon the fireplace for warmth and comfort. While today the fireplace is no longer a heating necessity, it is a popular amenity. The use of a single chimney for the first- and second- floor fireplaces is a common, cost-saving practice.

Two-story houses also make the most effective use of building sites. This is a significant economic factor when deciding between a one- or two-story house. The exterior dimensions of a two-story can be much smaller than those of a one-story house with the same square footage. Because of this, a smaller and consequently less expensive site can be purchased. Narrow or modest-size sites are used to full advantage when two-story units are built upon them. With today's inflated land prices, utilizing a smaller, more affordable lot allows direction of money to the actual construction of a larger home.

Like one-story structures, two-story houses can be in-line, L-shaped, U-shaped or even angular. Two-stories can also be part one-story. And sometimes it is sensible to add only a one-story wing for a family or living room. Winged two-story houses provide a spacious low-cost alternative.

While the rectangular two-story configuration is the most economical to build for the amount of livable square footage it delivers, there are other popular shapes that can be wisely constructed. Consider, for example, the L-shaped two-story with a front-projecting garage. This plan fits on a smaller site than if the garage were appended to the side of the main house structure.

Two-story houses become even more affordable when attic space is completed, or when the basement is developed into bonus recreational, hobby or storage areas.

As presented in the plans in this section, elegant features may complement the two-story design: grand full-height foyers and sweeping staircases. For those who like a more open feeling, two-stories easily accommodate second-story bridges, interior balconies and upstairs lounges. With a sloping site, the basement can often be exposed and windows and door-walls installed to allow for the creation of light, airy living spaces. This can turn a two-story house into a three-story house in a most cost-effective manner.

Design S2733 First Floor: 1,177 square feet; Second Floor: 1,003 square feet; Total: 2,180 square feet

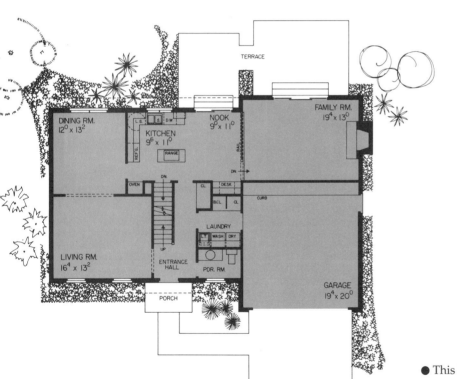

DINING RM.
12⁰ x 13²

KITCHEN
9⁶ x 11⁰

NOOK
9⁰ x 11⁰

FAMILY RM.
19⁴ x 13⁰

TERRACE

RANGE

OVEN

DESK

CURB

LAUNDRY

LIVING RM.
16⁴ x 13²

ENTRANCE HALL

PDR. RM.

PORCH

GARAGE
19⁴ x 20⁰

Width 54'
Depth 33'

Design by
Home Planners

Cost to build? See page 216
to order complete cost estimate
to build this house in your area!

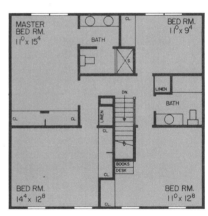

MASTER
BED RM.
11⁰ x 15⁴

BATH

BED RM.
11⁰ x 9⁴

LINEN

BATH

BED RM.
14⁴ x 12⁸

BED RM.
11⁰ x 12⁸

BOOKS DESK

● This is definitely a four-bedroom Colonial with charm galore. The kitchen features an island range and a sunny breakfast nook with outdoor access. All will enjoy the sunken family room with its fireplace and sliding glass doors leading to the terrace. The laundry room is found on the first floor for added convenience while the basement provides space for future recreational activities.

Photo by Carl Socolow

This home, as shown in the photograph, may differ from the actual blueprints. For more detailed information, please check the floor plans carefully.

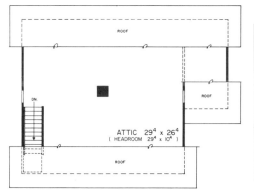

ATTIC 29⁴ x 26⁴
(HEADROOM 29⁴ x 10⁴)

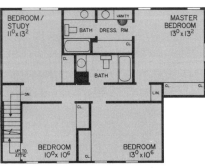

BEDROOM / STUDY 11⁰ x 13²

BATH   DRESS. RM.   VANITY

MASTER BEDROOM 13⁰ x 13²

BATH

BEDROOM 10⁰ x 10⁶

BEDROOM 13⁰ x 10⁶

LIN.

Design S2774

First Floor: 1,366 square feet
Second Floor: 969 square feet
Total: 2,335 square feet
Attic: 969 square feet

● Beginning with the formal areas, this design offers pleasures for the entire family. There is the quiet corner living room which has an opening to the sizable dining room. This room will enjoy plenty of natural light from the delightful bay window overlooking the rear yard. It is also conveniently located with the efficient U-shaped kitchen just a step away. The kitchen features many built-ins with a pass-through to the beam-ceilinged breakfast room. Sliding glass doors to the terrace are fine attractions in both the sunken family room and the breakfast room. The service entrance to the garage is flanked by a clothes closet and a large, walk-in pantry. There is a secondary entrance through the laundry room. Four bedrooms and two baths are located upstairs.

TERRACE

RAISED HEARTH

FAMILY RM. 21⁴ x 13⁶

BREAKFAST RM. 14⁰ x 11⁶

KITCHEN 10⁰ x 11⁸

PASS THRU

DINING RM. 13⁰ x 11⁶ + BAY

RANGE

LAUNDRY RM. 10⁰ x 7⁶

DESK   BRM. CL.   REF'G   OVEN

DN.

DN.

DRY. WASH. LT.

CL.

PANTRY

POR. RM.

CL.

CURB

DN.

FOYER

LIVING RM. 17⁰ x 13⁶

UP

COVERED PORCH

GARAGE 21⁴ x 21⁸

Width 59'-6"
Depth 46'

Quote One™
Cost to build? See page 216 to order complete cost estimate to build this house in your area!

Design by
Home Planners

Design S2622

First Floor: 624 square feet
Second Floor: 624 square feet
Total: 1,248 square feet

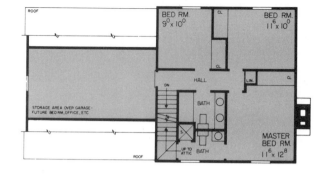

● This Colonial adaptation provides a functional design that allows for expansion in the future. A cozy fireplace in the living room adds warmth to this space as well as the adjacent dining area. The roomy L-shaped kitchen features a breakfast nook and an over-the-sink window. The upstairs holds two secondary bedrooms that share a full bath with a double vanity. The master bedroom is on this floor as well. Its private bath contains access to attic storage. An additional storage area over the garage can become a bedroom, office or study in the future.

Design by
Home Planners

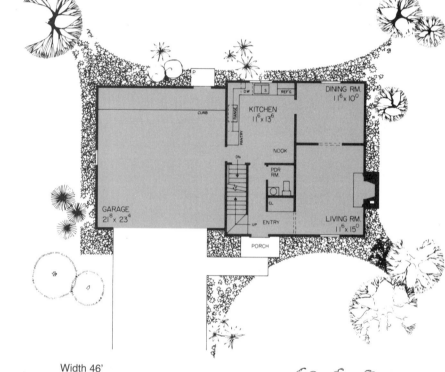

Width 46'
Depth 26'

Photo by Andrew D. Lautman

This home, as shown in the photograph, may differ from the actual blueprints. For more detailed information, please check the floor plans carefully.

QUOTE ONE®

Cost to build? See page 216 to order complete cost estimate to build this house in your area!

Design S1956 First Floor: 990 square feet
Second Floor: 728 square feet; Total: 1,718 square feet

● The blueprints for this home include details for both the three-bedroom and four-bedroom options. The first-floor livability does not change.

Design by Home Planners

4 BEDROOM PLAN

OPTIONAL 3 BEDROOM PLAN

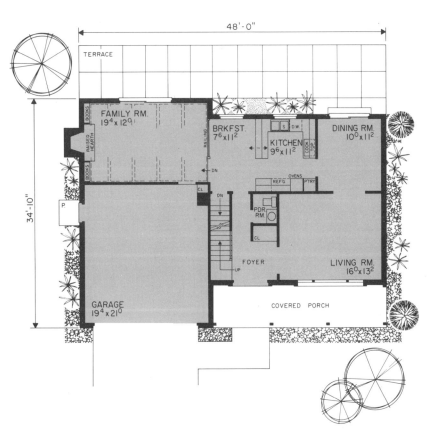

This home, as shown in the photograph, may differ from the actual blueprints.
For more detailed information, please check the floor plans carefully.

Photo by Bob Greenspan

Design S2974

First Floor: 911 square feet
Second Floor: 861 square feet
Total: 1,772 square feet

● Victorian houses are well known for their orientation on narrow building sites. From the front covered porch, the foyer directs traffic all the way to the back of the house with its open living and dining rooms. The U-shaped kitchen conveniently services both the dining room and the front breakfast room. Well worth mentioning is the veranda and the screened porch which both highlight the

outdoor livability presented in this design. Three bedrooms are contained on the second floor, while recreational, hobby and storage space is offered by the basement and the attic.

Cost to build? See page 216
to order complete cost estimate
to build this house in your area!

Design by
Home Planners

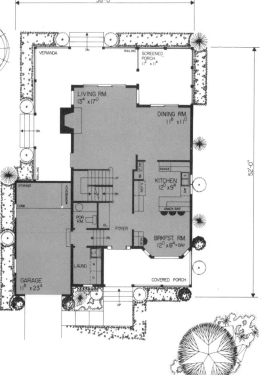

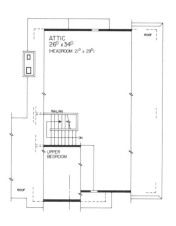

This home, as shown in the photograph, may differ from the actual blueprints.
For more detailed information, please check the floor plans carefully.

Photo by Andrew D. Lautman

Design S3309

First Floor: 1,375 square feet
Second Floor: 1,016 square feet
Total: 2,391 square feet

● Covered porches, front and back, are a fine preview to the livable nature of this Victorian. Living areas are defined in a family room with a fireplace, formal living and dining rooms and a kitchen with a breakfast room. An ample laundry room, a garage with a storage area and a powder room round out the first floor. Three second-floor bedrooms are joined by a study and two full baths.

Design by
Home Planners

Cost to build? See page 216
to order complete cost estimate
to build this house in your area!

143

● Covered porches front and rear are the first signal that this is a fine example of Folk Victorian styling. Complementing the exterior is a grand plan for family living. A formal living room and attached dining room provide space for entertaining guests. The large family room with fireplace is a gathering room for everyday. Both areas have access to outdoor spaces. Four bedrooms occupy the second floor. The master suite features two lavatories, a window seat and three closets. One of the family bedrooms has its own private balcony and could be used as a study. Note the open staircase and convenient linen storage.

Design S3385

First Floor: 1,096 square feet
Second Floor: 900 square feet
Total: 1,996 square feet

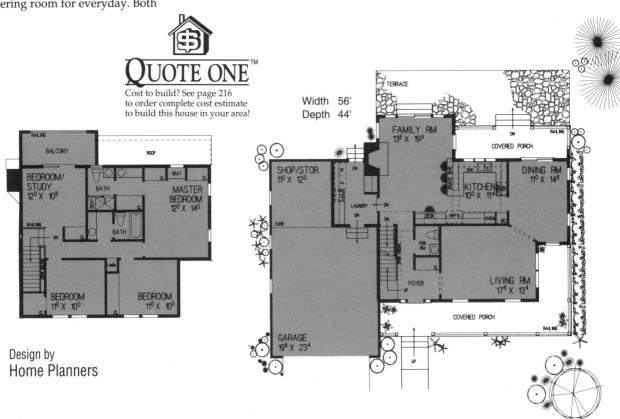

QUOTE ONE™

Cost to build? See page 216 to order complete cost estimate to build this house in your area!

Width 56'
Depth 44'

Design by
Home Planners

This home, as shown in the photograph, may differ from the actual blueprints.
For more detailed information, please check the floor plans carefully.

Photos by Andrew D. Lautman

Design by
Home Planners

Design S3316

First Floor: 1,111 square feet
Second Floor: 886 square feet
Total: 1,997 square feet

Cost to build? See page 216
to order complete cost estimate
to build this house in your area!

● Don't be fooled by a small-looking exterior. This plan offers three bedrooms and plenty of living space. Notice that the screened porch leads to a rear terrace with access to the breakfast room. A living room/dining room combination adds spaciousness to the first floor.

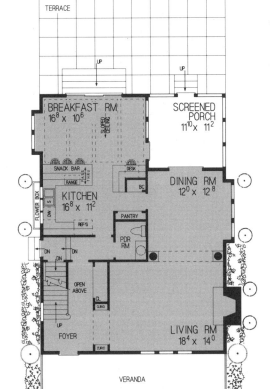

Width 34'-1"
Depth 50'

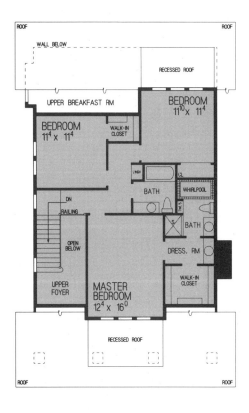

Design S9414

First Floor: 1,007 square feet
Second Floor: 803 square feet
Total: 1,810 square feet

● This efficient plan is traditionally styled and just made for narrow lots. Special features include extra space over the garage for storage or a workshop, a nook with bay window, a large family room with fireplace and a kitchen with expansive corner-window treatment. The spacious master suite includes a "tray" vaulted ceiling, spa tub, large shower and double vanity. Two additional bedrooms round out the upper floor, one featuring a vaulted ceiling and half-round window.

Design by
Alan Mascord
Design Associates, Inc.

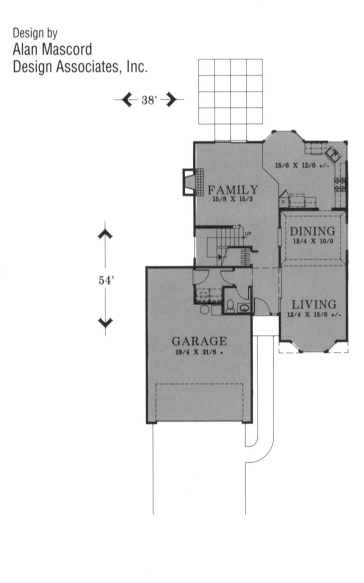

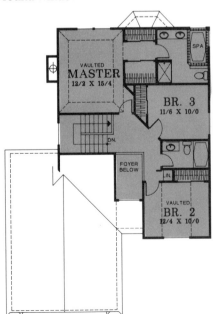

NOOK
10/0 X 12/6
(9' CLG)

10/4 X 12/6 +/-

**VAULTED
FAMILY**
13/0 X 12/8

DESK

D.W.

REF.

PAN O

DINING
12/0 x 9/0
(9' CLG)

GARAGE
19/0 x 22/0

LIVING
12/0 x 12/0
(9' CLG)

UP

PORCH

Design S9593
First Floor: 968 square feet
Second Floor: 837 square feet
Total: 1,805 square feet

Width 40'
Depth 46'

**VAULTED
MASTER**
13/0 X 12/6

LINEN

BR. 3
10/8 x 11/0

DN

D W

BR. 2
12/0 x 10/0

Design by
**Alan Mascord
Design Associates, Inc.**

● Stone piers add character to the charming covered porch that welcomes you into this three-bedroom home. Inside, a columned hallway provides a graceful entrance into the formal living and dining rooms from the two-story foyer. An L-shaped kitchen located nearby conveniently serves both the formal dining room and the casual bay-windowed breakfast nook. Board games, good books and lively conversation are just a few of the family pursuits that will be enjoyed in a comfortable family room warmed by the glow of the fireplace. Upstairs, two fine, secondary bedrooms share a full hall bath. Double doors provide entry into a luxurious master suite designed to transport you into a world of relaxation. A walk-in closet and a soothing master bath complete this quiet retreat. Laundry facilities handily accommodate the family and complete the second floor.

Design S9413

First Floor: 1,076 square feet
Second Floor: 819 square feet
Total: 1,895 square feet

● Consider this compact
contemporary with a flair for
the dramatic. The entry, den
and great room feature
impressive vaulted ceilings.
Note that the great room has
a floor that is sunken two
steps; the den is accessed
through French doors from
the entry. An elegant master
suite features a spa tub, large
shower and walk-in closet.
Don't miss the additional
shop or storage area built out
along one side of the garage.

Design by
Alan Mascord
Design Associates, Inc.

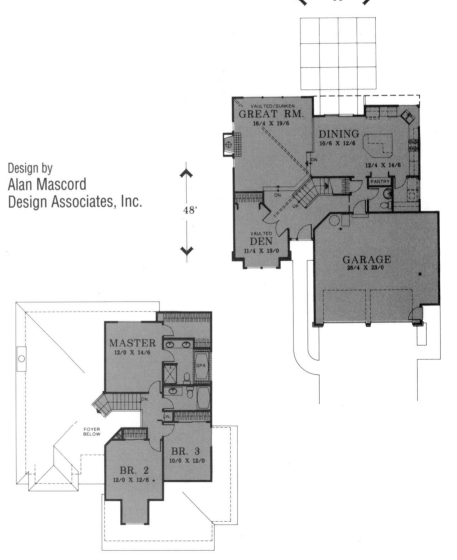

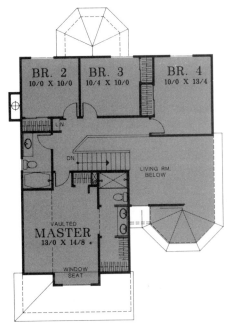

BR. 2
10/0 X 10/0

BR. 3
10/4 X 10/0

BR. 4
10/0 X 13/4

LIN.

DN.

LIVING RM.
BELOW

VAULTED
MASTER
13/0 X 14/8 +

WINDOW
SEAT

Design by
Alan Mascord
Design Associates, Inc.

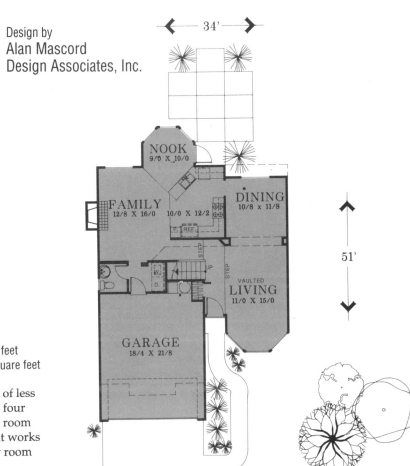

34'

NOOK
9/0 X 10/0

FAMILY
12/8 X 16/0

10/0 X 12/2

DINING
10/8 x 11/8

REF.

STEP

STEP

W.

UP

D.

VAULTED
LIVING
11/0 X 15/0

GARAGE
18/4 X 21/8

51'

Design S9467 First Floor: 899 square feet
Second Floor: 871 square feet; Total: 1,770 square feet

● Try packing more features into a plan of less
than 1,800 square feet! This plan includes four
bedrooms, a separate family room, living room
and eating nook all in a compact plan that works
well on even the smallest lots. The family room
shares a breakfast bar with an efficiently
designed kitchen that overlooks the charming
nook with its bay windows projecting into the
rear yard. The master bedroom upstairs is
spacious.

Design S9509

Main Level: 1,022 square feet
Upper Level: 813 square feet
Total: 1,835 square feet

● This house not only accommodates a narrow lot, but it also fits a sloping site. Notice how the two-car garage is tucked away under the first level of the house. The angled corner entry gives way to a two-story living room with a tiled hearth. The dining room shares an interesting angled space with this area and enjoys easy service from the efficient kitchen. A large pantry and an angled corner sink add character to this area. The family room offers double doors to a refreshing balcony. A powder room and a laundry room complete the main level. Upstairs, three bedrooms include a vaulted master suite with a private bath. Bedrooms 2 and 3 each take advantage of direct access to a full bath.

Design by
Alan Mascord
Design Associates, Inc.

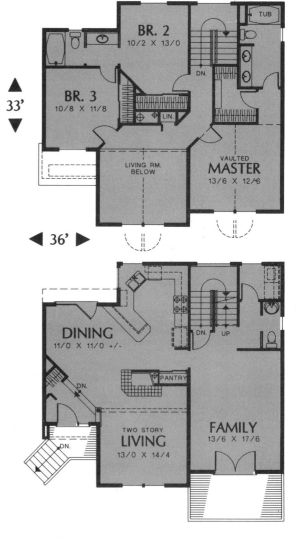

Design S9490

First Floor: 1,150 square feet
Second Floor: 1,213 square feet
Total: 2,363 square feet

● Symmetry is the key to the appeal of this wood-sided two-story. Its beauty is well matched by a most livable interior. The formal living room to the front of the plan is enhanced by a bay window and opens directly to the formal dining room. An L-shaped kitchen has a cooking island and attached nook. The family room features a fireplace flanked by windows. Upstairs are four bedrooms. The master suite has a vaulted ceiling and a huge closet and spa tub in its bath. Three family bedrooms share a full bath with double-bowl vanity.

◄ 50' ►

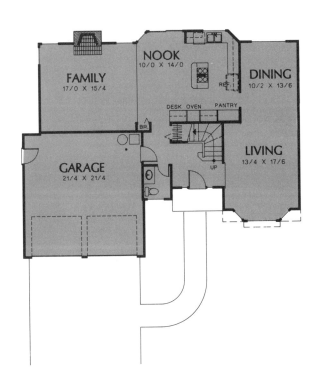

40'

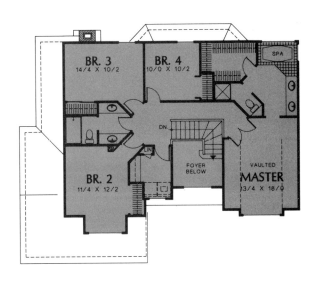

Design by
Alan Mascord
Design Associates, Inc.

ALTERNATE ELEVATION

Design S9437

First Floor: 1,009 square feet
Second Floor: 1,049 square feet
Total: 2,058 square feet

● This efficient two-story home incorporates all of the features demanded by today's discriminating home buyer. Check out the gracious two-story foyer featuring a comfortable L-shaped stair and dormered window filling the area with an abundance of natural light. The spacious kitchen includes an island, large pantry, desk and bayed-out nook area. Opening directly off the nook is a large family room with fireplace and glass doors leading to the outdoor living space. The upper floor of this home includes four generous bedrooms. Note the large walk-in closet in the master suite as well as the alternate master bath layout featuring spa tub in a tiled platform. An alternate plan, S9437-A, provides the same wonderful floor plan with a different exterior look.

Design S9437A

First Floor: 1,009 square feet
Second Floor: 1,082 square feet
Total: 2,091 square feet

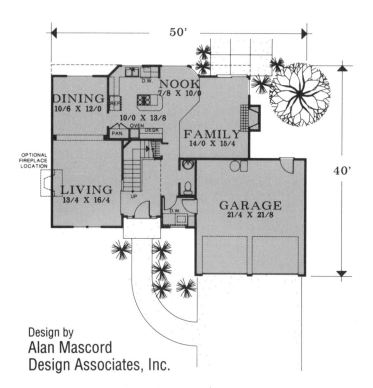

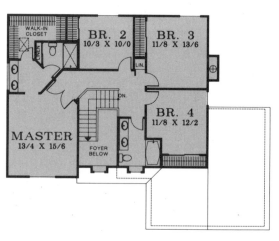

ALTERNATE MASTER W/ SPA TUB

Design by
Alan Mascord Design Associates, Inc.

Design S9421

First Floor: 1,157 square feet
Second Floor: 980 square feet
Total: 2,137 square feet

● Country style comes home in this great farmhouse with front porch. The dramatic two-story foyer with its angled stairway forms the circulation hub for this efficient home. Upstairs, a large master suite includes a spa tub, large shower and walk-in closet. Three other bedrooms round out the upper floor.

Design by
Alan Mascord
Design Associates, Inc.

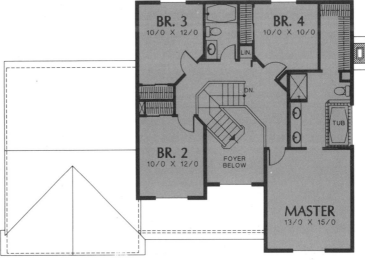

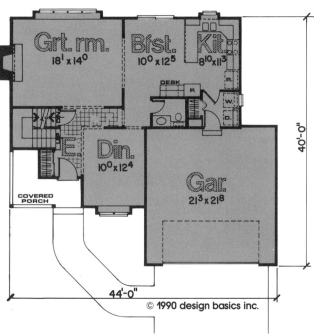

Design S9260

First Floor: 891 square feet
Second Floor: 759 square feet
Total: 1,650 square feet

● A quaint covered porch leads to a volume entry with decorator plant ledge above the closet in this home. The formal dining room has a boxed window that can be seen from the entry. A fireplace in the large great room adds warmth and coziness to the attached breakfast room and well-planned kitchen. Notice the nearby powder room for guests. Upstairs are three bedrooms. Bedroom 3 has a beautiful arched window under a volume ceiling. The master bedroom has a walk-in closet and pampering dressing area with double vanity and a whirlpool under a window. The upstairs landing overlooks the entry below.

Design by
Design Basics, Inc.

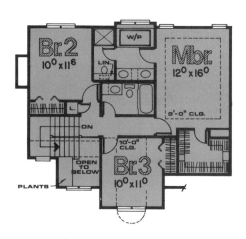

154

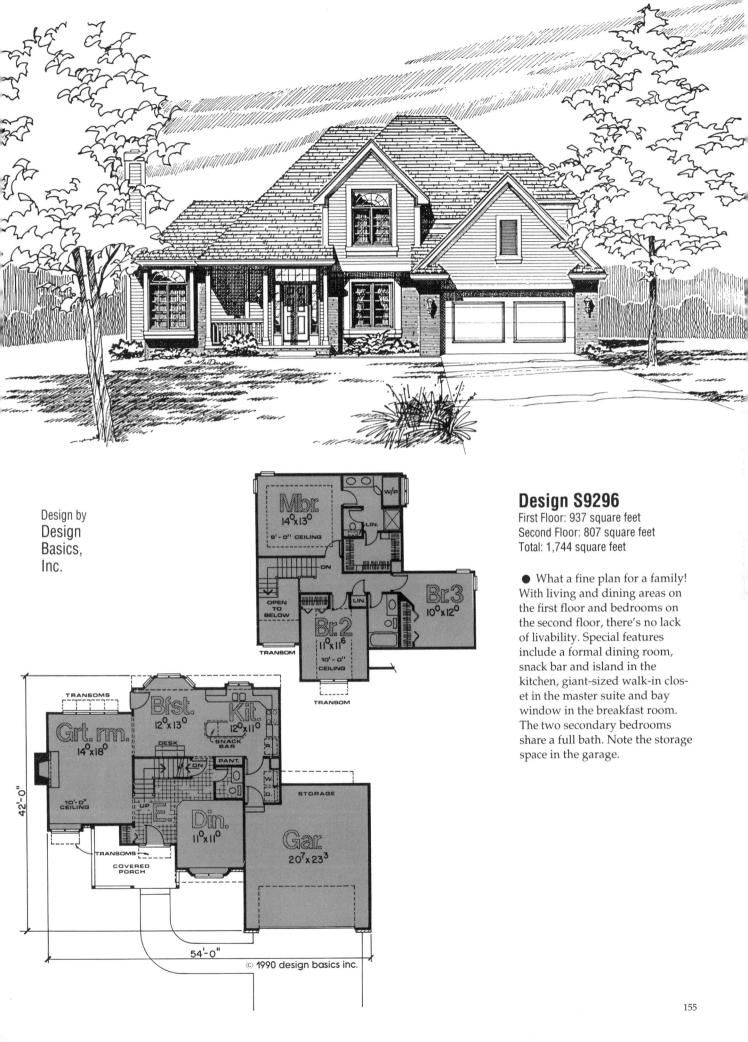

Design by
Design
Basics,
Inc.

TRANSOMS

Grt. rm.
14⁰x18⁰

10'-0"
CEILING

Bfst.
12⁰x13⁰

Kit.
12⁰x11⁰

SNACK BAR

DESK

DN

PANT.

UP

TRANSOMS

COVERED
PORCH

Din.
11⁰x11⁰

STORAGE

W.
D.

Gar.
20⁷x23³

42'-0"

54'-0"

© 1990 design basics inc.

Mbr.
14⁰x13⁰

9'-0" CEILING

W/P

LIN.

OPEN
TO
BELOW

DN

LIN.

Br.2
11⁰x11⁶

10'-0"
CEILING

Br.3
10⁰x12⁰

TRANSOM

TRANSOM

Design S9296

First Floor: 937 square feet
Second Floor: 807 square feet
Total: 1,744 square feet

● What a fine plan for a family!
With living and dining areas on
the first floor and bedrooms on
the second floor, there's no lack
of livability. Special features
include a formal dining room,
snack bar and island in the
kitchen, giant-sized walk-in closet in the master suite and bay
window in the breakfast room.
The two secondary bedrooms
share a full bath. Note the storage
space in the garage.

155

Design S9259

First Floor: 1,224 square feet
Second Floor: 950 square feet
Total: 2,174 square feet

● Abundant windows throughout this home add light and a feeling of openness. The front entry separates formal from informal living patterns: living room and dining room on the left, den and family room on the right. If desired, the den can be made to open up to the family room with French doors. To the rear is the kitchen which opens to the bayed breakfast room. Notice the fireplace in the family room. Upstairs there are four bedrooms. Three secondary bedrooms share a full bath. Bedroom 2 has a volume ceiling and half-round window. The master suite features a plant shelf, whirlpool, skylight above the vanity and a walk-in closet.

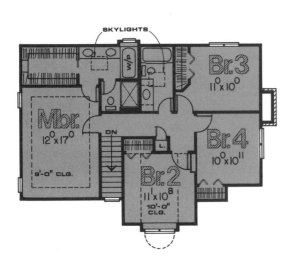

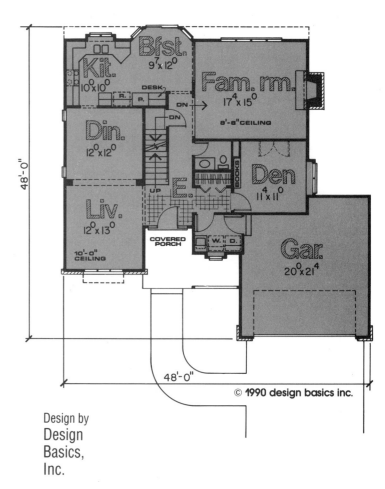

Design by
Design
Basics,
Inc.

© 1990 design basics inc.

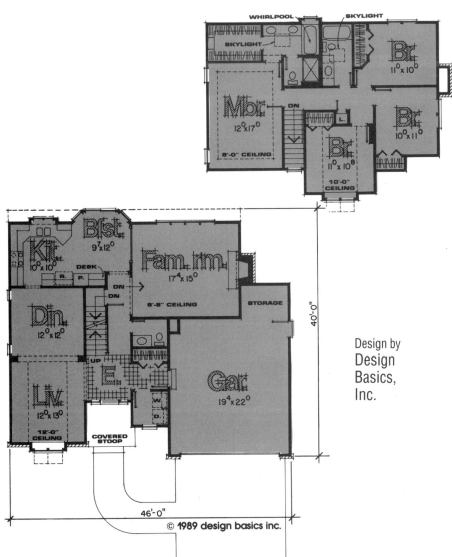

Design by
Design
Basics,
Inc.

© 1989 design basics inc.

Design S9233

First Floor: 1,081 square feet
Second Floor: 950 square feet
Total: 2,031 square feet

● Cherished traditional exterior styling gives way to a most livable floor plan in this home. The volume living room with raised ceiling opens to a large dining room for entertaining. An efficient kitchen with pantry and planning desk is open to the bay-windowed dinette. The sunken family room features a fireplace and plenty of windows. Be sure to notice the large master bedroom with an elaborate skylit master bath which includes a walk-in closet, double vanity and compartmented stool and shower. Three secondary bedrooms which are segregated for privacy share a skylit hall bath. Extra storage space is available in the garage.

Photo by Kevin McAndrews

Design S9232

First Floor: 1,551 square feet
Second Floor: 725 square feet
Total: 2,276 square feet

● This narrow-lot plan features a wraparound porch at the two-story entry, which opens to the formal dining room with beautiful bay windows. The great room features a handsome fireplace and a ten-and-a-half foot ceiling. A well-equipped island kitchen with pantry and built-in desk is available for the serious cook. The large master bedroom has a vaulted ceiling and a luxury master bath with two-person whirlpool, skylight and large walk-in closet. Three secondary bedrooms with ample closet space share a compartmented bath including double vanity and a large linen closet.

Design by
Design Basics, Inc.

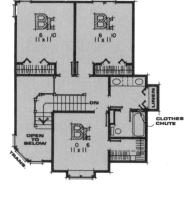

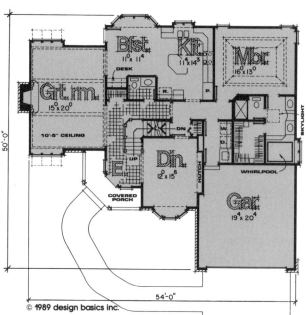

© 1989 design basics inc.

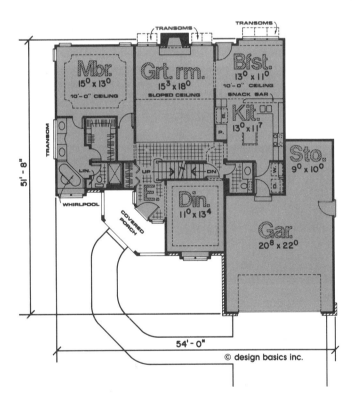

Design by
Design
Basics,
Inc.

Design S7236

First Floor: 1,413 square feet
Second Floor: 563 square feet
Total: 1,976 square feet

● With its angled porch, wood railing and shutter treatments, this home inspires a picturesque country atmosphere. The majestic great room beckons with a high ceiling and sunny, tall windows framing the fireplace. The well-designed kitchen offers daily cooking ease while the bright breakfast area includes access to the outdoors. The spacious master bedroom features a tray ceiling and a master bath with an angled whirlpool, dual lavs, a shower and a large walk-in closet. Three bedrooms and a shared bath complete the second floor. Notice the abundant storage space in the garage.

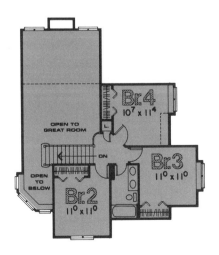

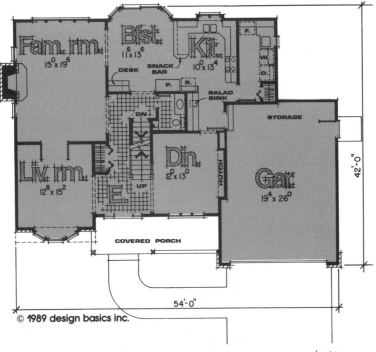

© 1989 design basics inc.

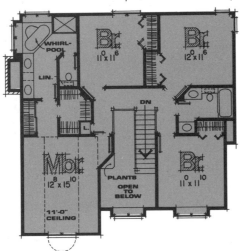

Design S9230

First Floor: 1,303 square feet
Second Floor: 1,084 square feet
Total: 2,387 square feet

● It's hard to get beyond the covered front porch of this home, but doing so reveals a bright two-story entry open to the central hall. Just to the left, an enticing bay window enlivens the living room, featuring French doors which connect to the family room. The efficient kitchen with snack bar and pantry is open to the bay-windowed breakfast area with planning desk. The salad sink and counter space double as a service for the formal dining room. The master bedroom features a raised ceiling and arched window. Its adjoining bath contains a walk-through closet/transition area and a corner whirlpool.

Design by
Design
Basics,
Inc.

Design S9235

First Floor: 919 square feet
Second Floor: 927 square feet
Total: 1,846 square feet

● Wonderful country design begins with the wraparound porch of this plan. Explore further and find a two-story entry with a coat closet and plant shelf above and a strategically placed staircase alongside. The island kitchen with a boxed window over the sink is adjacent to a large bay-windowed dinette. The great room includes many windows and a fireplace. A powder bath and laundry room are both conveniently placed on the first floor. Upstairs, the large master suite contains His and Hers walk-in closets, corner windows and a bath area featuring a double vanity and whirlpool tub. Two pleasant secondary bedrooms have interesting angles and a third bedroom in the front features a volume ceiling and arched window.

© 1989 design basics inc.

Design by
Design
Basics,
Inc.

Cost to build? See page 216 to order complete cost estimate to build this house in your area!

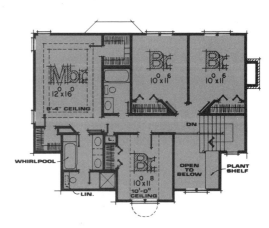

DECK

SUN RM.
11-10 × 10-0

DINING
14-0 × 12-0

fireplace

GREAT RM.
14-0 × 20-0

MASTER
BED RM.
14-0 × 14-0

bath

balcony above

KITCHEN
14-0 × 13-8

FOYER
6-0 × 8-0

cl

pd.
rm.

walk-in
closet

down

up

sta.

wash dry

storage

UTILITY

GARAGE
20-0 × 19-8

60-6

52-8

Design S9650

First Floor: 1,352 square feet
Second Floor: 576 square feet
Sun Room: 127 square feet
Total: 2,055 square feet

● This striking contemporary home retains some
traditional flavor at the front exterior. Inside, the
mood is modern and efficient. The formal dining
room and the great room open to the sun room
which has four skylights for passive solar heating.
A spacious kitchen allows for a breakfast bar or
separate table. The sun room, great room and master bedroom offer direct access to the deck which
provides space for a hot tub. The luxurious master
bath has a double-bowl vanity, shower and
whirlpool tub. The second level has two spacious
bedrooms sharing a full bath and a loft area overlooking the great room below. Ample attic storage
space is provided over the garage.

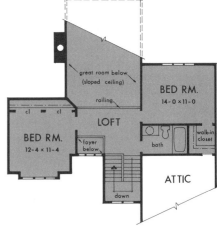

great room below
(sloped ceiling)

railing

BED RM.
14-0 × 11-0

cl   cl

LOFT

BED RM.
12-4 × 11-4

foyer
below

bath

walk-in
closet

down

ATTIC

Design by
**Donald A.
Gardner,
Architect, Inc.**

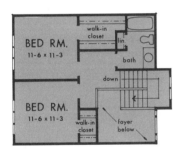

Design by
**Donald A.
Gardner,
Architect, Inc.**

Design S9610

First Floor: 1,209 square feet
Second Floor: 525 square feet
Total: 1,734 square feet

● A well-proportioned, compact house such as this never feels cramped, and its special floor plan makes it seem larger than it really is. From the two-story entrance foyer move to the living/dining area with cathedral ceiling and skylights. The master suite features its own bath with double-bowl vanity, whirlpool tub and shower. Look for walk-in closets here as well as in the two family bedrooms upstairs. A large deck off the living area allows space for a hot tub.

Design S9616

First Floor: 1,734 square feet
Second Floor: 958 square feet
Total: 2,692 square feet

● A wraparound covered porch at the front and sides of this home and the open deck with spa and seating provide plenty of outside living area. A central great room features a vaulted ceiling, fireplace and clerestory windows above. The loft/study on the second floor overlooks this gathering area. Besides a formal dining room, kitchen, breakfast room and sun room on the first floor, there is also a generous master suite with garden tub. Three second-floor bedrooms complete sleeping accommodations. The plan includes a crawl-space foundation.

Design by
Donald A.
Gardner,
Architect, Inc.

FRONT

REAR

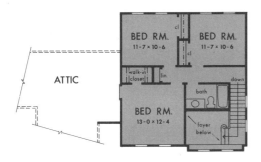

ATTIC

BED RM.
11-7 × 10-6

BED RM.
11-7 × 10-6

walk-in closet | lin.

bath

down

BED RM.
13-0 × 12-4

foyer below

Design S9672

First Floor: 1,410 square feet
Second Floor: 613 square feet
Total: 2,023 square feet

● This four-bedroom, 1½-story farmhouse offers special features in an up-to-date plan. Windows at the second level of the two-story foyer allow penetration of natural light. The generous great room with fireplace is accessible to a covered porch and carefully designed deck with seating and spa location. A kitchen with island counter services the breakfast and dining rooms while a wet bar provides an added dimension. Located on the first level for convenience, the master bedroom offers a large walk-in closet and a spacious master bath with double-bowl vanity, whirlpool tub and shower. The second level includes three bedrooms sharing a full bath and ample storage space.

Design by
Donald A. Gardner, Architect, Inc.

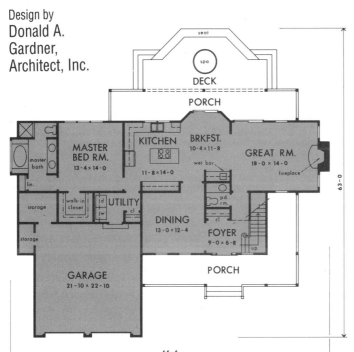

seat

spa

DECK

PORCH

KITCHEN
11-8 × 14-0

MASTER BED RM.
13-4 × 14-0

master bath

lin.

storage

storage

walk-in closet

UTILITY

DINING
13-0 × 12-4

BRKFST.
10-4 × 11-8

wet bar

pd. rm.

GREAT RM.
18-0 × 14-0

fireplace

FOYER
9-0 × 6-8

up

PORCH

GARAGE
21-10 × 22-10

63-0

66-6

B. NATHAN

Design S9614

First Floor: 1,345 square feet
Second Floor: 536 square feet
Total: 1,881 square feet

● An elegant exterior combines with a functional interior to offer an exciting design for the contemporary minded. Notice the cheery sun room that captures the heat of the sun. The master suite and great room both have access to this bright space through sliding glass doors. A U-shaped kitchen has a window garden, a breakfast bar and ample cabinet space. Note how the great room ceiling with exposed wood beams slopes from the deck up to operable clerestory windows at the study/play area on the second level. Also notice bonus storage space in the attic over the garage. Order Design S9614 for crawl-space foundation; order Design S9614-A for basement foundation.

FRONT

Design by
**Donald A.
Gardner,
Architect, Inc.**

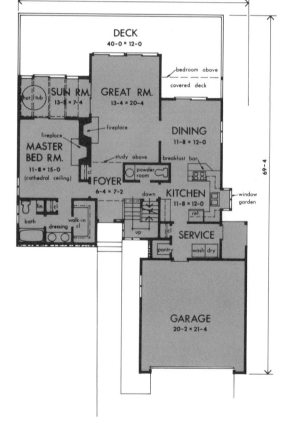

REAR

FRONT

Design S9613

First Floor: 1,340 square feet
Second Floor: 504 square feet
Total: 1,844 square feet

● Because this home's sun room is a full two stories high, it acts as a solar collector when oriented to the south. Enjoying the benefits of this warmth are the dining and great rooms on the first floor and the master suite on the second floor. A spacious deck further extends the outdoor living potential. Special features to be found in this house include: sloping ceiling with exposed wood beams and a fireplace in the great room; cathedral ceiling, fireplace, built-in shelves and ample closet space in the master bedroom; clerestory windows and a balcony overlook in the upstairs study; and convenient storage space in the attic over the garage. Order Design S9613 for a crawl-space foundation; order Design S9613-A for a basement foundation.

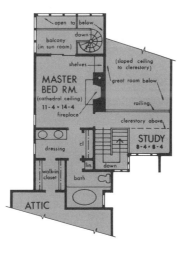

45-4

DECK
27-8 × 12-0

balcony above

SUN RM.
13-4 × 8-0

GREAT RM.
13-4 × 25-0

BED RM.
10-4 × 11-4

DINING
11-4 × 12-4

fireplace

storage

study above

cl

window planter

KITCHEN
11-4 × 8-0

down

FOYER
6-0 × 5-0

bath

SERVICE

dry wash   cl   pantry

BED RM.
10-4 × 11-4

cl

up

60-0

GARAGE
20-2 × 21-4

open to below

down

balcony
(in sun room)

shelves

(sloped ceiling to clerestory)

MASTER
BED RM.
(cathedral ceiling)
11-4 × 14-4

great room below

fireplace

railing

clerestory above

dressing

cl

STUDY
8-4 × 8-4

walk-in closet

bath

down

ATTIC

Design by
Donald A.
Gardner,
Architect, Inc.

REAR

Design S2711

First Floor: 975 square feet
Second Floor: 1,024 square feet
Total: 1,999 square feet

● Sleek, affordable style is apparent in this design. The large dining area, the kitchen, the mudroom off the garage and the spacious bedrooms are key selling points for the young family. Also notice the private balcony off the master suite, the cozy study with lots of storage space, the terrace to the rear of the house and the sizable snack bar for the kids, and the adults.

Design by
Home Planners

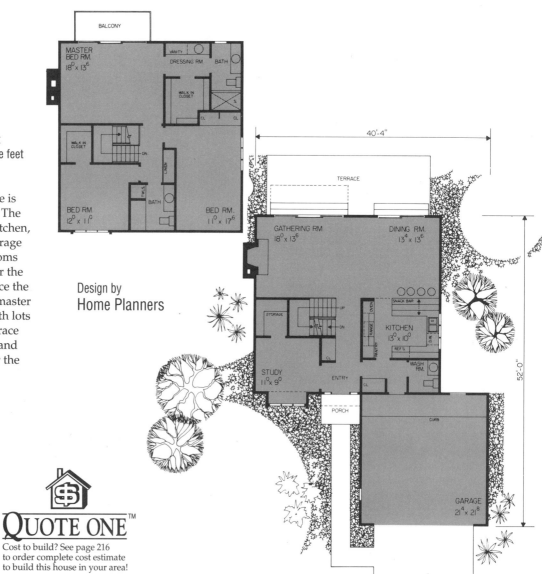

QUOTE ONE™

Cost to build? See page 216
to order complete cost estimate
to build this house in your area!

This home, as shown in the photograph, may differ from the actual blueprints.
For more detailed information, please check the floor plans carefully.

Design S2488
First Floor: 1,113 square feet; Second Floor: 543 square feet; Total: 1,656 square feet

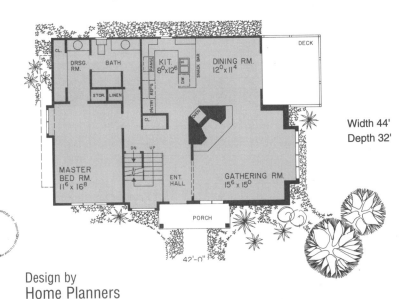

Width 44'
Depth 32'

Design by
Home Planners

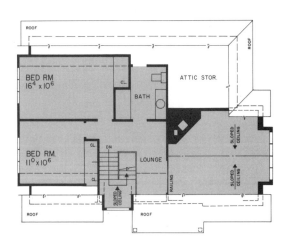

● Whether serving the young active family as a leisure-time retreat, or the retired couple as a year-round home, the flexibility of this design provides both efficiency and comfort. As a vacation home, the plan's two sizable bedrooms, full bath and lounge accommodate youngsters or guests. When functioning as a retirement home, the second floor fulfills the need for additional space and privacy or caters to visiting family and friends.

169

This home, as shown in the photograph, may differ from the actual blueprints. For more detailed information, please check the floor plans carefully.

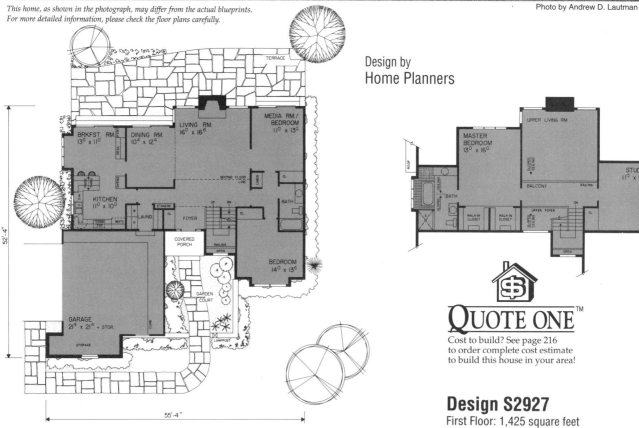

Design by
Home Planners

QUOTE ONE™

Cost to build? See page 216
to order complete cost estimate
to build this house in your area!

Design S2927

First Floor: 1,425 square feet
Second Floor: 704 square feet
Total: 2,129 square feet

● This charming Early American design is just as warm on the inside. The first floor features a convenient kitchen with a pass-through to the breakfast room. There's also a formal dining room just steps away in the rear of the house. An adjacent rear living room enjoys its own fireplace. Other features include a rear media room (or optional third bedroom) and a complete second-floor master suite. A downstairs bedroom enjoys an excellent front view. Other highlights include a garden court, a covered porch and a large garage with extra storage.

This home, as shown in the photograph, may differ from the actual blueprints.
For more detailed information, please check the floor plans carefully.

Design S2826 First Floor: 1,112 square feet
Second Floor: 881 square feet; Total: 1,993 square feet

ALTERNATE KITCHEN / DINING RM. /
BREAKFAST RM. FLOOR PLAN

● This is an outstanding example of the type of informal, traditional-style architecture that has captured the modern imagination. The interior plan houses all of the features that people want most: a spacious gathering room, formal and informal dining areas, an efficient U-shaped kitchen, a master bedroom, two children's bedrooms, a second-floor lounge, an entrance court and a rear terrace and deck.

Cost to build? See page 216
to order complete cost estimate
to build this house in your area!

Design by
Home Planners

Quote One™

Cost to build? See page 216 to order complete cost estimate to build this house in your area!

Design by
Home Planners

Design S2854

First Floor: 1,261 square feet
Second Floor: 950 square feet
Total: 2,211 square feet

● A fine sight, indeed. This is a story-and-a-half, but the second floor has so much livability, it's more like a two-story plan. In addition to a large master suite, two kids' rooms and a second full bath, the second floor has a cozy spot that could serve as a lounge, a nursery or a play area. The first floor is solidly utilitarian with a living room with a fireplace, a large separate dining room, a family room, an efficient U-shaped kitchen, a study with a nifty bay window and a covered porch.

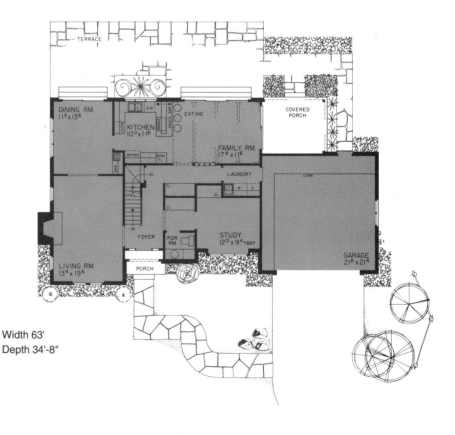

Width 63'
Depth 34'-8"

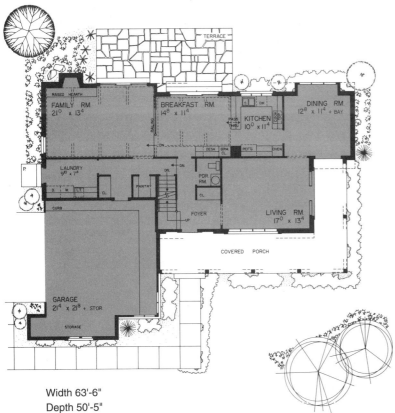

Design by
Home Planners

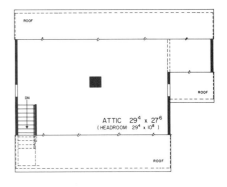

Width 63'-6"
Depth 50'-5"

Design S2939 First Floor: 1,409 square feet; Second Floor: 1,020 square feet; Total: 2,429 square feet

● Here's a Tudor adaptation with plenty of warmth and comfort for the entire family! Start with the big wrap-around covered porch in front. Then there's a large attic with headroom, a bonus for bulk storage and even possible expansion. An efficient U-shaped kitchen features many built-ins with also a pass-thru to a beamed-ceiling breakfast room. Sliding glass doors to a terrace are highlights in both the sunk-en family room and the breakfast room. A service entrance to the garage has a storage closet on each side, plus a secondary entrance through the laun-dry area. Recreational activities and hobbies can be enjoyed in the base-ment area. There are four bedrooms plus two baths upstairs, isolated from household noise and activity. A quiet corner living room opens to a sizable formal dining room. This room enjoys natural light from a bay window that overlooks the backyard.

Design S9142

First Floor: 839 square feet
Second Floor: 769 square feet
Total: 1,608 square feet

● A beautiful Tudor facade is further enhanced by a great floor plan. The front entry leads to a foyer that separates the huge living room and dining room. The living room is warmed by a fireplace and well-lighted by corner windows. A galley-style kitchen has an attached breakfast area and nearby utility room. Three bedrooms and two baths dominate the second floor. The

Design by
Larry W.
Garnett &
Associates, Inc.

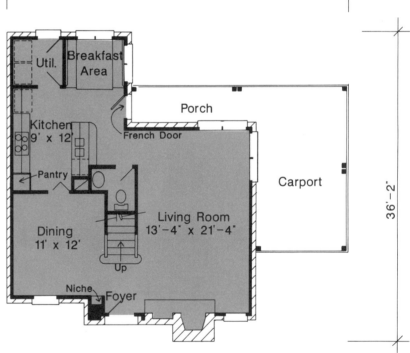

master bedroom has an oversized closet and bath with double-bowl vanity. Notice how the rear porch leads directly to the side carport. Special extras include a built-in niche in the foyer and large pantry in the kitchen.

Design by
**Larry W.
Garnett &
Associates, Inc.**

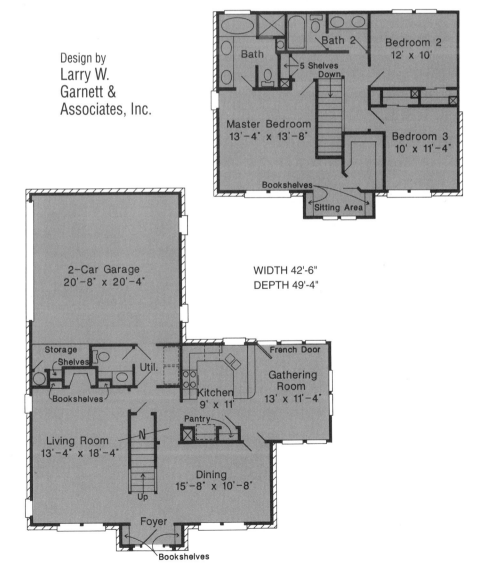

WIDTH 42'-6"
DEPTH 49'-4"

Design S9141

First Floor: 987 square feet
Second Floor: 857 square feet
Total: 1,844 square feet

● Tudor design makes a beautiful move in this appealing two-story plan. The floor plan offers formal living and dining to the right and left of the entry foyer. Bookshelves in the living room flank a cozy fireplace. The gathering room is just off the efficient kitchen and has a French door to the rear yard. The second floor features three bedrooms, one of which is a grand master suite with sitting area and pampering bath. Two family bedrooms share a compartmented bath. A two-car garage provides a large storage area with built-in shelves.

Design by
Larry W.
Garnett &
Associates, Inc.

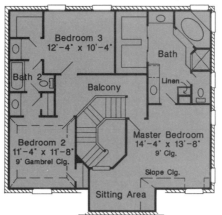

Design S9029

First Floor: 1,208 square feet
Second Floor: 1,066 square feet
Total: 2,274 square feet

WIDTH 60'
DEPTH 36'-8"

● This quaint little plan works so
well on narrow lots that you might
never suspect all the livability that
can be found inside. From the front
foyer turn right to the wonderfully
open living room that has as its
focus an open hearth through to
the rear family room. A left turn
from the foyer leads to a formal dining room with
bay window. Another bay window can be found
in the breakfast room which is next to an efficient
L-shaped kitchen. Upstairs are three lovely bedrooms. Be sure to investigate all the features of the
master suite: a sitting room, double walk-in closet,
and separate tub and shower.

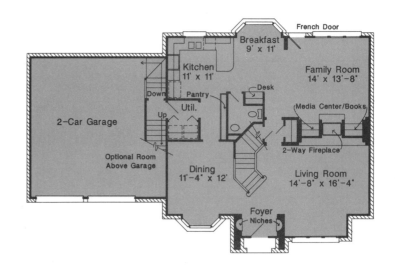

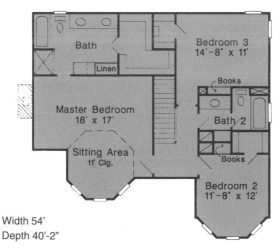

Width 54'
Depth 40'-2"

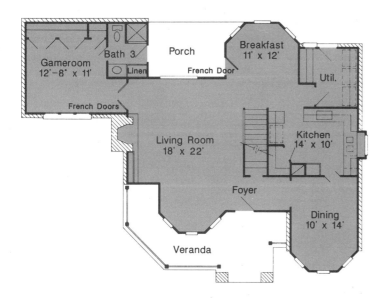

Design S9059

First Floor: 1,299 square feet
Second Floor: 1,069 square feet
Total: 2,368 square feet

● With a veranda wrapping around an octagon-shaped turret, decorative shingle siding, and double posts placed on brick pedestals, this home recalls the grand Queen Anne Style designs of the late 19th Century. The foyer offers access to both the bay-windowed dining room and the living area. French doors lead from the living area to a game room which can easily become a guest room with a private bath. The second floor features two children's bedrooms, each with a walk-in closet and a built-in bookcase. The master bedroom has a sitting area with an eleven-foot-high octagon-shaped ceiling. Plenty of linen storage, along with a dressing table, combine with a separate glass-enclosed shower to create a superb master bath. Plans are included for a detached, two-car garage.

Design by
Larry W.
Garnett &
Associates, Inc.

Photo by Andrew D. Lautman

This home, as shown in the photograph, may differ from the actual blueprints. For more detailed information, please check the floor plans carefully.

Design S9055

First Floor: 997 square feet
Second Floor: 1,069 square feet
Total: 2,066 square feet

● With its exceptional detail and proportions, this home is reminiscent of the Queen Anne Style. Turned posts resting on brick pedestals support a raised-gable entry to the veranda. The foyer opens to a living area with a bay-windowed alcove and a fireplace with flanking bookshelves. A large walk-in pantry and box window at the sink are special features in the kitchen. Natural light fills the breakfast area with a full-length bay window and a French door. Upstairs, the master bedroom offers unsurpassed elegance and convenience. The sitting area has an eleven-foot ceiling with arch-top windows. The bath area features a large walk-in closet, His and Hers lavatories, and plenty of linen storage. Plans for a two-car detached garage are included.

Design by
Larry W.
Garnett &
Associates, Inc.

Width 39'-8"
Depth 39'-2"

QUOTE ONE®

Cost to build? See page 216
to order complete cost estimate
to build this house in your area!

Design S9196

First Floor: 1,525 square feet
Second Floor: 795 square feet
Total: 2,320 square feet

● An L-shaped covered porch provides a happy marriage of indoor-
outdoor living relationships. The
foyer opens onto a living room that
presents opportunities to curl up in
front of the fire with a good book,
use state-of-the-art electronics
housed in the built-in media center
and access the porch through a
French door. A kitchen designed
for efficiency combines with the
breakfast area for informal meals
and serves the nearby dining room
for formal occasions. Located on
the first floor for privacy, the master suite provides a relaxing retreat.
A built-in book case stores your
favorite novels and a spacious master bath features a whirlpool tub
and a separate shower. Three bedrooms and a full bath complete the
second floor.

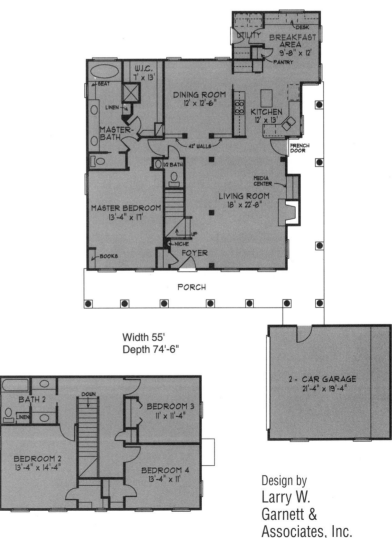

Width 55'
Depth 74'-6"

Design by
Larry W.
Garnett &
Associates, Inc.

Design S9849

First Floor: 780 square feet
Second Floor: 915 square feet
Total: 1,695 square feet

● The lines of this home are very clean, as well as traditional. Inside, contemporary priorities reign. To the left of the foyer is the powder room. Opposite is a formal dining room with passage to the kitchen, which is open to the breakfast area and great room. This area is particularly well-suited to entertaining both formally and informally, with an open, airy design to the kitchen. The large fireplace is well placed and framed by glass and light. Opening from the great room is a

two-car garage and a staircase to the second level. The master suite's double-door entrance, tray ceiling and fireplace are of special interest. The adjoining master bath and walk-in closet complement this area well. The laundry room is found on this level, convenient to any of the bedrooms. Bedrooms 2 and 3 complete this level with a shared bath.

Width 41'
Depth 41'

Design by
Design Traditions

Design S9848 First Floor: 915 square feet
Second Floor: 935 square feet; Total: 1,850 square feet

● The appearance of this home at once suggests classic values. On entry, the foyer opens to a hallway leading to the kitchen and the main-level powder room and to a generous great room with a fireplace, opening onto a large deck. The dining room is adjacent to the great room and is framed by columns. In the kitchen, the design maximizes convenience. The staircase off the foyer leads to the upper level where the master suite and two family bedrooms are found. A bonus room completes the second floor. This home is designed with a basement foundation.

Design by
Design Traditions

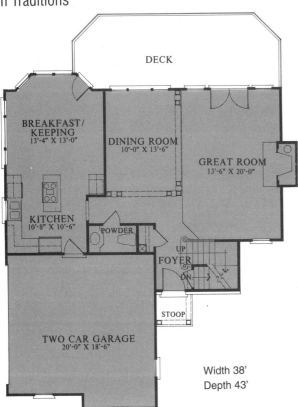

Width 38'
Depth 43'

Design S9845 First Floor: 1,020 square feet
Second Floor: 1,175 square feet; Total: 2,195 square feet

● A picture of European style, this elegant beauty features state-of-the-art floor planning. Formal living and dining areas are found to the right of the two-story foyer. A family room with bay window and fireplace is the casual counterpart. The kitchen is large enough to accommodate gourmet cooking and has an attached breakfast bay. Upstairs there are four bedrooms—one a master suite with all the favored appointments. The family bedrooms share a full bath with double lavatories.

WIDTH 54'
DEPTH 39'

Design by
Design Traditions

Design S9847 First Floor: 1,225 square feet
Second Floor: 565 square feet; Total: 1,790 square feet

● The exterior of this home is intriguing and inviting. The combination of materials and shapes is reminiscent of an English country home. Beyond the columned entry is a classic raised foyer which leads to the sunken dining room and the great room. The openness of the plan is evident in the kitchen and the breakfast area. The bay-windowed master bedroom boasts a tray ceiling, a walk-in closet and a sumptuous bath. The open gallery staircase overlooks the great room and provides entry to two more bedrooms as well as an unfinished bonus room. The home is designed with a basement foundation.

Design by
Design Traditions

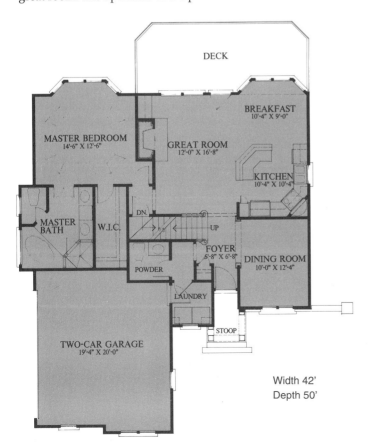

Width 42'
Depth 50'

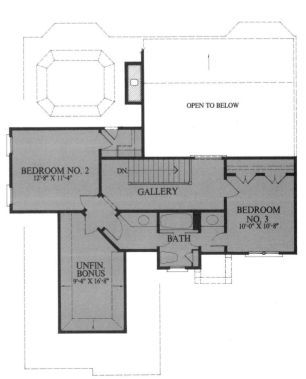

Design S9842 First Floor: 1,053 square feet; Second Floor: 1,053 square feet; Total: 2,106 square feet

● Brick takes a bold stand in grand traditional style in this treasured design. From the front entry to rear deck, the floor plan serves family needs in just over 2,000 square feet. The front study has a nearby full bath, making it a handy guest bedroom. The family room with fireplace opens to a cozy breakfast area. For more formal entertaining there's a dining room just off the entry. The kitchen features a prep island and huge pantry. Upstairs, the master bedroom has its own sitting room and a giant-sized closet. Two family bedrooms share a full bath.

Design by
Design Traditions

Quote One®

Cost to build? See page 216 to order complete cost estimate to build this house in your area!

WIDTH 52'
DEPTH 34'

Copyright 1992 Stephen S. Fuller, Inc.

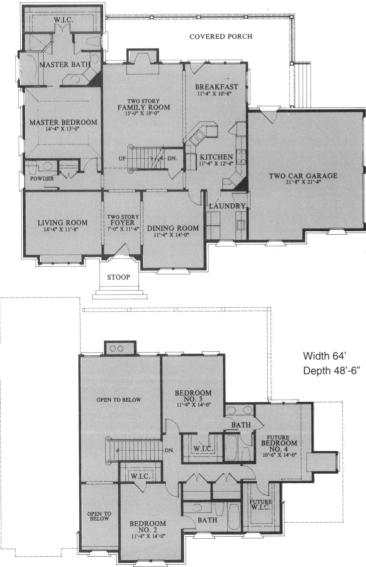

COVERED PORCH

W.I.C.

MASTER BATH

TWO STORY
FAMILY ROOM
15'-0" X 19'-0"

BREAKFAST
11'-4" X 10'-8"

MASTER BEDROOM
14'-4" X 13'-0"

KITCHEN
11'-4" X 12'-4"

UP — DN.

TWO CAR GARAGE
21'-8" X 21'-4"

POWDER

LAUNDRY

LIVING ROOM
14'-4" X 11'-8"

TWO STORY
FOYER
7'-0" X 11'-4"

DINING ROOM
11'-4" X 14'-0"

STOOP

OPEN TO BELOW

BEDROOM
NO. 3
11'-4" X 14'-0"

BATH

FUTURE
BEDROOM
NO. 4
10'-6" X 14'-0"

DN.

W.I.C.

W.I.C.

FUTURE
W.I.C.

OPEN TO
BELOW

BEDROOM
NO. 2
11'-4" X 14'-0"

BATH

Width 64'
Depth 48'-6"

Design S9877

First Floor: 1,660 square feet
Second Floor: 665 square feet
Total: 2,325 square feet

● This stately two-story home echoes tradition with the use of brick and jack arch detailing. The center of the home opens with a protective recess entry. Once inside, the foyer is flanked by a spacious dining room to the right and study on the left; with the addition of French doors this room can also function as a guest room if needed. Beyond the foyer lies a two-story family room accented by a warming fireplace and open railing staircase. This room flows casually into the spacious breakfast room and well-planned kitchen located near the laundry room and garage. The secluded master bedroom with a tray ceiling and master bath including His and Hers vanities, garden tub and walk in closet completes the main level of this home. Upstairs, three additional bedrooms with roomy closets and two baths combine to finish this traditional country home.

Design by
Design Traditions

Cost to build? See page 216
to order complete cost estimate
to build this house in your area!

Copyright 1992 Stephen S. Fuller, Inc.

Design S9878

First Floor: 1,205 square feet
Second Floor: 1,160 square feet
Total: 2,365 square feet

● This home draws its inspiration from the stately homes on the English countryside, offering the same formality, elegance and comfort. The two-story foyer begins with the open-rail staircase and then flows into the dining room, living room and family room. The family room leads to the well-lit breakfast room and step-saving kitchen, making this truly the focal point of family activity. In addition, the family room offers passage to the formal living room and relaxing veranda, providing a wonderful setting for outdoor entertaining. Upstairs are four generously sized bedrooms. The master bedroom enjoys privacy with its position at the rear of the home. Entering through double doors, the visual appeal of the tray ceiling and window treatments make the room a restful retreat. Three additional bedrooms share two baths.

Design by
Design Traditions

Width 52'-6"
Depth 44'-6"

Copyright 1992 Stephen S. Fuller, Inc.

Design S9857

First Floor: 1,156 square feet
Second Floor: 1,239 square feet
Total: 2,395 square feet

● This Traditional home combines an attractive classic exterior with an open and sophisticated interior design. On approach, notice the use of brick and siding, Palladian and box bay windows, flower boxes and a covered entrance flanked by columns. The two-story foyer has a staircase to the left and a coat closet and powder room straight ahead. Proceeding right from the foyer, we see both the living and dining rooms with their individual window treatments. Entering the kitchen from the dining room we pass a corner butler pantry for added convenience while entertaining. The open design flowing to the breakfast area and family room features two large bay windows. The open foyer staircase leads to the upper level, beginning with the master suite. The bay window extends the eye beyond the attractive master bedroom. The master bath contains a luxurious tub, separate shower and dual vanities, as well as a large linen closet. A large walk-in master closet completes the suite. Bedroom two is inviting with its bay window and large closet. All three secondary bedrooms share a hall bath with separate vanity and bathing areas.

Design by
Design Traditions

Width 54'
Depth 39'-5"

Design S8618

First Floor: 1,352 square feet
Second Floor: 1,000 square feet
Total: 2,352 square feet

Design by
Home Design
Services, Inc.

● A covered patio shades the entry to the foyer of this home—it is lit by an arched window. Double doors to the right open to a guest room with arched picture window. The great room, open to the level above, has a wet bar; a large rear patio also offers a wet bar. The tiled kitchen provides a serving bar for the breakfast room. French doors in the master bed-room open onto a deck. The spacious bath here includes a walk-in closet, twin vanities and spa tub. Two additional bed-rooms and a bath complete the second level. The front bed-room includes a study and opens onto a deck. The plan can be built with a flat-tiled or barrel roof.

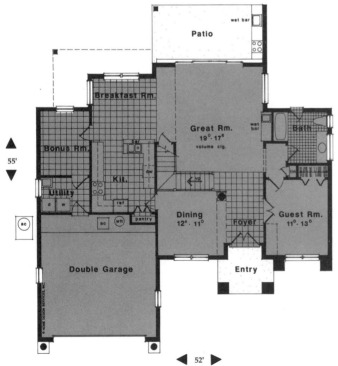

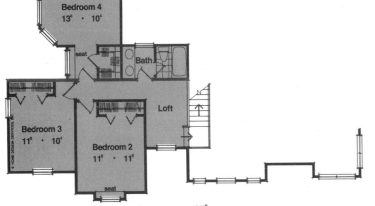

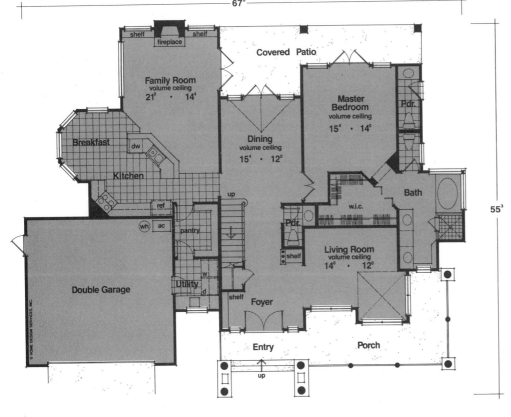

Design S8622

First Floor: 1,820 square feet
Second Floor: 700 square feet
Total: 2,520 square feet

● Expansive interior space, a porch and a patio are found in this country-style plan. Front-to-back views begin at the double doors that open to the foyer and extend through the dining room to the covered patio. To the right, the foyer spreads into the living room, which opens to a tower. The pass-through kitchen—notice the large walk-through pantry—is linked to the sunny bayed breakfast area. The family room includes a fireplace flanked by windows and built-in shelves. French doors provide access to the covered patio from the family room, the dining room, and the master bedroom. The lower-level master suite includes a private bath with double vanities, a spa tub and a spacious walk-in closet. Three additional bedrooms and a loft are located upstairs.

Design by
Home Design
Services, Inc.

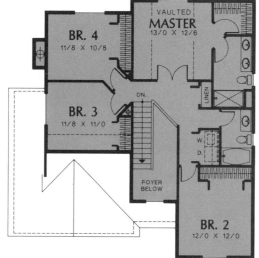

Design by
Alan Mascord
Design Associates, Inc.

◀ 40' ▶

Design S9518

First Floor: 944 square feet
Second Floor: 1,013 square feet
Total: 1,957 square feet

● The true meaning of "less is more" is apparent in this two-story narrow lot home. Creative use of space makes this home appear much larger than it actually is. Enter the formal living areas—a bayed living room and a columned dining room—to the right of the foyer. Informal living areas occupy the rear of the plan. A family room with a warming fireplace shares space with an efficient, L-shaped kitchen with a cooktop island and a sunny eating nook that provides access to the rear grounds. The second floor contains the sleeping zone with three family bedrooms and the master suite. The master bedroom is highlighted by a vaulted ceiling and a walk-in closet. The master bath features a shower and a double-bowl vanity.

▲
42'
▼

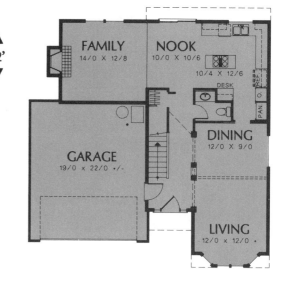

Design S8898

First Floor: 1,075 square feet
Second Floor: 816 square feet
Total: 1,891 square feet

● The vaulted entry area of this home will impress visitors. The great room features a vaulted ceiling shared with the dining room. The U-shaped kitchen serves the family room with a pass-through. A bay window and deck access make the family room extra special, as does a warming hearth. A utility room and a powder room lead to the two-car garage. Upstairs, three bedrooms include a master bedroom suite with an efficient, private bath and two closets. The secondary bedrooms share a full hall bath.

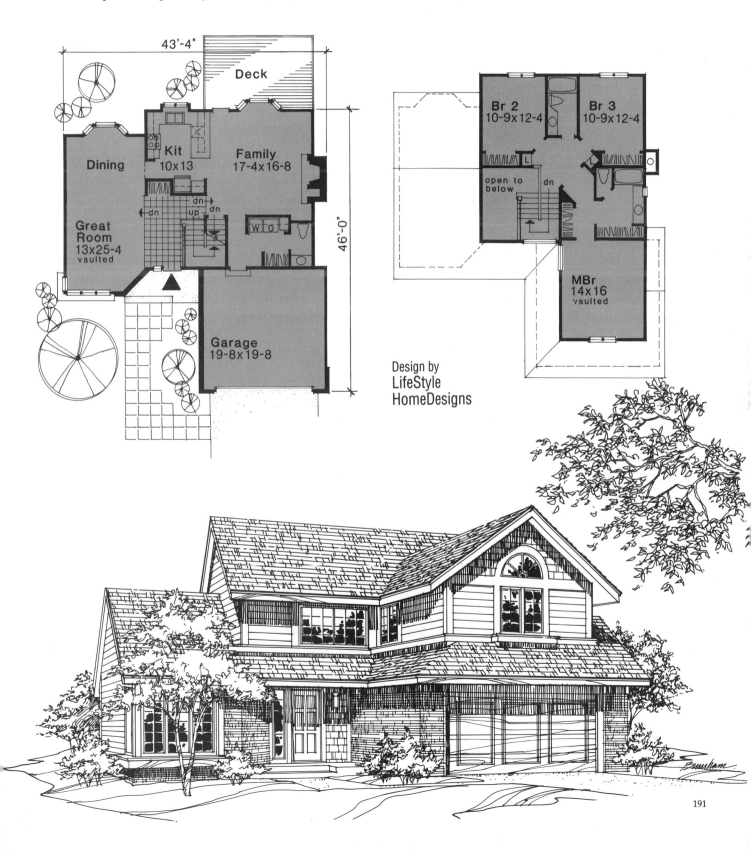

Design by
LifeStyle
HomeDesigns

Design S9474

First Floor: 1,180 square feet
Second Floor: 1,084 square feet
Total: 2,264 square feet

● Details and amenities make a home so much more than just a place to live—this plan has its share. The first floor has living and working areas surrounding a central hallway and staircase. The family room has a fireplace and sliding glass doors to the rear yard. Formal occasions are handled easily in the living room/dining room area. The kitchen is centrally located for convenience. Upstairs there are four bedrooms, each with plenty of closet space. Don't overlook the sumptuous bath in the master suite. Choose a two-car garage or three-car garage depending on your needs.

Design by
Alan Mascord
Design Associates, Inc.

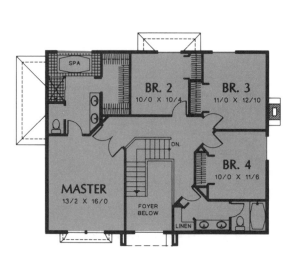

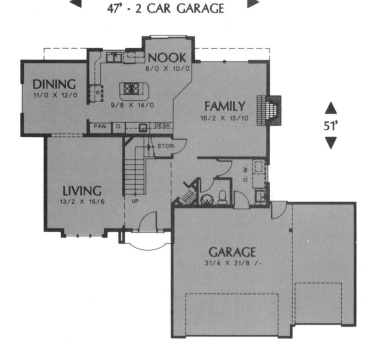

Design S9477

First Floor: 1,308 square feet
Second Floor: 1,141 square feet
Total: 2,449 square feet

Design by
Alan Mascord
Design Associates, Inc.

◀ 56' ▶

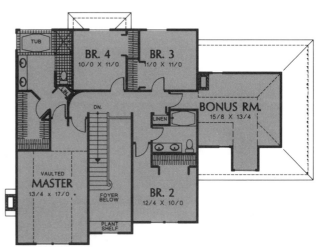

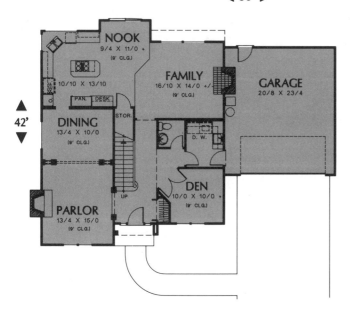

● Quietly stated elegance is the key to this home's attraction. Its floor plan allows plenty of space for formal and informal occasions. Note that the rear of the first floor is devoted to an open area serving as family room, breakfast nook and island kitchen. This area is complemented by a formal parlor/dining room combination. A private den could function as a guest room with the handy powder room nearby. There are four bedrooms on the second floor. Bonus room over the garage could become an additional bedroom or study.

Design by
**Alan Mascord
Design Associates, Inc.**

◄ 49' ►

SPA

DEN/BR. 2
10/3 X 9/10

BR. 3
11/6 X 13/4

LIN.

LINEN

MASTER
13/0 X 16/8

DN.

FOYER
BELOW

BR. 4
11/0 X 12/6

DINING
10/4 X 11/10

NOOK
7/8 X 10/0

▲
40'
▼

FAMILY
13/6 X 15/2

PAN.   DESK

LIVING
13/0 X 16/2

UP

GARAGE
19/4 X 21/4

D. W.

PORCH

Design S9524

First Floor: 1,032 square feet
Second Floor: 1,075 square feet
Total: 2,107 square feet

● This stylish country farmhouse is enhanced by the classically rounded columns supporting the covered front porch. Formal living and dining rooms are found to the left of the entry. To the right rests the informal living area. A family room warmed by a cheerful fireplace shares space with the eating nook, offering access to the rear grounds. This provides a winning combination with the efficient kitchen, which features an L-shaped counter and an island cooktop. This area will quickly become a favorite place for family gatherings. The second floor is reserved for the sleeping quarters. Bedrooms 3 and 4 are separated from the master suite by Bedroom 2 which may also serve as an optional den. The master suite provides a relaxing retreat. The pampering bath features a soothing spa tub, a separate shower and a large walk-in closet.

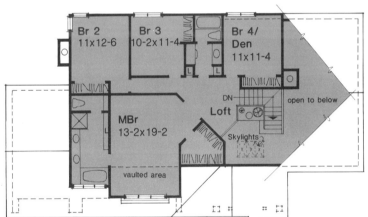

Br 2
11x12-6

Br 3
10-2x11-4

Br 4/
Den
11x11-4

MBr
13-2x19-2

DN

Loft

open to below

Skylights

vaulted area

Design by
**LifeStyle
HomeDesigns**

Design S8899

First Floor: 1,290 square feet
Second Floor: 1,155 square feet
Total: 2,445 square feet

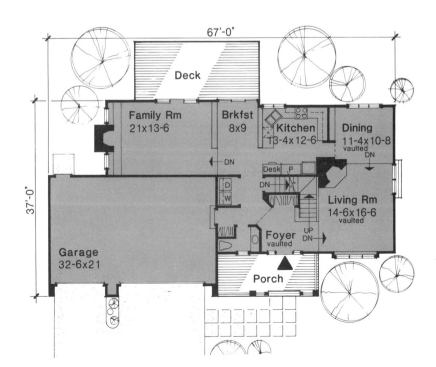

67'-0"

Deck

Family Rm
21x13-6

Brkfst
8x9

Kitchen
13-4x12-6

Dining
11-4x10-8
vaulted

37'-0"

DN

Desk

DN

P

DN

Living Rm
14-6x16-6
vaulted

Foyer
vaulted

UP
DN

Garage
32-6x21

Porch

● A vaulted, skylit foyer with a
dramatic staircase opens this plan.
To the right, a gracious living room
with a fireplace opens to a dining
room. The full kitchen is conveniently located between the dining
room and the breakfast room. The
family room features a central
hearth and built-in cabinets. A rear
deck enhances outdoor livability.
On the second floor, four bedrooms–or three and a den–include
a spacious master suite. Its bath
extends a separate shower and tub
and dual lavatories.

195

Design S9311

First Floor: 1,032 square feet
Second Floor: 865 square feet
Total: 1,897 square feet

● Combining lap siding, a covered front porch and brick accents, the exterior of this home exudes country charm. Just off the tiled entry, the volume living room shares an open arrangement with the formal dining room. Meals prepared in the generous kitchen will be enjoyed in the bayed dinette with large pantry. After dinner, relax in the spacious family room with raised-hearth fireplace. Upstairs, the master bedroom suite contains His and Hers closets which separate the bedroom from the master bath with double vanity. The whirlpool tub is brightened by an arch-top window. Three secondary bedrooms are served by their own convenient bath and linen closet.

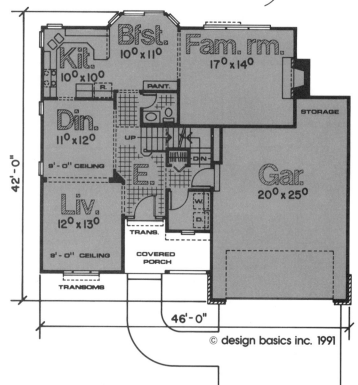

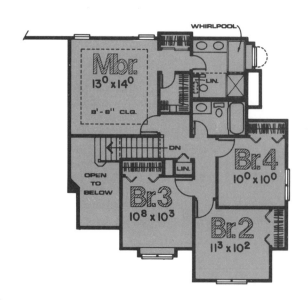

Design by
Design Basics, Inc.

196

Design S9269

First Floor: 1,081 square feet; Second Floor: 1,136 square feet
Total: 2,217 square feet

● Victorian charm and detailing radiate from the elevation of this four-bedroom, two-story design. Inside, formal living spaces, visible from the entry, begin with a dining room with hutch space and a parlor highlighted by a bayed window and alluring angles. the T-shaped staircase allows quick access to the informal spaces at the rear, such as the comfortable gathering room with a fireplace, built-in bookcase and many windows. Casual traffic patterns flow through a sunny, open breakfast area and island kitchen. Upstairs, a compartmented bath is shared by the secondary sleeping quarters. Gracing the master sleeping quarters is an elegant vaulted ceiling and private dressing/bath area offering an oval whirlpool, angled vanity and walk-in wardrobe.

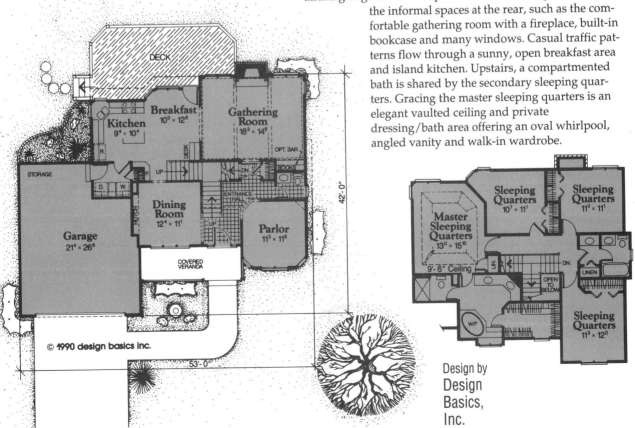

Design by
Design Basics, Inc.

Design S9343

First Floor: 1,000 square feet
Second Floor: 993 square feet
Total: 1,993 square feet

● At less than 2,000 square feet, this plan captures the heritage and romance of an authentic Colonial home with many modern amenities. Stylish, yet economical to build, here's a classic design for move-up buyers. A central hall leads to the formal rooms at the front where showpiece furnishings can be displayed. For daily living, the informal rooms can't be beat. A bookcase and large linen cabinet are thoughtful touches upstairs. Further evidence of tasteful design is shown in the master suite. A volume ceiling, large walk-in closet and whirlpool tub await the fortunate homeowner. Each secondary bedroom has bright windows to add natural lighting and comfort.

Cost to build? See page 216 to order complete cost estimate to build this house in your area!

Design by
Design Basics, Inc.

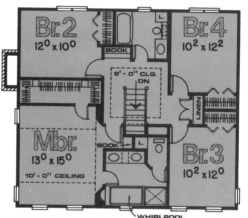

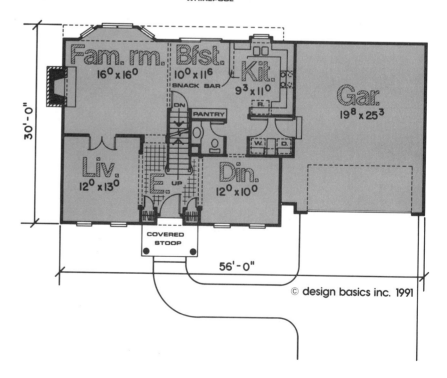

© design basics inc. 1991

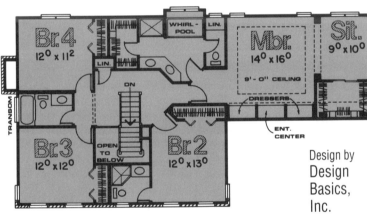

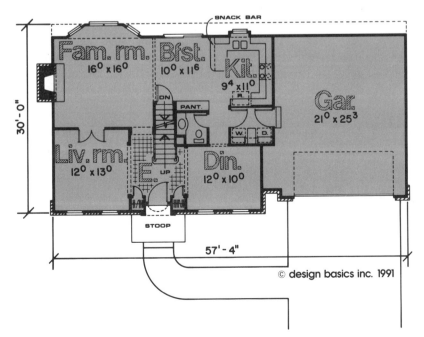

Design by
Design
Basics,
Inc.

© design basics inc. 1991

Design S9344

First Floor: 1,000 square feet
Second Floor: 1,345 square feet
Total: 2,345 square feet

● Repeating window detailing, an arched entry and a brick facade highlight the exterior of this modern, two-story Colonial home. Formal rooms at the front provide entertaining ease. The dining room is served by a convenient passageway for quick kitchen service while bright windows and French doors add appeal to the living room. A relaxing family room has a bayed conversation area plus a clear view through the sunny dinette into the gourmet kitchen. Features include wrapping counters, a snack bar, two Lazy Susans and a generous pantry. Upstairs, a U-shaped hall with a view to below offers separation to all four bedrooms. Bedroom 2 has its own bath. Homeowners will love the expansive master retreat. This oasis features a private sitting room, two walk-in closets, compartmented bath, separate vanities and a window-brightened whirlpool tub.

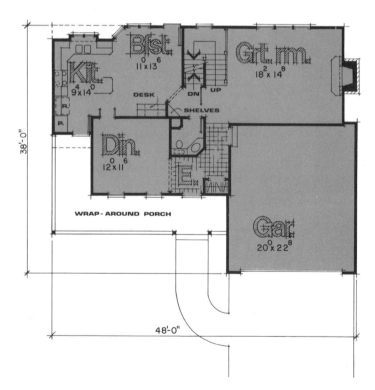

WRAP-AROUND PORCH

38'-0"

48'-0"

Design by
**Design
Basics,
Inc.**

Design S9289
First Floor: 927 square feet
Second Floor: 1,163 square feet
Total: 2,090 square feet

● If you've ever dreamed of living in a country home, you'll love the wrapping porch on this four-bedroom, two-story home. Comfortable living begins in the great room with windows and nearby staircase. Just off the entry, a formal dining room was designed to make entertaining a pleasure. The large kitchen includes a pantry, island counter, roll-top desk and Lazy Susan. A private door accesses the wraparound porch from the kitchen. Be sure to take a good look at the bright dinette. Upstairs, secondary bedrooms share a centrally located bath with double vanity. For convenience, the laundry room is located on the same level as the bedrooms. The deluxe master bedroom is accessed by double doors. In the master bath, you'll enjoy the whirlpool, transom window and sloped ceiling.

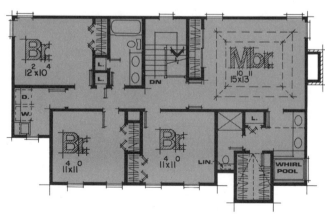

MULTI-LEVEL & HILLSIDE HOMES

Affordable Choices

Versatility of form is the key to multi-level houses. Among their many faces are the split-level, bi-level and hillside house. Each of these types shares a common feature — complete livability achieved by the "stacking" of living areas or zones. Like 1½-story and two-story structures, such stacking minimizes site size requirements, the size of the roof area and the expanse of the foundation.

The split-level house may have its living levels arranged in several ways. The most common are the side-to-side split and the front-to-back split. The levels are usually identified as the main living level, the upper sleeping level and the lower recreation level. When a fourth level is added — generally the basement — the structure is often called a quad-level.

The bi-level (also referred to a split-foyer) is characterized by a central foyer, or entry hall, from which two flights of stairs originate. Usually one flight of several steps leads to the living level; the other with a similar number of steps leads to the sleeping level, most often located above the lower living level. Variations of the popular split-foyer house may have these levels reversed.

The hillside house is designed to take advantage of a sloping building site. It may take the form of a one- or two-story structure with an exposed lower level.

Because of their unique structure, multi-levels often incorporate a garage into the perimeter of the house. This design not only achieves convenience but results in a lower initial expense — such houses can be constructed on smaller, less costly sites.

However, the main cost-effective aspect of the split-level is that it features a lower level which is raised above ground, easily accommodating living areas. Such amenities as large window walls and sliding glass doors with access to patios and terraces are often found in such a design. It is also common to find bedrooms on the lower level.

Another cost savings is realized in areas where sloping or uneven sites are found. Considered "problem" sites or, at least, less desirable sites, they may be available for sale at prices far below those of flatter sites. Building an appropriate multi-level on a bargain lot may make an otherwise unaffordable house within range even though engineering costs may be a bit more expensive than with a flat site. And building on such sites will often result in a striking and unique finished product.

While each of the three types of multi-levels adapt well to sloping sites, the split-level and bi-level can also be effectively built on flat sites, making the multi-level one of the most popular styles for any region of the country. The homes in this section display the best in multi-level design, including such special features as interior and exterior balconies, overlooks and great views. For cost-effective housing with a variety of options, the multi-level is a wise choice.

Design S7229

Square Footage: 1,696

● This convenient split-entry ranch design features a great room with a volume ceiling, a fireplace flanked by bookcases and a floor-to-ceiling view of the back yard. The efficient double-L kitchen includes a sunny bay-windowed breakfast area. Box ceilings grace both the breakfast nook and the formal dining room. The laundry room is strategically located near the sleeping wing. Two secondary bedrooms offer abundant closet space and a shared full bath. The deluxe master bedroom includes a vaulted ceiling, a large walk-in closet and a bath with a whirlpool tub and a skylit dual vanity.

Design by
Design Basics, Inc.

Width 54'
Depth 34'

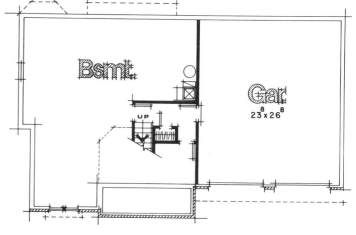

Design S9949

Square Footage: 1,770

● Wood frame, weatherboard siding and stacked stone give this home its country cottage appeal. The concept is reinforced by the double elliptical arched front porch, the Colonial balustrade and the roof-vent dormer. Inside, the foyer leads to the great room and the dining room. The well-planned kitchen easily serves the breakfast room. A rear deck makes outdoor living extra-enjoyable. Three bedrooms include a master suite with a tray ceiling and a luxurious bath. The two secondary bedrooms share a compartmented bath. This home is designed with a basement foundation.

Design by
Design Traditions

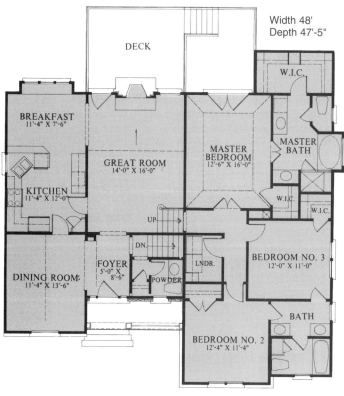

Width 48'
Depth 47'-5"

DECK

BREAKFAST
11'-4" X 7'-6"

GREAT ROOM
14'-0" X 16'-0"

KITCHEN
11'-4" X 12'-0"

MASTER BEDROOM
12'-6" X 16'-0"

MASTER BATH

W.I.C.

W.I.C.

UP

DINING ROOM
11'-4" X 13'-6"

FOYER
5'-0" X 8'-6"

DN

POWDER

LNDR.

BEDROOM NO. 3
12'-0" X 11'-0"

BEDROOM NO. 2
12'-4" X 11'-4"

BATH

203

Design S9345

Main Level: 1,499 square feet
Lower Level: 57 square feet
Total: 1,556 square feet

● A high-impact entry defines the exterior of this special multi-level home design. A formal dining room with interesting ceiling detail and a boxed window is open to the entry. In the volume great room, homeowners will enjoy a handsome brick fireplace and large windows to the back. Wrapping counters, a corner sink, Lazy Susan and pantry add convenience to the thoughtful kitchen. The adjoining bayed breakfast area has a sloped ceiling and arched transom window. The three bedrooms in this home provide privacy from the main living areas. Two secondary bedrooms share the hall bath. Last, but not least, the master suite offers a vaulted ceiling, skylit dressing/bath area with double vanity, walk-in closet and whirlpool tub.

Design by
Design
Basics,
Inc.

© 1987 design basics inc.

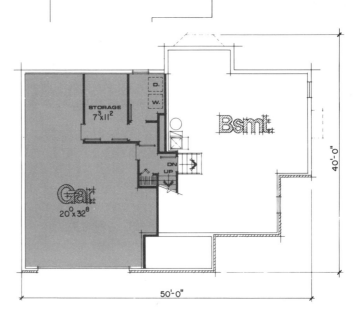

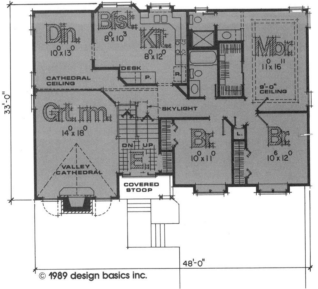

© 1989 design basics inc.

33'-0"

48'-0"

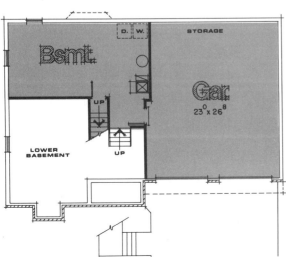

Design by
Design
Basics,
Inc.

Design S9291
Square Footage: 1,458

● From the volume entry, expansive views of the great room and dining room captivate home owners and guests. The great room with a fireplace centered under the valley cathedral ceiling beckons. An efficient kitchen which serves the bright dinette has a pantry and planning desk. The cathedral ceiling in the dining room adds to the atmosphere of meals and entertaining. Two secondary bedrooms with boxed windows are accessed by the corridor hallway. Comfort abounds in the master suite with 9-foot tiered ceiling plus mirrored bi-pass doors for the walk-in closet and private bath.

Design S9841

Square Footage: 1,725 (without basement)

● European style takes beautifully to a sloped lot. This design tames a slight grade by making use of a hillside garage. The upper level is split into two levels accessed from the foyer. The entry level holds living and dining space; the lower level houses bedrooms.

Design by
Design Traditions

WIDTH 47'-6"
DEPTH 45'-6"

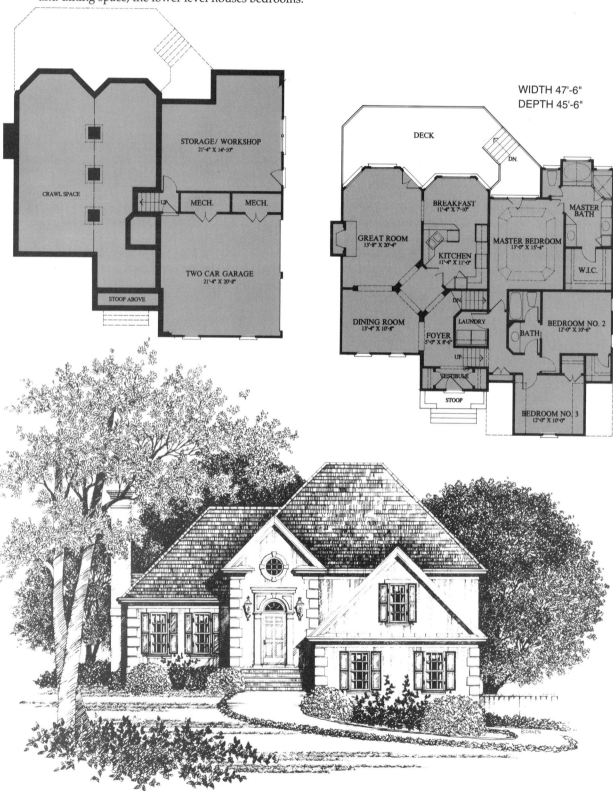

Copyright 1992 Stephen S. Fuller, Inc.

Design S9879

Square Footage: 1,770

● The country cottage styling of this stately brick home includes brick detailing framing the front entry and windows. Gambles and a multi-level roof help create the soft charm of this design. The foyer provides views into both the large great room with warming hearth and the dining room with vaulted ceiling, making a tremendous first impression. From the great room, one enters the kitchen with spacious work area and adjacent breakfast room including a boxed bay window. The second level offers two bedrooms and a bath in an arrangement well-suited for children. The master bedroom is entered through large double doors and features a tray ceiling and French doors leading to a private deck.

Design by
Design Traditions

QUOTE ONE®

Cost to build? See page 216 to order complete cost estimate to build this house in your area!

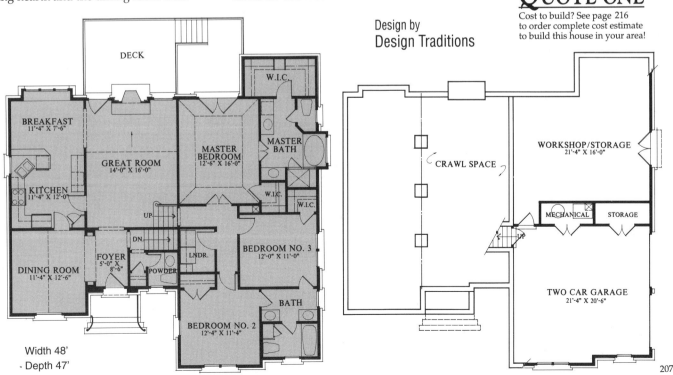

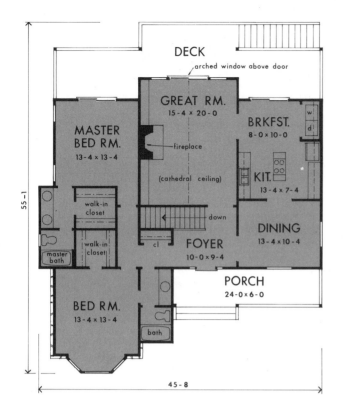

DECK

arched window above door

GREAT RM.
15-4 × 20-0

BRKFST.
8-0 × 10-0

MASTER
BED RM.
13-4 × 13-4

fireplace

(cathedral ceiling)

KIT.
13-4 × 7-4

walk-in
closet

walk-in
closet

master
bath

c1

down

FOYER
10-0 × 9-4

DINING
13-4 × 10-4

BED RM.
13-4 × 13-4

bath

PORCH
24-0 × 6-0

55-1

45-8

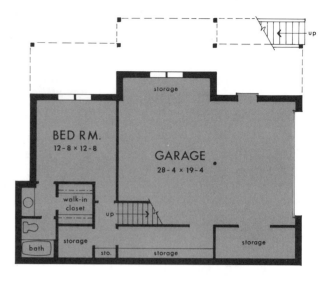

storage

BED RM.
12-8 × 12-8

GARAGE
28-4 × 19-4

walk-in
closet

bath

up

storage

sto.

storage

storage

up

Design by
**Donald A.
Gardner,
Architect, Inc.**

Design S9684
Square Footage: 1,528
Basement (heated): 394; (unheated): 851

● Loaded with charm, this compact plan has plenty of livability within its walls. The main floor contains a great room, a formal dining room, an island kitchen with an attached breakfast nook, a grand master suite and one family bedroom. On the garage level is a wealth of storage in addition to the bedroom with a full bath. A rear deck adds great outdoor livability. Please specify basement or crawlspace foundation when ordering.

B. NATHAN

Design by
Home Planners, Inc.

Design S2485

Main Level: 1,108 square feet
Lower Level: 983 square feet
Total: 2,091 square feet

● This hillside vacation home gives the appearance of being a one-story from the road. However, since it is built off the edge of a slope, the rear exterior is a full two-story structure. Notice the projecting deck and how it shelters the terrace. Each of the generous glass areas is protected from the summer sun by the overhangs and the extended walls. The clerestory windows of the front exterior provide natural light to the center of the plan.

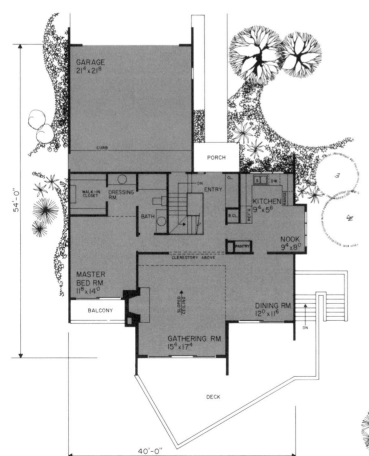

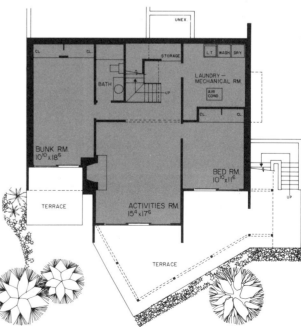

Design S2761 Main Level: 1,242 square feet
Lower Level: 1,242 square feet; Total: 2,484 square feet

● Here is another one-story that doubles its livability by exposing the lowest level at the rear. Formal living on the main level and informal living, the activity room and study, on the lower level. Observe the wonderful outdoor living facilities. The deck acts as a cover for the terrace.

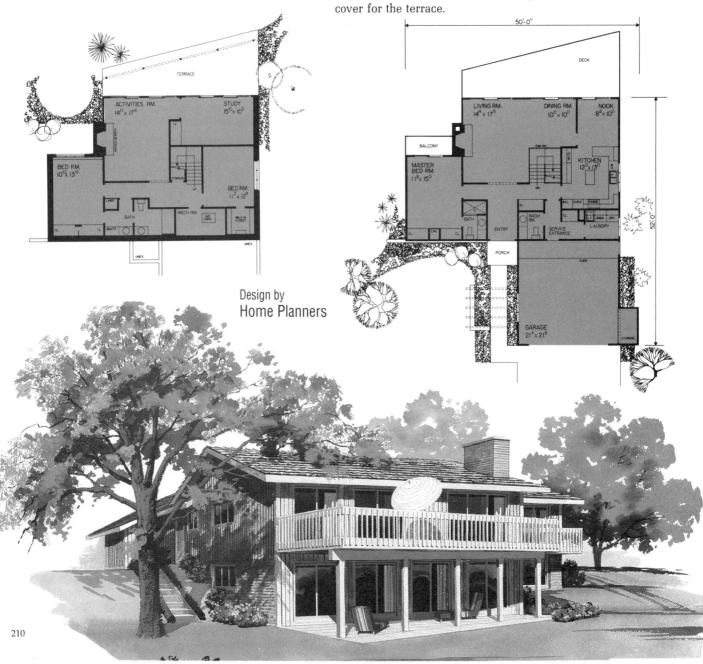

TERRACE

ACTIVITIES RM.
14⁰ x 17⁶

STUDY
15⁵ x 10⁰

BED RM.
10⁰ x 13¹⁰

BED RM.
11² x 12⁸

STORAGE
UP

BATH
MECH. RM.
AIR COND.
WALK IN CLOSET

VANITY
CL
CL

UNEX
UNEX

Design by
Home Planners

50'-0"

DECK

LIVING RM.
14² x 17⁶

DINING RM.
10⁰ x 10⁰

NOOK
8⁸ x 10⁰

BALCONY

MASTER BED RM.
11⁸ x 15⁰

KITCHEN
12⁰ x 13⁰

BATH
ENTRY

WASH RM.

OVEN RANGE
WASH DRY
LAUNDRY

SERVICE ENTRANCE

PORCH

52'-0"

GARAGE
21⁴ x 21⁸

STORAGE

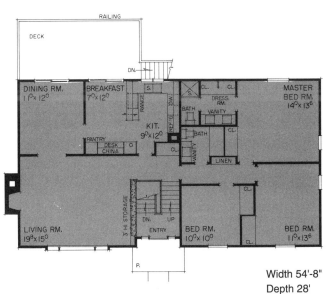

DECK

RAILING

DN.

DINING RM.
11⁰x12⁰

BREAKFAST
7⁰x12⁰

KIT.
9⁰x12⁰

PANTRY

DESK
CHINA

RANGE

REF'G.

D.W.

S.

BATH

DRESS. RM.

VANITY

BATH

VANITY

CL.

LINEN

MASTER BED RM.
14⁰x13⁶

LIVING RM.
19⁸x15⁰

3' HI STORAGE

DN. UP

ENTRY

BED RM.
10⁰x10⁰

BED RM.
11⁰x13⁶

CL.

P.

Width 54'-8"
Depth 28'

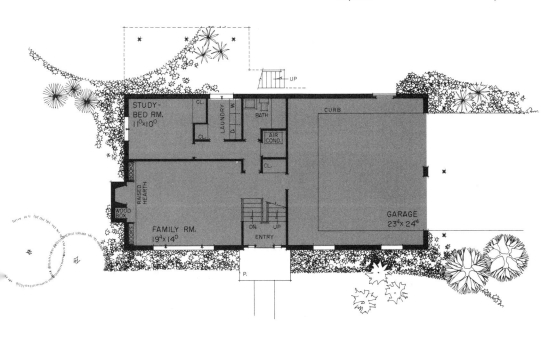

UP

STUDY-
BED RM.
11⁰x10⁰

LAUNDRY

W

D

BATH

AIR COND.

CL.

CURB

RAISED HEARTH

WOOD BOX

FAMILY RM.
19⁴x14⁰

DN. UP

ENTRY

GARAGE
23⁴x24⁴

P.

Design S1850

Main Level: 1,456 square feet
Lower Level: 728 square feet
Total: 2,184 square feet

● A perfect rectangle, this split-level is comparatively inexpensive to build and very appealing to live in. It features a large upper-level living room with fireplace, formal dining room, three bedrooms (with two full baths nearby), and an outdoor deck. Another fireplace warms the family room on the lower level, which also has a full bath and room for a study or fourth bedroom.

QUOTE ONE™

Cost to build? See page 216 to order complete cost estimate to build this house in your area!

Design by
Home Planners

Design S2823

First Floor: 1,370 square feet
Second Floor: 927 square feet
Total: 2,297 square feet

Quote One™

Cost to build? See page 216
to order complete cost estimate
to build this house in your area!

● The street view of this contemporary design features a small courtyard entrance as well as a private terrace off the study. Inside the livability will be outstanding. This design features spacious first-floor activity areas that flow smoothly into each other. In the gathering room a raised-hearth fireplace creates a dramatic focal point. An adjacent covered terrace, featuring a skylight, is ideal for outdoor dining and could be screened in later for an additional room.

Design by
Home Planners,
Inc.

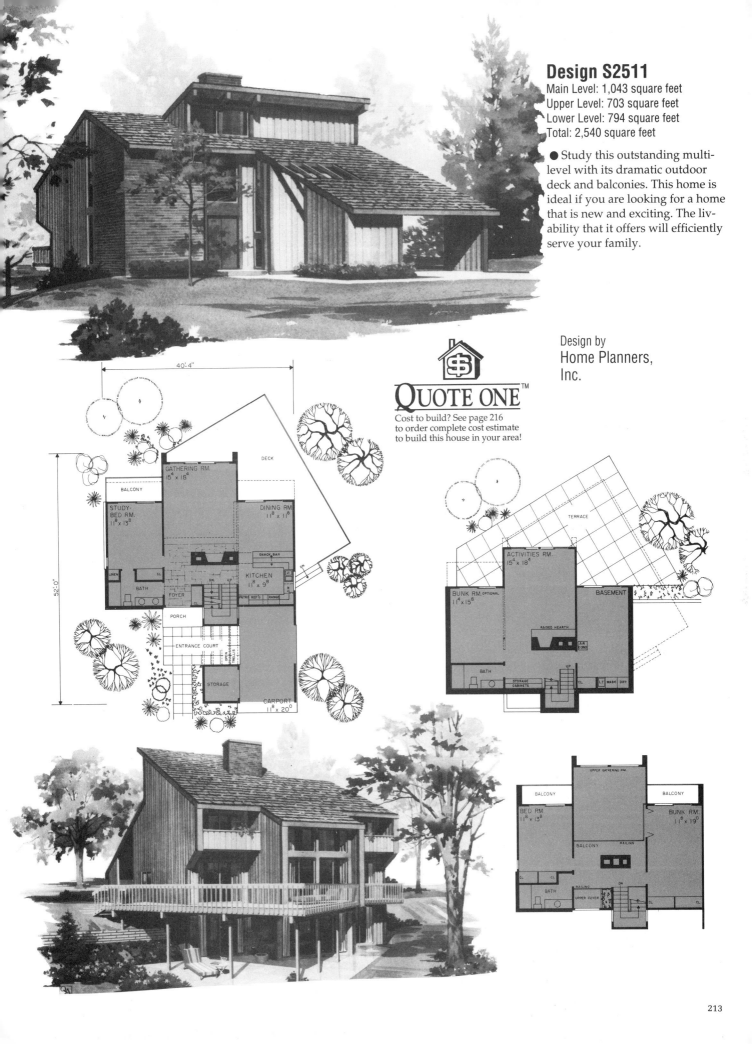

Design S2511

Main Level: 1,043 square feet
Upper Level: 703 square feet
Lower Level: 794 square feet
Total: 2,540 square feet

● Study this outstanding multi-level with its dramatic outdoor deck and balconies. This home is ideal if you are looking for a home that is new and exciting. The livability that it offers will efficiently serve your family.

QUOTE ONE™

Cost to build? See page 216
to order complete cost estimate
to build this house in your area!

Design by
Home Planners,
Inc.

LET US SHOW YOU OUR HOME BLUEPRINT PACKAGE.

Building a home? Planning a home? Our Blueprint Package has nearly everything you need to get the job done right, whether you're working on your own or with help from an architect, designer, builder or subcontractors. Each Blueprint Package is the result of many hours of work by licensed architects or professional designers.

QUALITY

Hundreds of hours of painstaking effort have gone into the development of your blueprint set. Each home has been quality-checked by professionals to insure accuracy and buildability.

VALUE

Because we sell in volume, you can buy professional quality blueprints at a fraction of their development cost. With our plans, your dream home design costs only a few hundred dollars, not the thousands of dollars that architects charge.

SERVICE

Once you've chosen your favorite home plan, you'll receive fast, efficient service whether you choose to mail or fax your order to us or call us toll free at 1-800-521-6797. For customer service, call toll free 1-888-690-1116.

SATISFACTION

Over 50 years of service to satisfied home plan buyers provide us unparalleled experience and knowledge in producing quality blueprints.

ORDER TOLL FREE 1-800-521-6797

After you've looked over our Blueprint Package and Important Extras on the following pages, simply mail the order form on page 221 or call toll free on our Blueprint Hotline: 1-800-521-6797. We're ready and eager to serve you. For customer service, call toll free 1-888-690-1116.

Each set of blueprints is an interrelated collection of detail sheets which includes components such as floor plans, interior and exterior elevations, dimensions, cross-sections, diagrams and notations. These sheets show exactly how your house is to be built.

AMONG THE SHEETS INCLUDED MAY BE:

FRONTAL SHEET

This artist's sketch of the exterior of the house gives you an idea of how the house will look when built and landscaped. Large floor plans show all levels of the house and provide an overview of your new home's livability, as well as a handy reference for deciding on furniture placement.

FOUNDATION PLANS

This sheet shows the foundation layout including support walls, excavated and unexcavated areas, if any, and foundation notes. If slab construction rather than basement, the plan shows footings and details for a monolithic slab. This page, or another in the set, may include a sample plot plan for locating your house on a building site.

DETAILED FLOOR PLANS

These plans show the layout of each floor of the house. Rooms and interior spaces are carefully dimensioned and keys are given for cross-section details provided later in the plans. The positions of electrical outlets and switches are shown.

HOUSE CROSS-SECTIONS

Large-scale views show sections or cut-aways of the foundation, interior walls, exterior walls, floors, stairways and roof details. Additional cross-sections may show important changes in floor, ceiling or roof heights or the relationship of one level to another. Extremely valuable for construction, these sections show exactly how the various parts of the house fit together.

INTERIOR ELEVATIONS

Many of our drawings show the design and placement of kitchen and bathroom cabinets, laundry areas, fireplaces, bookcases and other built-ins. Little "extras," such as mantelpiece and wainscoting drawings, plus molding sections, provide details that give your home that custom touch.

EXTERIOR ELEVATIONS

These drawings show the front, rear and sides of your house and give necessary notes on exterior materials and finishes. Particular attention is given to cornice detail, brick and stone accents or other finish items that make your home unique.

SAMPLE PACKAGE

FRONTAL SHEET

FOUNDATION PLANS

DETAILED FLOOR PLANS

EXTERIOR ELEVATIONS

INTERIOR ELEVATIONS

HOUSE CROSS-SECTIONS

IMPORTANT EXTRAS TO DO THE JOB RIGHT!

INTRODUCING EIGHT IMPORTANT PLANNING AND CONSTRUCTION AIDS DEVELOPED BY OUR PROFESSIONALS TO HELP YOU SUCCEED IN YOUR HOME-BUILDING PROJECT

MATERIALS LIST

(Note: Because of the diversity of local building codes, our Materials List does not include mechanical materials.)

For many of the designs in our portfolio, we offer a customized materials take-off that is invaluable in planning and estimating the cost of your new home. This Materials List outlines the quantity, type and size of materials needed to build your house (with the exception of mechanical system items). Included are framing lumber, windows and doors, kitchen and bath cabinetry, rough and finish hardware, and much more. This handy list helps you or your builder cost out materials and serves as a reference sheet when you're compiling bids. A Materials List cannot be ordered before blueprints are ordered.

SPECIFICATION OUTLINE

This valuable 16-page document is critical to building your house correctly. Designed to be filled in by you or your builder, this book lists 166 stages or items crucial to the building process. It provides a comprehensive review of the construction process and helps in choosing materials. When combined with the blueprints, a signed contract, and a schedule, it becomes a legal document and record for the building of your home.

QUOTE ONE®

SUMMARY COST REPORT / MATERIALS COST REPORT

A new service for estimating the cost of building select designs, the Quote One® system is available in two separate stages: The Summary Cost Report and the Materials Cost Report.

The **Summary Cost Report** is the first stage in the package and shows the total cost per square foot for your chosen home in your zip-code area and then breaks that cost down into various categories showing the costs for building materials, labor and installation. The report includes three grades: Budget, Standard and Custom. These reports allow you to evaluate your building budget and compare the costs of building a variety of homes in your area.

Make even more informed decisions about your home-building project with the second phase of our package, our **Materials Cost Report.** This tool is invaluable in planning and estimating the cost of your new home. The material and installation (labor and equipment) cost is shown for each of over 1,000 line items provided in the Materials List (Standard grade), which is included when you purchase this estimating tool. It allows you to determine building costs for your specific zip-code area and for your chosen home design. Space is allowed for additional estimates from contractors and subcontractors, such as for mechanical materials, which are not included in our packages. This invaluable tool includes a Materials List. For most plans, a Materials Cost Report cannot be ordered before blueprints are ordered. Call for details. In addition, ask about our Home Planners Estimating Package.

The Quote One® program is continually updated with new plans. If you are interested in a plan that is not indicated as Quote One®, please call and ask our sales reps. They will be happy to verify the status for you. To order these invaluable reports, use the order form on page 221 or call 1-800-521-6797.

CONSTRUCTION INFORMATION

If you want to know more about techniques—and deal more confidently with subcontractors—we offer these useful sheets. Each set is an excellent tool that will add to your understanding of these technical subjects. These helpful details provide general construction information and are not specific to any single plan.

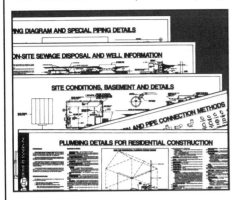

PLUMBING

The Blueprint Package includes locations for all the plumbing fixtures, including sinks, lavatories, tubs, showers, toilets, laundry trays and water heaters. However, if you want to know more about the complete plumbing system, these Plumbing Details will prove very useful. Prepared to meet requirements of the National Plumbing Code, these fact-filled sheets give general information on pipe schedules, fittings, sump-pump details, water-softener hookups, septic system details and much more. Sheets also include a glossary of terms.

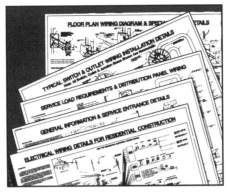

ELECTRICAL

The locations for every electrical switch, plug and outlet are shown in your Blueprint Package. However, these Electrical Details go further to take the mystery out of household electrical systems. Prepared to meet requirements of the National Electrical Code, these comprehensive drawings come packed with helpful information, including wire sizing, switch-installation schematics, cable-routing details, appliance wattage, doorbell hook-ups, typical service panel circuitry and much more. A glossary of terms is also included.

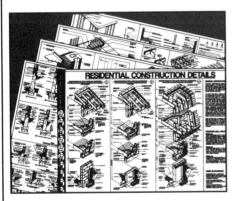

CONSTRUCTION

The Blueprint Package contains everything an experienced builder needs to construct a particular house. However, it doesn't show all the ways that houses can be built, nor does it explain alternate construction methods. To help you understand how your house will be built—and offer additional techniques—this set of Construction Details depicts the materials and methods used to build foundations, fireplaces, walls, floors and roofs. Where appropriate, the drawings show acceptable alternatives.

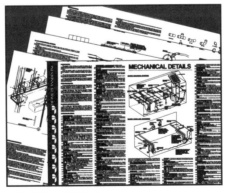

MECHANICAL

These Mechanical Details contain fundamental principles and useful data that will help you make informed decisions and communicate with subcontractors about heating and cooling systems. Drawings contain instructions and samples that allow you to make simple load calculations, and preliminary sizing and costing analysis. Covered are today's most commonly used systems from heat pumps to solar fuel systems. The package is filled with illustrations and diagrams to help you visualize components and how they relate to one another.

PLAN-A-HOME®

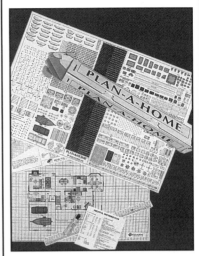

PLAN-A-HOME® is an easy-to-use tool that helps you design a new home, arrange furniture in a new or existing home, or plan a remodeling project. Each package contains:

✓ **MORE THAN 700 REUSABLE PEEL-OFF PLANNING SYMBOLS** on a self-stick vinyl sheet, including walls, windows, doors, all types of furniture, kitchen components, bath fixtures and many more.

✓ **A REUSABLE, TRANSPARENT, ¼" SCALE PLANNING GRID** that matches the scale of actual working drawings (¼" equals one foot). This grid provides the basis for house layouts of up to 140'x92'.

✓ **TRACING PAPER** and a protective sheet for copying or transferring your completed plan.

✓ **A FELT-TIP PEN**, with water-soluble ink that wipes away quickly.

Plan-A-Home® lets you lay out areas as large as a 7,500 square foot, six-bedroom, seven-bath house.

To Order, Call Toll Free 1-800-521-6797

To add these important extras to your Blueprint Package, simply indicate your choices on the order form on page 221. Or call us toll free 1-800-521-6797 and we'll tell you more about these exciting products. For customer service, call toll free 1-888-690-1116.

HOUSE BLUEPRINT PRICE SCHEDULE

Prices guaranteed through December 31, 2000

TIERS	1-SET STUDY PACKAGE	4-SET BUILDING PACKAGE	8-SET BUILDING PACKAGE	1-SET REPRODUCIBLE	HOME CUSTOMIZER® PACKAGE
P1	$20	$50	$90	$140	N/A
P2	$40	$70	$110	$160	N/A
P3	$60	$90	$130	$180	N/A
P4	$80	$110	$150	$200	N/A
P5	$100	$130	$170	$230	N/A
P6	$120	$150	$190	$250	N/A
A1	$400	$440	$500	$600	$650
A2	$440	$480	$540	$660	$710
A3	$480	$520	$580	$720	$770
A4	$520	$560	$620	$780	$830
C1	$560	$600	$660	$840	$890
C2	$600	$640	$700	$900	$950
C3	$650	$690	$750	$950	$1000
C4	$700	$740	$800	$1000	$1050
L1	$750	$790	$850	$1050	$1100
L2	$800	$840	$900	$1100	$1150
L3	$900	$940	$1000	$1200	$1250
L4	$1000	$1040	$1100	$1300	$1350

OPTIONS FOR PLANS IN TIERS A1–L4

Additional Identical Blueprints in same order for "A1–L4" price plans ....$50 per set

Reverse Blueprints (mirror image) with 4- or 8-set order
for "A1–L4" price plans ....$50 fee per order

Specification Outlines ....$10 each

Materials Lists for "A1–C3" price plans ....$60 each

Materials Lists for "C4–L4" price plans ....$70 each

OPTIONS FOR PLANS IN TIERS P1–P6

Additional Identical Blueprints in same order for "P1–P6" price plans ....$10 per set

Reverse Blueprints (mirror image) for "P1–P6" price plans ....$10 per set

1 Set of Deck Construction Details ....$14.95 each

Deck Construction Package ....add $10 to Building Package price
(includes 1 set of "P1–P6" price plans, plus
1 set Standard Deck Construction Details)

1 Set of Gazebo Construction Details ....$14.95 each

Gazebo Construction Package ....add $10 to Building Package price
(includes 1 set of "P1–P6" price plans, plus
1 set Standard Gazebo Construction Details)

IMPORTANT NOTES

The 1-set study package is marked "not for construction."
Prices for 4- or 8-set Building Packages honored only at time of original order. All Donald A. Gardner basement foundations will incur a $225 surcharge. Right-reading reverse blueprints, if available, will incur a $165 surcharge.

INDEX

To use the Index below, refer to the design number listed in numerical order (a helpful page reference is also given). Note the price index letter and refer to the House Blueprint Price Schedule above for the cost of one, four or eight sets of blueprints or the cost of a reproducible drawing. Additional prices are shown for identical and reverse blueprint sets, as well as a very useful Materials List for some of the plans. Also note in the Index below those plans that have matching or complementary Deck Plans or Landscape Plans. Refer to the schedules above for prices of these plans. All plans in this publication are customizable. However, only Home Planners plans can be customized with the Home Planners Home Customizer® Package. These plans are indicated below with the letter "Y." See page 221 for more information. The letter "Y" also identifies plans that are part of our Quote One® estimating service and those that offer Materials Lists. See page 216 for more information.

To Order: Fill in and send the order form on page 221—or call toll free 1-800-521-6797 or 520-297-8200. FAX: 1-800-224-6699 or 520-544-3086

DESIGN	PRICE	PAGE	MATERIALS LIST	CUSTOMIZABLE®	QUOTE ONE®	DECK	DECK PRICE	LANDSCAPE	LANDSCAPE PRICE	REGIONS
S1850	C1	211	Y	Y						
S1920	A4	71	Y	Y	Y			OLA026	P3	123568
S1956	A3	141	Y	Y	Y	ODA018	P3			
S2145	A3	103	Y	Y	Y			OLA010	P3	1234568
S2485	A4	209	Y	Y						
S2488	A4	169	Y	Y	Y	ODA003	P2			
S2490	C2	123	Y	Y	Y					
S2511	C1	213	Y	Y	Y	ODA009	P2	OLA030	P3	12345678
S2563	C1	101	Y	Y	Y	ODA015	P2	OLA002	P3	123568
S2606	A3	51	Y	Y	Y			OLA022	P3	123568
S2622	A3	140	Y	Y	Y	ODA004	P2	OLA001	P3	123568
S2657	A4	102	Y	Y	Y			OLA001	P3	123568
S2661	A4	100	Y	Y	Y	ODA014	P2	OLA003	P3	123568
S2707	A3	78	Y	Y	Y	ODA018	P3	OLA027	P3	12345678
S2711	A4	168	Y	Y	Y	ODA006	P2	OLA030	P3	12345678
S2733	A4	138	Y	Y	Y	ODA001	P2	OLA006	P3	123568
S2761	C1	210	Y	Y	Y			OLA030	P3	12345678
S2774	C1	139	Y	Y	Y	ODA001	P2	OLA008	P4	1234568
S2776	A4	105	Y	Y	Y	ODA014	P2	OLA008	P4	1234568
S2822	A3	104	Y	Y	Y			OLA030	P3	12345678
S2823	A4	212	Y	Y	Y	ODA013	P2	OLA030	P3	12345678
S2826	A4	171	Y	Y	Y	ODA017	P2			
S2854	C1	172	Y	Y	Y	ODA013	P2	OLA021	P3	123568
S2864	A3	79	Y	Y	Y	ODA001	P2	OLA026	P3	123568
S2875	A4	75	Y	Y	Y	ODA014	P2	OLA037	P4	347
S2878	A4	76	Y	Y	Y	ODA013	P2	OLA001	P3	123568
S2927	C1	170	Y	Y	Y	ODA001	P2			
S2939	A4	173	Y	Y	Y	ODA009	P2			
S2947	A4	70	Y	Y	Y	ODA013	P2	OLA001	P3	123568
S2962	C1	50	Y	Y	Y					
S2974	A4	142	Y	Y	Y			OLA024	P4	123568
S3309	C1	143	Y	Y	Y			OLA010	P3	1234568
S3314	A4	52	Y	Y	Y			OLA001	P3	123568
S3316	A3	145	Y	Y	Y			OLA003	P3	123568
S3332	C1	72	Y	Y	Y			OLA001	P3	123568
S3340	A4	73	Y	Y	Y			OLA025	P3	123568
S3355	A2	74	Y	Y	Y	ODA018	P3	OLA021	P3	123568
S3385	A3	144	Y	Y	Y	ODA001	P2	OLA008	P4	1234568
S3431	A4	89	Y	Y	Y					
S3438	C2	122	Y	Y	Y			OLA010	P3	1234568
S3443	C1	120	Y	Y	Y	ODA011	P2	OLA021	P3	123568
S3444	C1	121	Y	Y	Y	ODA006	P2	OLA021	P3	123568
S3460	A3	77	Y	Y	Y			OLA001	P3	123568
S3486	A3	88	Y	Y	Y					
S3488	C1	84	Y	Y	Y	ODA013	P2	OLA021	P3	123568
S3497	C2	96	Y	Y	Y					

DESIGN	PRICE	PAGE	MATERIALS LIST	CUSTOMIZABLE	QUOTE ONE	DECK	DECK PRICE	LANDSCAPE	LANDSCAPE PRICE	REGIONS
S3569	A3	53	Y	Y	Y	ODA006	P2	OLA039	P3	3478
S3600	A4	49	Y	Y	Y			OLA001	P3	123568
S3601	A4	49	Y	Y	Y			OLA001	P3	123568
S7229	A3	202	Y							
S7236	A4	159	Y							
S7282	A4	131	Y							
S8601	C1	86								
S8604	A4	90								
S8605	C1	22								
S8606	A4	24								
S8610	A3	19								
S8611	A3	18								
S8612	A4	20								
S8613	A3	21								
S8614	A4	85								
S8618	A4	188								
S8622	C1	189								
S8638	A4	87								
S8645	C1	25								
S8667	A4	23								
S8890	A3	48								
S8898	A3	191								
S8899	A4	195								
S8923	A4	17	Y		Y					
S8927	A4	111								
S9006	A3	58	Y		Y					
S9023	A2	7								
S9027	A3	14	Y		Y					
S9028	A3	13	Y		Y					
S9029	A4	176								
S9034	A2	56								
S9038	A3	59								
S9041	A2	108								
S9044	A2	106								
S9045	A2	55								
S9055	A4	178	Y		Y					
S9059	A4	177								
S9088	C1	12	Y		Y					
S9089	A3	16	Y		Y					
S9096	A2	6								
S9098	A3	15	Y		Y					
S9117	A2	107								
S9118	A3	11								
S9119	A4	110								
S9123	A2	54								
S9131	A2	109	Y		Y					
S9136	A3	10								
S9141	A3	175								
S9142	A3	174								
S9143	A3	9								
S9144	A2	57	Y		Y					
S9178	A3	8								
S9196	A4	179								
S9200	A4	29	Y		Y					
S9202	A4	33	Y							
S9204	A4	30	Y							
S9206	A4	128	Y		Y					
S9230	C1	160	Y							
S9232	A4	158	Y							
S9233	C1	157	Y							
S9235	A4	161	Y							
S9236	A2	28	Y							
S9237	A3	31	Y							
S9251	C1	135	Y		Y					
S9256	A4	26	Y							
S9257	A3	32	Y							
S9259	C1	156	Y							
S9260	A4	154	Y							
S9265	A3	126	Y							
S9269	A4	197	Y							
S9281	C1	132	Y							
S9289	A4	200	Y							
S9291	A2	205	Y							
S9296	A4	155	Y							
S9311	A4	196	Y							
S9315	A4	129	Y							
S9324	C1	130	Y							
S9328	A2	27	Y							
S9332	A3	134	Y	Y						
S9339	A4	127	Y							
S9340	C1	133	Y							

DESIGN	PRICE	PAGE	MATERIALS LIST	CUSTOMIZABLE	QUOTE ONE	DECK	DECK PRICE	LANDSCAPE	LANDSCAPE PRICE	REGIONS
S9341	C1	136	Y							
S9343	A4	198	Y		Y					
S9344	C1	199	Y							
S9345	A3	204	Y							
S9403	A3	37	Y					OLA001	P3	123568
S9413	A3	148	Y					OLA001	P3	123568
S9414	A3	146	Y					OLA001	P3	123568
S9421	A4	153	Y					OLA001	P3	123568
S9427	A3	38	Y					OLA001	P3	123568
S9429	A2	36	Y					OLA001	P3	123568
S9430	A3	97	Y					OLA001	P3	123568
S9431	A2	34	Y					OLA001	P3	123568
S9437	C1	152	Y					OLA001	P3	123568
S9437A	C1	152	Y					OLA001	P3	123568
S9451	A4	39	Y					OLA005	P3	123568
S9464	A4	98	Y					OLA005	P3	123568
S9467	A3	149	Y					OLA001	P3	123568
S9474	A4	192	Y					OLA001	P3	123568
S9477	A4	193	Y					OLA004	P3	123568
S9487	A4	99	Y					OLA001	P3	123568
S9490	A4	151	Y					OLA001	P3	123568
S9508	A3	35	Y					OLA001	P3	123568
S9509	A3	150	Y					OLA004	P3	123568
S9518	A3	190	Y					OLA001	P3	123568
S9524	A4	194	Y					OLA001	P3	123568
S9526	A3	95	Y		Y					
S9593	A3	147	Y							
S9602	A3	66	Y							
S9604	A3	64	Y							
S9605	A4	116	Y							
S9606	A3	115	Y		Y					
S9607	A2	65	Y							
S9608	A3	94	Y							
S9610	A3	163	Y							
S9611	A3	80	Y							
S9612	A3	81	Y							
S9613	A3	167	Y							
S9614	A3	166	Y							
S9616	C1	164	Y							
S9620	A2	63	Y							
S9621	A3	112	Y		Y					
S9623	A4	117	Y		Y					
S9625	A4	114	Y							
S9634	A4	83	Y							
S9639	A3	60	Y							
S9645	A3	113	Y		Y					
S9650	A4	162	Y							
S9651	A4	68	Y							
S9654	A4	118	Y							
S9655	A4	82	Y							
S9663	A2	93	Y							
S9664	A2	61	Y		Y					
S9666	A3	92	Y		Y					
S9670	A4	69	Y							
S9672	A4	165	Y							
S9682	A3	67	Y							
S9684	A2	208	Y							
S9726	A2	62	Y							
S9732	A4	119	Y							
S9831	C2	44	Y		Y					
S9839	C1	40								
S9840	C1	41	Y		Y					
S9841	C1	206								
S9842	C2	184	Y		Y					
S9843	C2	42								
S9844	C2	42	Y		Y					
S9845	C2	182								
S9847	C1	183								
S9848	C1	181								
S9849	C1	180	Y		Y					
S9853	C2	47	Y		Y					
S9857	C2	187								
S9862	C2	46	Y		Y					
S9872	C1	43	Y		Y					
S9874	C2	45	Y		Y					
S9875	C2	124								
S9876	C2	125	Y		Y					
S9877	C2	185	Y		Y					
S9878	C2	186								
S9879	C1	207	Y		Y					
S9949	C1	203								

BEFORE YOU ORDER...

BEFORE FILLING OUT THE COUPON AT RIGHT OR CALLING US ON OUR TOLL-FREE BLUEPRINT HOTLINE, YOU MAY WANT TO LEARN MORE ABOUT OUR SERVICES AND PRODUCTS. HERE'S SOME INFORMATION YOU WILL FIND HELPFUL.

OUR EXCHANGE POLICY

Since blueprints are printed in response to your order, we cannot honor requests for refunds. However, we will exchange your entire first order for an equal or greater number of blueprints within our plan collection within 90 days of the original order. The entire content of your original order must be returned to our offices before an exchange will be processed. If the returned blueprints look used, redlined or copied, we will not honor your exchange. Fees for exchanging your blueprints are as follows: 20% of the amount of the original order...*plus* the difference in cost if exchanging for a design in a higher price bracket or *less* the difference in cost if exchanging for a design in lower price bracket. **(Reproducible blueprints are not exchangeable.)** Please add $25 for postage and handling via Regular Service; $35 via Priority Service; $45 via Express Service. Shipping and handling charges are not refundable.

ABOUT REVERSE BLUEPRINTS

If you want to build in reverse of the plan as shown, we will include any number of reverse blueprints (mirror image) from a 4- or 8-set package for an additional fee of $50. Although lettering and dimensions will appear backward, reverses will be a useful aid if you decide to flop the plan.

REVISING, MODIFYING AND CUSTOMIZING PLANS

The wide variety of designs available in this publication allows you to select ideas and concepts for a home to fit your building site and match your family's needs, wants and budget. Like many homeowners who buy these plans, you and your builder, architect or engineer may want to make changes to them. Some changes may be made by your builder, but we recommend that most changes be made by a licensed architect or engineer. If you need to make alterations to a design that is customizable, you need only order our Home Customizer® Package to get you started. As set forth below, we cannot assume any responsibility for blueprints which have been changed, whether by you, your builder or by professionals selected by you or referred to you by us, because such individuals are outside our supervision and control.

ARCHITECTURAL AND ENGINEERING SEALS

Some cities and states are now requiring that a licensed architect or engineer review and "seal" a blueprint, or officially approve it, prior to construction due to concerns over energy costs, safety and other factors. Prior to application for a building permit or the start of actual construction, we strongly advise that you consult your local building official who can tell you if such a review is required.

ABOUT THE DESIGNS

The architects and designers whose work appears in this publication are among America's leading residential designers. Each plan was designed to meet the requirements of a nationally recognized model building code in effect at the time and place the plan was drawn. Because national building codes change from time to time, plans may not comply with any such code at the time they are sold to a customer. In addition, building officials may not accept these plans as final construction documents of record as the plans may need to be modified and additional drawings and details added to suit local conditions and requirements. We strongly advise that purchasers consult a licensed architect or engineer, and their local building official, before starting any construction related to these plans.

LOCAL BUILDING CODES AND ZONING REQUIREMENTS

At the time of creation, our plans are drawn to specifications published by the Building Officials and Code Administrators (BOCA) International, Inc.; the Southern Building Code Congress (SBCCI) International, Inc.; the International Conference of Building Officials (ICBO); or the Council of American Building Officials (CABO). Our plans are designed to meet or exceed na-

tional building standards. Because of the great differences in geography and climate throughout the United States and Canada, each state, county and municipality has its own building codes, zone requirements, ordinances and building regulations. Your plan may need to be modified to comply with local requirements regarding snow loads, energy codes, soil and seismic conditions and a wide range of other matters. In addition, you may need to obtain permits or inspections from local governments before and in the course of construction. Prior to using blueprints ordered from us, we strongly advise that you consult a licensed architect or engineer—and speak with your local building official—before applying for any permit or beginning construction. We authorize the use of our blueprints on the express condition that you strictly comply with all local building codes, zoning requirements and other applicable laws, regulations, ordinances and requirements. **Notice: Plans for homes to be built in Nevada must be re-drawn by a Nevada-registered professional. Consult your building official for more information on this subject.**

FOUNDATION AND EXTERIOR WALL CHANGES

Depending on your specific climate or regional building practices, you may wish to change a full basement to a slab or crawlspace foundation. Most professional contractors and builders can easily adapt your plans to alternate foundation types. Likewise, most can easily change 2x4 wall construction to 2x6, or vice versa.

DISCLAIMER

We and the designers we work with have put substantial care and effort into the creation of our blueprints. However, because we cannot provide on-site consultation, supervision and control over actual construction, and because of the great variance in local building requirements, building practices and soil, seismic, weather and other conditions, WE CANNOT MAKE ANY WARRANTY, EXPRESS OR IMPLIED, WITH RESPECT TO THE CONTENT OR USE OF OUR BLUEPRINTS, INCLUDING BUT NOT LIMITED TO ANY WARRANTY OF MERCHANTABILITY OR OF FITNESS FOR A PARTICULAR PURPOSE.

TERMS AND CONDITIONS

These designs are protected under the terms of United States Copyright Law and may not be copied or reproduced in any way, by any means, unless you have purchased Sepias or Reproducibles which clearly indicate your right to copy or reproduce. We authorize the use of your chosen design as an aid in the construction of one single family home only. You may not use this design to build a second or multiple dwellings without purchasing another blueprint or blueprints or paying additional design fees.

HOW MANY BLUEPRINTS DO YOU NEED?

A single set of blueprints is sufficient to study a home in greater detail. However, if you are planning to obtain cost estimates from a contractor or subcontractors—or if you are planning to build immediately—you will need more sets. Because additional sets are cheaper when ordered in quantity with the original order, make sure you order enough blueprints to satisfy all requirements. The following checklist will help you determine how many you need:

__ Owner

__ Builder (generally requires at least three sets; one as a legal document, one to use during inspections, and at least one to give to subcontractors)

__ Local Building Department (often requires two sets)

__ Mortgage Lender (usually one set for a conventional loan; three sets for FHA or VA loans)

__ TOTAL NUMBER OF SETS

ORDER FORM

The Home Customizer®

"This house is perfect...if only the family room were two feet wider." Sound familiar? In response to the numerous requests for this type of modification, Home Planners has developed **The Home Customizer® Package**. This exclusive package offers our top-of-the-line materials to make it easy for anyone, anywhere to customize any Home Planners design to fit their needs. Check the index on page 218-219 for those plans which are customizable.

Some of the changes you can make to any of our plans include:

- exterior elevation changes
- kitchen and bath modifications
- roof, wall and foundation changes
- room additions and more!

The Home Customizer® Package includes everything you'll need to make the necessary changes to your favorite Home Planners design. The package includes:

- instruction book with examples
- architectural scale and clear work film
- erasable red marker and removable correction tape
- ¼"-scale furniture cutouts
- 1 set reproducible drawings
- 1 set study blueprints for communicating changes to your design professional
- a copyright release letter so you can make copies as you need them
- referral letter with the name, address and telephone number of the professional in your region who is trained in modifying Home Planners designs efficiently and inexpensively.

The Home Customizer® Package will not only save you 25% to 75% of the cost of drawing the plans from scratch with an architect or engineer, it will also give you the flexibility to have your changes and modifications made by our referral network or by the professional of your choice. Now it's even easier and more affordable to have the custom home you've always wanted.

ORDER TOLL FREE!
FOR INFORMATION ABOUT ANY OF OUR SERVICES OR TO ORDER CALL

1-800-521-6797 OR 520-297-8200
Browse our website:
www.homeplanners.com

BLUEPRINTS ARE NOT REFUNDABLE EXCHANGES ONLY

FOR CUSTOMER SERVICE,
CALL TOLL FREE **1-888-690-1116.**

HOME PLANNERS, LLC wholly owned by Hanley-Wood, LLC
3275 WEST INA ROAD, SUITE 110 • TUCSON, ARIZONA • 85741

THE BASIC BLUEPRINT PACKAGE
Rush me the following (please refer to the Plans Index and Price Schedule in this section):

___Set(s) of blueprints for plan number(s) _____. $_____
___Set(s) of reproducibles for plan number(s) _____. $_____
___Home Customizer® Package for plan(s)_____ $_____
___Additional identical blueprints (standard or reverse) in same order @ $50 per set. $_____
___Reverse blueprints @ $50 fee per order. Right-reading reverse @ $165 surcharge $_____

IMPORTANT EXTRAS
Rush me the following:

___Materials List: $60 (Must be purchased with Blueprint set.) Add $10 for Schedule C4–L4 plans. $_____
___**Quote One®** Summary Cost Report @ $29.95 for one, $14.95 for each additional,
for plans _____ $_____
Building location: City _____ Zip Code _____
___**Quote One®** Materials Cost Report @ $120 Schedules P1–C3; $130 Schedules C4–L4,
for plan_____(Must be purchased with Blueprints set.) $_____
Building location: City _____ Zip Code _____
___Specification Outlines @ $10 each. $_____
___Detail Sets @ $14.95 each; any two $22.95; any three $29.95; all four for $39.95 (save $19.85). $_____
___❏ Plumbing ❏ Electrical ❏ Construction ❏ Mechanical
___Plan-A-Home® @ $29.95 each. $_____

DECK BLUEPRINTS
(Please refer to the Plans Index and Price Schedule in this section)

___Set(s) of Deck Plan _____. $_____
___Additional identical blueprints in same order @ $10 per set. $_____
___Reverse blueprints @ $10 per set. $_____
___Set of Standard Deck Details @ $14.95 per set. $_____
___Set of Complete Deck Construction Package (Best Buy!) Add $10 to Building Package
Includes Custom Deck Plan _____ Plus Standard Deck Details

LANDSCAPE BLUEPRINTS
(Please refer to the Plans Index and Price Schedule in this section)

___Set(s) of Landscape Plan _____. $_____
___Additional identical blueprints in same order @ $10 per set. $_____
___Reverse blueprints @ $10 per set. $_____
Please indicate the appropriate region of the country for Plant & Material List.

POSTAGE AND HANDLING	1–3 sets	4+ sets
Signature is required for all deliveries. **DELIVERY** No CODs (Requires street address—No P.O. Boxes)		
•Regular Service (Allow 7–10 business days delivery)	❏ $20.00	❏ $25.00
•Priority (Allow 4–5 business days delivery)	❏ $25.00	❏ $35.00
•Express (Allow 3 business days delivery)	❏ $35.00	❏ $45.00
OVERSEAS DELIVERY	fax, phone or mail for quote	

Note: All delivery times are from date Blueprint Package is shipped.

POSTAGE (From box above) $_____
SUBTOTAL $_____
SALES TAX (AZ & MI residents, please add appropriate state and local sales tax.) $_____
TOTAL (Subtotal and tax) $_____

YOUR ADDRESS (please print)

Name _____

Street_____

City _____State_____Zip _____

Daytime telephone number (_____) _____

FOR CREDIT CARD ORDERS ONLY

Credit card number _____ Exp. Date: (M/Y) _____
Check one ❏ Visa ❏ MasterCard ❏ Discover Card ❏ American Express

Signature_____

Please check appropriate box: ❏ Licensed Builder-Contractor ❏ Homeowner

ORDER TOLL FREE!
1-800-521-6797 or 520-297-8200

Order Form Key

HPT13

HOME PLANNERS WANTS YOUR BUILDING EXPERIENCE TO BE AS PLEASANT AND TROUBLE-FREE AS POSSIBLE.

That's why we've expanded our library of Do-It-Yourself titles to help you along. In addition to our beautiful plans books, we've added books to guide you through specific projects as well as the construction process. In fact, these are titles that will be as useful after your dream home is built as they are right now.

BIGGEST & BEST  1001 of our best-selling plans in one volume. 1,074 to 7,275 square feet. 704 pgs $12.95 1K1	**ONE-STORY**  450 designs for all lifestyles. 800 to 4,900 square feet. 384 pgs $9.95 OS	**MORE ONE-STORY**  475 superb one-level plans from 800 to 5,000 square feet. 448 pgs $9.95 MOS	**TWO-STORY**  443 designs for one-and-a-half and two stories. 1,500 to 6,000 square feet. 448 pgs $9.95 TS
VACATION  465 designs for recreation, retirement and leisure. 448 pgs $9.95 VSH	**HILLSIDE**  208 designs for split-levels, bi-levels, multi-levels and walkouts. 224 pgs $9.95 HH	**FARMHOUSE**  200 country designs from classic to contemporary by 7 winning designers. 224 pgs $8.95 FH	**COUNTRY HOUSES**  208 unique home plans that combine traditional style and modern livability. 224 pgs $9.95 CN
BUDGET-SMART  200 efficient plans from 7 top designers, that you can really afford to build! 224 pgs $8.95 BS	**BARRIER FREE**  Over 1,700 products and 51 plans for accessible living. 128 pgs $15.95 UH	**ENCYCLOPEDIA**  500 exceptional plans for all styles and budgets—the best book of its kind! 528 pgs $9.95 ENC	**ENCYCLOPEDIA II**  500 completely new plans. Spacious and stylish designs for every budget and taste. 352 pgs $9.95 E2
AFFORDABLE  Completely revised and updated, featuring 300 designs for modest budgets. 256 pgs $9.95 AF	**VICTORIAN**  160 striking Victorian & Farmhouse designs from three leading designers. 192 pgs $12.95 VDH	**ESTATE**  Dream big! Twenty-one designers showcase their biggest and best plans. 208 pgs $15.95 EDH	**LUXURY**  154 fine luxury plans—loaded with luscious amenities! 192 pgs $14.95 LD2
EUROPEAN STYLES  200 homes with a unique flair of the Old World. 224 pgs $15.95 EURO	**COUNTRY CLASSICS**  Donald Gardner's 101 best Country and Traditional home plans. 192 pgs $17.95 DAG	**WILLIAM POOLE**  70 romantic house plans that capture the classic tradition of home design. 160 pgs $17.95 WEP	**TRADITIONAL**  85 timeless designs from the Design Traditions Library. 160 pgs $17.95 TRA
COTTAGES  25 fresh new designs that are as warm as a tropical breeze. A blend of the best aspects of many coastal styles. 64 pgs $19.95 CTG	**CLASSIC**  Timeless, elegant designs that always feel like home. Gorgeous plans that are as flexible and up-to-date as their occupants. 240 pgs $9.95 CS	**CONTEMPORARY**  The most complete and imaginative collection of contemporary designs available anywhere. 240 pgs. $9.95 CM	**EASY-LIVING** 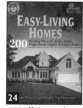 200 efficient and sophisticated plans that are small in size, but big on livability. 224 pgs $8.95 EL
SOUTHERN  207 homes rich in Southern styling and comfort. 240 pgs $8.95 SH	**SOUTHWESTERN**  138 designs that capture the spirit of the Southwest. 144 pgs $10.95 SW	**WESTERN**  215 designs that capture the spirit and diversity of the Western lifestyle. 208 pgs $9.95 WH	**NEIGHBORHOOD**  170 designs with the feel of main street America. 192 pgs $12.95 TND
CRAFTSMAN  170 Home plans in the Craftsman and Bungalow style. 192 pgs $12.95 CC	**COLONIAL HOUSES**  181 Classic early American designs. 208 pgs $9.95 COL	**DUPLEX & TOWNHOMES**  Over 50 designs for multi-family living. 64 pgs $9.95 DTP	**WATERFRONT**  200 designs perfect for your waterside wonderland. 208 pgs $10.95 WF

PROJECT GUIDES

WINDOWS	STREET OF DREAMS	MOVE-UP	OUTDOOR	GARAGES	DECKS	HOME BUILDING	BOOK & CD-ROM

   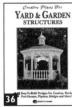    

| Discover the power of windows with over 160 designs featuring Pella's best. 192 pgs $9.95 WIN | Over 300 photos showcase 54 prestigious homes. 256 pgs $19.95 SOD | 200 stylish designs for today's growing families from 9 hot designers. 224 pgs $8.95 MU | 42 unique outdoor projects—gazebos, strombellas, bridges, sheds, playsets and more! 96 pgs $7.95 YG | 101 multi-use garages and outdoor structures to enhance any home. 96 pgs $7.95 GG | 25 outstanding single-, double- and multi-level decks you can build. 112 pgs $7.95 DP | Everything you need to know to work with contractors and subcontractors. 212 pgs $14.95 HBP | Both the Home Planners Gold book and matching Windows™ CD-ROM with 3D floorplans. $24.95 HPGC Book only $12.95 HPG |

LANDSCAPE DESIGNS

SOFTWARE	EASY-CARE	FRONT & BACK	BACKYARDS	BUYER'S GUIDE	FRAMING	BASIC WIRING	TILE

| Home design made easy! View designs in 3D, take a virtual reality tour, add decorating details and more. $59.95 PLANSUITE | 41 special landscapes designed for beauty and low maintenance. 160 pgs $14.95 ECL | The first book of do-it-yourself landscapes. 40 front, 15 backyards. 208 pgs $14.95 HL | 40 designs focused solely on creating your own specially themed backyard oasis. 160 pgs $14.95 BYL | A comprehensive look at 2700 products for all aspects of landscaping & gardening. 128 pgs $19.95 LPBG | For those who want to take a more hands-on approach to their dream. 319 pgs $21.95 SRF | A straightforward guide to one of the most misunderstood systems in the home. 160 pgs $12.95 CBW | Every kind of tile for every kind of application. Includes tips on use, installation and repair. 176 pgs $12.95 CWT |

BATHROOMS	KITCHENS	HOUSE CONTRACTING	VISUAL HANDBOOK	ROOFING	WINDOWS & DOORS	PATIOS & WALKS	TRIM & MOLDING

| An innovative guide to organizing, remodeling and decorating your bathroom. 96 pgs $10.95 CDB | An imaginative guide to designing the perfect kitchen. Chock full of bright ideas to make your job easier. 176 pgs $16.95 CKI | Everything you need to know to act as your own general contractor, and save up to 25% off building costs. 134 pgs $14.95 SBC | A plain-talk guide to the construction process; financing to final walk-through, this book covers it all. 498 pgs $19.95 RVH | Information on the latest tools, materials and techniques for roof installation or repair. 80 pgs $7.95 CGR | Installation techniques and tips that make your project easier and more professional looking. 80 pgs $7.95 CGD | Clear step-by-step instructions take you from the basic design stages to the finished project. 80 pgs $7.95 CGW | Step-by-step instructions for installing baseboards, window and door casings and more. 80 pgs $7.95 CGT |

Additional Books Order Form

To order your books, just check the box of the book numbered below and complete the coupon. We will process your order and ship it from our office within two business days. Send coupon and check (in U.S. funds).

YES! Please send me the books I've indicated:

❏ 1:IKI $12.95	❏ 20:TRA $17.95	❏ 39:HBP $14.95
❏ 2:OS $9.95	❏ 21:CTG $19.95	❏ 40:HPG $12.95
❏ 3:MOS $9.95	❏ 22:CS $9.95	❏ 40:HPGC $24.95
❏ 4:TS $9.95	❏ 23:CM $9.95	❏ 41:PLANSUITE ..$59.95
❏ 5:VSH $9.95	❏ 24:EL $8.95	❏ 42:ECL $14.95
❏ 6:HH $9.95	❏ 25:SH $8.95	❏ 43:HL $14.95
❏ 7:FH $8.95	❏ 26:SW $10.95	❏ 44:BYL $14.95
❏ 8:CN $9.95	❏ 27:WH $9.95	❏ 45:LPBG $19.95
❏ 9:BS $8.95	❏ 28:TND $12.95	❏ 46:SRF $21.95
❏ 10:UH $15.95	❏ 29:CC $12.95	❏ 47:CBW $12.95
❏ 11:ENC $9.95	❏ 30:COL $9.95	❏ 48:CWT $12.95
❏ 12:E2 ....$9.95	❏ 31:DTP $9.95	❏ 49:CDB $10.95
❏ 13:AF $9.95	❏ 32:WF $10.95	❏ 50:CKI $16.95
❏ 14:VDH $12.95	❏ 33:WIN $9.95	❏ 51:SBC $14.95
❏ 15:EDH $15.95	❏ 34:SOD $19.95	❏ 52:RVH $19.95
❏ 16:LD2 ....$14.95	❏ 35:MU $8.95	❏ 53:CGR $7.95
❏ 17:EURO $15.95	❏ 36:YG $7.95	❏ 54:CGD $7.95
❏ 18:DAG $17.95	❏ 37:GG $7.95	❏ 55:CGW $7.95
❏ 19:WEP $17.95	❏ 38:DP $7.95	❏ 56:CGT $7.95

Canadian Customers Order Toll Free 1-877-223-6389

Additional Books Subtotal (Please print) $ _____
ADD Postage and Handling (allow 4–6 weeks for delivery) $ 4.00
Sales Tax: (AZ & MI residents, add state and local sales tax.) $ _____
YOUR TOTAL (Subtotal, Postage/Handling, Tax) $ _____

YOUR ADDRESS (PLEASE PRINT)

Name _____
Street _____
City _____ State _____ Zip _____
Phone (_____) _____—_____

YOUR PAYMENT

Check one: ❏ Check ❏ Visa ❏ MasterCard ❏ Discover ❏ American Express
Required credit card information:

Credit Card Number _____
Expiration Date (Month/Year) _____ / _____
Signature Required _____

Home Planners, LLC
Wholly owned by Hanley-Wood, LLC
® 3275 W. Ina Road, Suite 110, Dept. BK, Tucson, AZ 85741

HPT13

223

Design S9621

OVER 3 MILLION BLUEPRINTS SOLD

"We instructed our builder to follow the plans including all of the many details which make this house so elegant… Our home is a fine example of the results one can achieve by purchasing and following the plans which you offer… Everyone who has seen it has assured us that it belongs in 'a picture book.' I truly mean it when I say that my home 'is a DREAM HOUSE.'"

S.P.
Anderson, SC

"We have had a steady stream of visitors, many of whom tell us this is the most beautiful home they've seen. Everyone is amazed at the layout and remarks on how unique it is. Our real estate attorney, who is a Chicago dweller and who deals with highly valued properties, told me this is the only suburban home he has seen that he would want to live in."

W. & P.S.
Flossmoor, IL

"Your blueprints saved us a great deal of money. I acted as the general contractor and we did a lot of the work ourselves. We probably built it for half the cost! We are thinking about more plans for another home. I purchased a competitor's book but my husband wants only your plans!"

K.M.
Grovetown, GA

"We are very happy with the product of our efforts. The neighbors and passersby appreciate what we have created. We have had many people stop by to discuss our house and kindly praise it as being the nicest house in our area of new construction. We have even had one person stop and make us an unsolicited offer to buy the house for much more than we have invested in it."

K. & L.S.
Bolingbrook, IL

"The traffic going past our house is unbelievable. On several occasions, we have heard that it is the 'prettiest house in Batvia.' Also, when meeting someone new and mentioning what street we live on, quite often we're told, 'Oh, you're the one in the yellow house with the wrap-around porch! I love it!'"

A.W.
Batvia, NY

"I have been involved in the building trades my entire life… Since building our home we have built two other homes for other families. Their plans from local professional architects were not nearly as good as yours. For that reason we are ordering additional plan books from you."

T.F.
Kingston, WA

"The blueprints we received from you were of excellent quality and provided us with exactly what we needed to get our successful home-building project underway. We appreciate your invaluable role in our home-building effort."

T.A.
Concord, TN